Music Therapy in Schools

by the same author

Music Therapy with Children and their Families
Edited by Amelia Oldfield and Claire Flower
Foreword by Vince Hesketh
ISBN 978 1 84310 581 7

Interactive Music Therapy – A Positive Approach
Music Therapy at a Child Development Centre
Amelia Oldfield
Foreword by Dr Fatima Janjua
ISBN 978 1 84310 309 7

of related interest

Arts Therapies in Schools
Research and Practice
Edited by Vicky Karkou
ISBN 978 1 84310 633 3

Adolescents, Music and Music Therapy
Methods and Techniques for Clinicians, Educators and Students
Katrina McFerran
Foreword by Tony Wigram
ISBN 978 1 84905 019 7

Music Therapy, Sensory Integration and the Autistic Child
Dorita S. Berger
Foreword by Donna Williams
ISBN 978 1 84310 700 2

Let's All Listen
Songs for Group Work in Settings that Include Students with Learning Difficulties and Autism
Pat Lloyd
Foreword by Adam Ockelford
ISBN 978 1 84310 583 1

Foreword by Dr Frankie Williams

EDITED BY JO TOMLINSON, PHILIPPA
DERRINGTON AND AMELIA OLDFIELD

Music
Therapy
in Schools

Working with Children of All Ages in
Mainstream and Special Education

Jessica Kingsley *Publishers*
London and Philadelphia

First published in 2012
by Jessica Kingsley Publishers
116 Pentonville Road
London N1 9JB, UK
and
400 Market Street, Suite 400
Philadelphia, PA 19106, USA

www.jkp.com

Library of Congress Cataloging in Publication Data
Music therapy in schools : working with children of all ages in mainstream and
special education / edited by Jo Tomlinson, Philippa Derrington, and Amelia
Oldfield ; foreword by Frankie Williams.
     p. cm.
  Includes bibliographical references and index.
  ISBN 978-1-84905-000-5 (alk. paper)
  1. Music therapy for children--Great Britain. 2. Music therapy for
teenagers--Great Britain. 3. School children--Mental health services--Great
Britain. I. Tomlinson, Jo. II. Derrington, Philippa. III. Oldfield, Amelia.
  ML3920.M89797 2012
  615.8'51540835--dc22
                    2011011123

British Library Cataloguing in Publication Data
A CIP catalogue record for this book is available from the British Library

ISBN 978 1 84905 000 5

Printed and bound in Great Britain

Contents

Foreword

I met Amelia Bolton (now Dr Amelia Oldfield) when she was a young newly qualified music therapist working at the Ida Darwin hospital, Cambridge in 1980. I have followed her successful work with children in Cambridgeshire for over 30 years. When she, Jo Tomlinson and Philippa Derrington asked me to read the draft and write a foreword to this book I echoed Pearl S. Buck's sentiments when she was asked to write the foreword to *Music Therapy in Special Education* (Nordoff and Robbins 1971a p.11): 'When I was invited to write a foreword for this remarkable book I accepted with pleasure. After such alacrity, however, I wondered if I could perform the task.' I also felt the same; however it was an invitation that allowed me to reflect over the last 40 years on the journey of music therapy for children and young people.

In 1970, as I started my music teaching career, little was known about music therapy. There were books by Juliette Alvin written in the 60s and in 1968 the Guildhall School of Music in London had started a training course in music therapy based on her work. There was also a book by Gaston in the USA (1968), and then in 1971 *Music Therapy in Special Education* by Nordoff and Robbins. In *Therapy in Music for Handicapped Children* (1971b) by the same authors published in the same year, Benjamin Britten wrote in the foreword:

> 'At this curious moment in musical history the validity of communication in art has itself been called into question, and it is wonderful to have a book where the concentration is entirely on just this, on communication pure and simple'

This I feel echoes once again with today's climate in the Arts and emphasises how important the chapters of this book are.

In 1971 an A level music pupil of mine was discussing her career options. She wanted to do something connected to music and medicine.

We looked at what was to both of us a new possibility called 'music therapy'. That pupil is now the Professor who has led music therapy at Anglia Ruskin University, Cambridge since 1994 – Helen Odell-Miller. Helen played in the Apollo Orchestra that I ran in the 1970s, alongside others who have become prime movers in music therapy, including Professor Tony Wigram, so my interest in music therapy was engaged and I was committed to developing the profession in educational settings. I visited Auriel Warwick in Oxfordshire and saw the inspirational work she was carrying out, and in 1984 Helen Odell-Miller and I drafted proposals for a music therapy service in Bedfordshire, where I was an advisory music teacher, employing Liz Clough from St John's Special School in Bedford to lead it in 1989. It had taken five years for the proposal to come to fruition. At this stage work was centred on special schools.

By 1989, when I moved to Cambridgeshire as General Inspector (Music), music therapy was a known but perhaps not well understood field in education. Again it took five years – until 1995 to set up a music therapy team led by Jo Storey (Tomlinson).

In 1994, the Head of Music, Peter Britton, at Anglia Polytechnic University (now Anglia Ruskin University) established the first MA Music Therapy course in the UK, appointing Helen Odell-Miller to lead it with Amelia Oldfield as co-designer. The partnership between the university and Cambridgeshire County Council has been invaluable in the development of music therapy in local schools. Dr Amelia Oldfield has provided the main source of supervision for the music therapists working in Cambridgeshire schools, many of whom have contributed chapters to this book.

This book shows examples of good practice and amply demonstrates a snapshot of much more work going on across the UK. The wonderful patience, passion and compassion, creativity, flexibility, rigor, humour and musical talent that the authors portray gives a picture of the place of music therapy in a range of different settings including children's centres, primary, secondary and special schools, hospices and even a garage! Whether it is giving eye-contact, sharing and turn-taking, finding order, expressing joy or anger, a means of communication, or having a time for being oneself in a safe and understood environment, these expressions fill the pages. I have been very fortunate to experience the work of some of the authors in this book and I feel it is essential to support the powerful intervention of music therapy and its research base. It is of vital importance to children, young people and families.

The chapters in this book take us forward to the 21st century and underline the importance and breadth of music therapy for children and young people in a range of educational and health settings. Music therapy is now an extremely important area of early intervention with children, which a number of the chapters address. The potential of the use of the double bass in music therapy is illustrated, as well as the need to match the energy of young people to motivate them, as one teenager comments, 'I couldn't be bothered when I came to school but (after music therapy sessions) I can now'

An imperative which runs through the book is the ability on the part of the practitioner to sustain an improvised musical encounter which is used in appropriate and effective ways. Music therapy is used as a means of communication and personal, social and emotional development, as opposed to music learning. One chapter pursues this and states that musical skills may be acquired along the way, but this may not be the aim. This argument is also extended to a discussion of music *in* therapy or music *as* therapy.

A recent report on Cambridgeshire Music's (the county music service) music therapy team comments: 'Fourteen therapists deliver 189 hours a week – this represents a significant contribution to vulnerable children and young people (in Cambridgeshire)' (Federation of Music Services – Smith 2010, p.5) But as I write, the music therapy services in Bedfordshire and Northern Ireland are under threat, to name but two.

Musicologists, neurologists, psychologists, psychotherapists and music therapists are now working together to discover the powerful effects of music on the brain; for example there is emerging evidence to show the specific effects that music therapy can have on those with acquired brain injury. In 1993 Anthony Storr observed at the end of his foreword to Margaret Heal and Tony Wigram's *Music Therapy in Health and Education:* 'Today, when at last more attention is given to the effects of music upon human beings, we have almost reached the depth of insight by the Greeks in the 5th century BC.' (p.xi) The speed of change is such that we do not know what future research will find, but in the field of education we must stay appraised of what is best and most appropriate for each child.

I can recommend this book wholeheartedly; we can all learn from it – all who are connected with children and young people in education, music, health and social care.

It has taken 40 years to build up this essential resource of music therapy in schools, local authorities and the health service, and it can take a few minutes to demolish this in a government or a council meeting. All those taking these decisions should read this book first.

Dr Frankie Williams
Cambridge
June 2011

Acknowledgements

The authors would like to thank:

- the children and the families who have taken part in music therapy sessions and have agreed to be included in this book
- the children and families who have contributed to the book through writing, commenting on the work or allowing photographs to be printed
- the schools' staff and multidisciplinary teams who have supported music therapy and in some cases contributed to chapters
- the clinical supervisors who have supported music therapy work in the schools
- the music therapy students who have been on placement with the authors and have provided practical help and inspiration for the writing.

The editors would like to thank:

- the authors, without whom the book could not exist. Working together has been rewarding and fulfilling
- Phyllis Champion for her thorough and always thoughtful editing.

Jo would like to thank her husband Hugh for his love, calmness and support. Thanks to her children Charlie and Natasha for being wonderful and providing creative inspiration!

Philippa would like to thank her friends and colleagues at Cottenham, head teacher Tony Cooper, and in particular, Sue Raven, head teacher of the Centre School, for making everything do-able. And thanks to Jo and Hugh for the ready supply of wine, log fires and delicious home-made brownies!

Amelia would like to thank her children, Daniel, Paul, Laura and Claire for their patience and help with their increasingly scatty mother. Thanks also to her husband, David, for his continuous and enduring support and love.

Introduction

Amelia Oldfield

Music therapy is still a relatively new and small profession. Nevertheless, at the beginning of the 21st century there are so many experienced music therapists working in schools around the world that this book could have easily been ten times as long as the present volume so the three editors decided to limit the choice of authors to those working in the UK. Even in the UK alone there are far more music therapists who could have contributed than there is space for in one book. When selecting authors, the editors have tried to include people working in different areas of the country, with a range of age groups, in different settings and with contrasting approaches. However, there will certainly be areas or types of work that have not been included. Perhaps this book will provide an incentive for many other future publications on this topic.

Although all the UK music therapy training courses prepare trainees to work with clients of all age groups, the proportion of music therapists who choose to work with children is high; according to the Association of Professional Music Therapists (APMT) around half those working in the UK spend at least part of their week working with children (APMT 2009). The vast majority of the work with children takes place in schools, but there are also a growing number of music therapists employed in children's hospices, a few work with children in private centres, and some work for the NHS in child development centres, children and adolescent psychiatric units and on children's wards in general hospitals.

Given that such a high percentage of music therapists do work in schools, it is surprising that there have been very few books devoted to this subject. One of the very first music therapy text books in the UK, *Music Therapy in Special Education*, was written by Paul Nordoff and Clive Robbins in 1971. The Nordoff and Robbins approach originated within the context of special schools where musician Paul Nordoff teamed up with special education teacher Clive Robbins to create a specific way of working. This approach was so successful that Nordoff-Robbins training courses have since opened up in a number of different countries. Forty years later the present book includes two chapters written by Nordoff-Robbins trained music therapists (Nicky O'Neill and Chris Achenbach) while the other 11 authors have trained on other courses in the UK. Vicky Karkou's (2010) book, *Arts Therapies in Schools: Research and Practice* is a welcome addition to the literature. A few chapters are written by music therapists but the emphasis is mainly on research rather than on describing clinical practice. There have been a number of chapters about music therapy in schools in more general music therapy text books such as Hibben (1991), Bull (2008) and Howden (2008). Bull and Howden reflect on the importance of working with the families of the children, a theme that is developed by a number of authors in the present book.

Much has changed in education in the UK since 1971. During the last ten years many special schools have closed and more children with special needs are being supported in both primary and secondary mainstream schools. Many of these children will have one-to-one support assistants and some attend specialist units such as pupil referral units (PRUs). Some special schools and mainstream primary schools in socially deprived areas now have nurseries or child care facilities and cater for the needs of parents and siblings as well as those of the children. As a result the role of music therapists in schools may differ greatly from one school to another, depending of course on the age and needs of the children, but also depending on whether the school is a mainstream school or a special school, and whether the school is working with families or not.

Music therapy has also changed and developed as a profession in the last 40 years. In 1971 there was only one music therapy training course in the UK, at the Guildhall School of Music, London, which had started three years previously in 1968. There are now seven training courses in the UK and the number of working music therapists has grown from around 40 to 700. In 1981 a career structure was set up for those working in the National Health Service. Initially this did not affect those working in schools who would often be employed as teachers or teaching assistants rather than music therapists, with varying working conditions and pay. In some instances this can mean that music therapists working in the same school will be working under varying contracts and have very different salaries. Many music therapists in schools have been, and continue to be, affected by inequalities and discrepancies in their employment conditions.

Nevertheless, the improved working conditions offered in the Health Service have gradually become more widespread, particularly since music therapists became state registered in 1999 and since the Agenda for Change salary reforms in the NHS in the last few years. There is still a discrepancy between pay and working conditions amongst music therapists working in schools but these are less marked than they were, and schools are increasingly using the NHS music therapy career structure as a guideline.

While some who work with children also work with adults, many decide early on in their careers that they only wish to work with children, become specialised and experienced in this area and do not envisage working elsewhere. This is the case for many of the authors in this book. It is interesting to reflect on why this is the case. It may be that there are sometimes more music therapy jobs available with children rather than with adults. It is often easier to secure funding for posts with children, particularly when money needs to be raised through charitable funding. Another answer is that music therapists who specialise in working with children particularly enjoy being with and working with children. Children grow and change, so the work can be rewarding and hopeful. Working with children can help therapists stay in touch with their playful, youthful and creative side, which helps to keep musical improvisations alive and fresh.

Working in schools may be reassuring to some therapists as it is an environment which everyone will have experienced as a child; some will also be experiencing schools through having their own children. As a result, working in a school may be less intimidating than working in a hospital or a clinical environment. However, this could also have disadvantages as therapists will have their own expectations of what a school environment should be like, as well as being influenced by their own positive and negative school experiences. Schools are busy places to work, where there will be many different members of staff with well-defined roles. The staff team may fit into established hierarchies and the music therapist will have to find his or her place as well as devote substantial amounts of time to getting to know the staff in each school. Those who have successfully worked in schools for a number of years will usually feel supported and respected, and have a sense of belonging to the school.

Many music therapists working in schools come from teaching backgrounds and may have worked first as teachers. This is the case for a number of the authors in this book, including Jo Tomlinson, Clare

Rosscornes and Jan Hall. Some music therapists who have previously been teachers enjoy going back to the school environment in a different role, although the transition from teacher to therapist may not always be smooth and adjustments have to be made. Other dually qualified people opt to teach part-time (either as classroom teachers or as instrumental teachers) and be music therapists part-time.

In this book music therapists from all over the UK, from a variety of backgrounds, with different experiences and varying theoretical orientations, will describe a wide range of work in children's centres (nursery age children), in mainstream primary and secondary schools, and in special schools. The chapters have been arranged to start with the youngest children in nursery school or children's centres and end with teenagers. The editors have encouraged authors to write about aspects of the work that they feel passionate about, and have not been prescriptive about the structure or content of the chapters. As a result, authors have approached the subject from different perspectives and written in varying ways, focusing particularly on different points. The first and the last chapters of the book give an overview of music therapy services that have been specially developed to match the needs of the children in a specific setting; Chapter 1, by Clare Rosscornes and Emma Davies, describes work with very young children in a children's centre, and Chapter 13, by Philippa Derrington, describes the work with teenagers in a learning support unit within a mainstream secondary school. In a similar way Nicky O'Neill (Chapter 2) describes the development of a service in an assessment nursery and Órla Casey (Chapter 11) looks at the role of music therapy with children with life-threatening illnesses and explores the links between services in schools and hospices. Other authors have chosen to describe in detail specific aspects of their clinical work: Jane Brackley investigates how music therapy can address the expression of anger and aggression (Chapter 6); Jo Tomlinson focuses on the use of imitation and reflection when interacting with children in sessions (Chapter 7) and Ian McTier explores the use of the double bass in his work with children with autistic spectrum disorder (Chapter 10). Jan Hall (Chapter 5) combines an interest in the setting she works in and her specific approach when she argues that the school she works in has particularly benefited from her dual role as both a music teacher and a music therapist. Other authors' work has been greatly influenced by the geographical and political circumstances of the schools they work in. This is the case for Karen Diamond's work in Belfast (Chapter 9) and also for the development of the school music therapy service in North Yorkshire, described by Angela Harrison (Chapter 8). The remaining three authors have all written about co-working and teamwork. Thus Anne Bruce and Suzie High (Chapter 4) give different professionals' views of music therapy work, and John Strange (Chapter 12) describes his joint work with teaching assistants. Chris Achenbach (Chapter 3) writes particularly about how he supports and trains students within his work.

All the chapters contain poignant and moving stories. In the case studies and vignettes, names and identifying details have been changed for reasons of confidentiality. The case work makes music therapy in the different schools come alive. There is great energy, commitment and enthusiasm, as well as an overall conviction that music therapy is useful in many different ways. This is no doubt why, in many schools, music therapists initially started working for a few hours a week and these hours were then slowly increased until in some cases they were employed full-time. Some music therapists have also described how their hours have been cut when school budgets have been reduced, but even in these cases optimism remains that the service will gradually develop and expand again. Appendix 1 describes how the service in Cambridgeshire has evolved during the last 14 years.

It is clear from this book that music therapists can adapt to the changing needs of different schools but can also provide specific approaches and techniques to fulfil the needs of individual children. It is also apparent that they work effectively with other staff and with parents, and are able to learn from as well as contribute to multidisciplinary teams. Every chapter in this book is an example of how music therapy has developed in a new way, or how a specific technique has evolved. Perhaps an overall trend is that while keeping a clear identity and role within the teaching team, music therapists have become increasingly flexible and creative, finding ways to adapt their skills and approaches to meet the changing needs of the children and the schools.

This book fills a gap in the literature and will be invaluable not only to music therapists working in schools but also to a wide range of professional colleagues in schools as well as to parents, relatives and carers of children receiving music therapy within the education environment.

Chapter 1

Setting up and Developing Music Therapy at a Children's Centre, for Pre-school Children and their Families and Carers

Emma Davies and Clare Rosscornes

Introduction

Emma Davies set up music therapy at The Fields Children's Centre in September 2002 and Clare Rosscornes took over the work in January 2008. In this chapter Emma will explain how she set up the post, after which Clare will describe how it currently works in practice.

The setting

The Fields Children's Centre is an educational and day-care setting for children aged three months to four years. It is situated within a multicultural community in a socio-economically diverse part of Cambridge. There are over 600 families with children aged under four in the catchment area of the centre. The centre provides 100 part-time educational places for three and four-year-olds and 74 full-time day-care places for children aged three months to four years. Forty-five per cent of the children are from ethnic groups other than white British, 37 per cent speak English as an additional language with 23 per cent at an early stage of language acquisition. There are currently 34 children who have special educational needs. Many parents are on a low income or unemployed and the centre is able to support those children through government and charitable funding. The centre is used by the community for the care and education of their children but it also provides support for families through various courses, activities and events, for example: new parent groups, parenting classes, baby and sleep clinics, antenatal classes and a range of activity groups for parents and children. There is also a community café which supports healthy eating and family well-being, and is used regularly by parents and families. The centre places an emphasis on families taking charge of their own learning within a framework of nurture and support.

The nursery caters for children aged three and four and has three class bases. Although the children belong to a particular base in the nursery, they can move freely from room to room and also into the large outdoor area where they have space to play, ride bikes and help to grow vegetables and plants during the spring and summer terms. It is a positive environment for children to interact, be creative and learn through play and activities. The day-care part of the centre cares for children aged three months to three years and there are two separate rooms where children are placed according to age. As with the nursery, these rooms provide a safe and stimulating environment for the children with both indoor and outdoor areas.

Emma describes how the post was set up

My first involvement with The Fields was on placement as a music therapy student in 2000. Music therapy students had been welcomed for some years as there was a consistently high percentage of children with special educational needs. At that point The Fields was solely a nursery school for three and four-year-olds and was in a very different setting to where it is now. It was located near a busy ring road next to a McDonald's and the majority of the school buildings were temporary, with little outside space. I worked in a small portakabin with a kitchenette at one end. At that point I felt that although some staff, including the head teacher, had a very positive attitude towards music therapy there was also a lack of understanding from others. Music therapy seemed to be perceived as quite separate from the children's nursery experience and there was confusion as to how something seemingly unquantifiable could be evaluated and assessed. In spite of these mixed feelings within the staff team, and even though at the time there were few music therapists working in this setting and very little literature available, it was still clear to me that music therapy could offer the school something complementary to the work it was achieving. However, it was not going to be easy to establish music therapy in this setting.

A year after I trained as a music therapist, the head teacher asked me to run a music project funded by 'Music for Youth'. It was designed to encourage every child attending a state nursery in Cambridgeshire to get involved with music. I ran music groups with an educational slant as well as an after-school music group for children and their parents and carers. Working with educational goals was particularly challenging for me because, as an already practising therapist, I often felt restricted to make my sessions achieve targets rather than allow the children to explore music in a more flexible and non-structured way. I also found it frustrating that in the process of the project I could clearly identify children who would benefit from music therapy but I could not carry out that work. However, it was precisely for this reason that I was motivated to begin the process of setting up a music therapy post at the nursery. I had the evidence to support the need which I think made more of an impact than if I had come to the nursery without this connection. The after-school music group was closer to some of the work I was already doing at the Croft Children's Unit for child and family psychiatry in Cambridge. For example, I had experienced the idea of using a group as an assessment tool to identify particular needs within families (Carter and Oldfield 2002) and therefore felt much clearer about what I was trying to achieve. Although not run as a therapy group, and with the main aim being for children and their parents and carers to interact within a relaxed setting and enjoy playing music together, it was also possible to identify families who might need extra support and to explain to the head teacher how music therapy could help. The journey from visiting music therapy student to in-house music therapist was a long, eventful one.

Reflections on the challenges of setting up the music therapy post

After various consultations, funding was found for me to continue running the after-school group and after a while additional funding was secured for one morning of music therapy (two individual sessions and a small group). At around this time, The Fields moved location to an existing primary school site with much more space and quieter surroundings. It also became a children's centre with better resources and a larger and more appropriate therapy room. However, this was also the time that I felt a crisis of professional confidence. My role was explicitly challenged by several members of staff and I found myself really contemplating what

I was doing. My sessions were often interrupted and I was told by one teacher that I was letting children run riot in my group. I did not view it at all like that, rather that I was allowing them to channel their energy in a free but contained way. I was in no doubt that the children were benefiting from the work but it still felt very disconnected from their nursery lives. My work felt as if it were in a bubble. At that point I was not working with the children's families (except for within the music group) and there was little opportunity to feed back to and involve the staff team. These last two points were key elements to the way I altered my style of working.

I started to discuss the possibility of bringing parents or carers into therapy where appropriate, for example, when I felt that the child's difficulties could be due to attachment or parenting issues. Again this approach was influenced by my work at the Croft Children's Unit, where I was working with families in very stressful circumstances. Music therapy was able to provide an alternative way to interact non-verbally and to empower families to find ways to express and process difficult issues (Oldfield and Flower 2008). It took time for some of the staff team to recognise the importance of involving parents, partly because it was a new idea and partly because the concept worked in contrast to the idea of children achieving states of independence and detachment from the family whilst at school. However, parents have increasingly become part of the life in the nursery as later sections in this chapter will demonstrate.

CASE STUDY 1.1: GUY

One case in particular made me realise that including parents and carers could be essential. Guy was two and half years old when I first met him and he had a diagnosis of autistic spectrum disorder. He had no speech and he presented as a very isolated and frustrated little boy. His parents were struggling to come to terms with the diagnosis. Guy was their first child and they talked about feeling at a loss as to how to help him. I felt strongly that in order to help Guy I had to first find ways to empower his parents with ways to communicate with him. As Guy's father was the main carer because his mother worked full-time, I asked him to attend music therapy for six months before Guy started his pre-school year, with the aim of Guy attending with his support assistant or alone once he was settled at nursery. During this period I encouraged Guy and his father to explore many different ways of communicating through improvisation. Guy particularly responded to familiar songs and also to ones we developed ourselves. He really listened when I sang about what he was doing, for example, 'Guy is playing the drum, Guy has stopped.' Guy's father was able to take some of these ideas away from the sessions and use them at home. When Guy's learning support assistant joined us, we also talked about ways in which she could use music to support Guy within the classroom. She created songs to help him understand what was happening during the day (a musical timetable) and also set up opportunities for Guy to play music with other children to help his social skills. The idea of music therapy offering something beyond the therapy door is particularly important because music therapists usually only provide sessions once a week.

To help the staff understand what I was trying to achieve in my work I suggested that I give a presentation about music therapy to the whole staff team during a teacher training session. I remember feeling terrified at the thought as it felt like a make-or-break situation. It was the case example I gave with video extracts that seemed to make the biggest impact, as it clearly demonstrated music therapy in action. I also ran a workshop and encouraged some of my critics to role-play some of the children in their classes. I encouraged a teacher to play a kazoo in such a way to represent a child with speech difficulties. I also played one and we had a long dialogue. Afterwards we discussed how beneficial it was to use a non-verbal way of communicating and expressing oneself, especially for children with speech and language difficulties. This was the first time that I was able to communicate with the whole team and, as a result, there was a real shift in the way people viewed my work. Staff from the day-care centre asked if I could do some work there which resulted in a regular singing session. However, more importantly it resulted in some of the staff introducing more music and singing time during the rest of the week. I realised at this point that the music therapy role did not simply involve coming in and doing music therapy within a closed room and leaving again. An essential element of my work was about sharing ideas and skills and encouraging others to find ways of using music when I was not there. I also explained how important it was to be included in meetings, particularly annual statement reviews, as this was the forum in which future recommendations were offered.

The presentation/workshop was a real turning point in the development of music therapy at The Fields. After the workshop I felt more included in the team and much more able to contribute ideas. As a result of the positive attitude towards music therapy, the centre decided to expand the hours from a half to a whole day. The time of the group was changed from after-school to lunchtime to cater for babies and younger children and numbers dramatically increased. I continued to run workshops and presentations not only to staff within the centre but also to professionals outside, such as speech therapists and local community leaders. After working at the centre for six years, I left on maternity leave and Clare took over the post.

The role of music therapy at the centre from Clare's perspective

I work at the centre one day a week during term time. My role is diverse and includes music therapy sessions, a drop-in community music group for parents and young children, singing in the classes and day-care rooms with the children, running ukulele workshops for parents and staff, and playing the piano for the Christmas concert. As Emma has described, the role of the music therapist grew from the needs of the children and music is now viewed by staff as an important part of the centre, supporting the children's development. This involves taking individuals and small groups for traditional music therapy in a contained setting, as well as opening up the idea of music to parents and their children, through the use of the community music group, singing sessions and workshops. For example, a ukulele workshop for staff was initiated following staff members' positive experiences of the day-care singing sessions and their desire to learn how to play themselves. In this way everyone can enjoy and benefit from music and I feel that I am very much working with the community. I have had to be adaptable and flexible in my approach and it has been a two-way learning process for myself and the staff. In this situation music therapy and community music seem to co-exist with natural overlaps between the two.

Music therapy sessions

At the start of each academic year, teachers in the nursery refer children to me for music therapy sessions, using a standard referral form. Children can be referred to me in the spring and summer terms as well, as children start at the centre throughout the year. Once they have been referred, I spend a few weeks observing them in the nursery and talking with teachers and teaching assistants about them. In this way I can see the children interacting with their peers and adults, which enhances the information given on the referral form. The reasons for referral include behavioural and emotional issues as well as learning difficulties. Some children have unspecified complex difficulties and others have a clear diagnosis, such as autistic spectrum disorder or Down syndrome. There are often many more referrals than I can see in the given time-frame and therefore I prioritise by liaising with the staff involved.

Once we have decided who I will work with, I contact parents to discuss the proposed music therapy and to gain their permission. A large room, which is used for various activities throughout the week, is set aside for music therapy on a Wednesday. There is a piano in the room and I can wheel in the music trolley, which has a variety of percussion instruments. In addition there are some large drums stored in a cupboard in the room and I also use my own ukulele and clarinet. There is a good understanding of music therapy, largely due to how Emma set up the post. The day is well structured, beginning with three or four music therapy sessions, with enough space in between for reflection, note writing and liaising with staff. At lunchtime I prepare the room for the community music group for parents and young children. I take one or two more music therapy sessions in the afternoon followed by a singing time with the children in day-care.

The sessions are mostly uninterrupted as the staff understand that it can be distracting for the children if someone enters the room and that we may be in the middle of an improvisation. I often work alongside a teaching assistant, because of the nature and age of the children. This provides a link between the class and the music therapy room and maintains good communication with staff. Once a child has begun music therapy sessions, I keep notes and assess progress towards their aims each term. As part of this process I will continually assess if music therapy is still a useful intervention. The children are generally only at the nursery for a year or two at the most which therefore often provides a clear ending. If, however, I feel that they should continue with music therapy, I will recommend this to the school that they are moving to in my report.

I liaise with teachers and teaching assistants on a weekly basis and in doing so gain a fuller picture of the child and their needs. I also link in with the speech therapist who may be working with a child who I am seeing and, if appropriate, with family workers who can provide an even broader picture of the child within the wider context. Due to the nature of the setting I tend to see parents as they drop off or collect their children and this provides a natural way of keeping regular contact with them. The centre is very community-based and parents are often there for different groups or to use the café. In the same way that Emma described, I find that when working with individual children in this setting I have become more open to working with families in the session if the need arises. The children are young and therefore there may be separation issues, particularly for a parent of a child who has special needs. This may mean working with the parent in the room or it may mean suggesting that the child comes with a teaching assistant.

Community music group

(In this section, the use of the word parent can mean parent, carer or grandparent). The group takes place each week and lasts for approximately 45 minutes. Parents and their children (aged up to three) sometimes come to the café before the group as it is held around lunchtime. As it is a drop-in group I am never sure how many parents and children will come, so numbers can vary greatly. However, it has proved to be a popular group, often with several regulars as well as new faces each week. Generally there are around eight to ten children with a parent. We all sit in a large circle on the mats with the children sitting together with their parent. I begin with a hello song – singing to each child in turn whilst they play small percussion instruments. I usually have a vague structure in my mind of songs that we will sing but I also adapt this to the needs of the children who are there and to the general feel of the group that week.

Figure 1.1 Parents and children enjoy sharing musical interaction during the community music group

During the course of the group we will usually sing some familiar nursery rhymes and action songs and play the large floor drums together, with several children sharing each drum. We also sometimes sing a song which involves using a light colourful cloth, under which each child takes a turn to sit as we float it up and down. The songs that we use present a mixture of familiarity, anticipation, suspense and many opportunities for bonding between the parent and child. Many parents naturally sing and play percussion along with the songs using lots of encouraging facial expressions. They are strengthening the bond between themselves and their child within this safe and contained environment. Several child development theorists (Bowlby 1988; Stern 1985; Winnicott 1964) have written about the importance of a parent developing secure attachments with their child, in particular in the child's first two years. A music group such as this presents an ideal opportunity for these attachments to develop healthily and for the child to begin to interact with others. In addition, it has also proved to be a place where parents can meet and form friendships. Indeed, after the group I always leave time for parents to chat with each other as we begin to pack away. Thus the group works on two levels, for the child and for the parent.

Figure 1.2 Siblings also often attend the group together and can explore musical exchanges

What do the parents say?

The community music group is a popular weekly group for many parents, and questionnaires were completed to receive feedback about the sessions (see Appendix 2). Many parents enjoy attending the group as it is interactive and fun for them as well as for their child. One parent commented: 'He interacts nicely with the other kids. Sharing seems to be easier for him at the group.' Several parents commented on the pleasure of seeing their child enjoying music, especially if there was no history of musical ability in the family. Parents felt it was important that the music was live and one parent said: 'It's great to see the many different ways Sara has enjoyed the group – from being a passive member of the group as a baby, to wanting to do actions at home and she now takes part enthusiastically.' The music group also seems to provide something that they may not ordinarily do with their child. It is bringing music to families who otherwise may not access it and gives the opportunity to develop communicative interaction, self-confidence and foster a positive early relationship with music. In the words of one parent: '[Jimmy] enjoys music at home too... a lot of inspiration from this group.' It may also be the parent's first contact with the centre and can lead to an easier transition into the nursery when the child is three years old, as illustrated in the following case study:

CASE STUDY 1.2: THEO

Attending the community music group

Theo and his mother regularly attended community music group at the centre. At this stage Theo was two years old and did not appear to use any speech when in the group. He was always very excited by being at the music group and would choose several different instruments throughout the session. He would often run around the outside of the group, sometimes crossing the mats everyone was sitting on, or coming very close to a child on the mat and looking intently at them. His mother did not have full mobility and therefore it was difficult for her to keep him with her all the time. I talked with her about how Theo was in the group and whilst we agreed that it was good for him to let off steam there was some concern about his own safety and the other children's. However, between us all this situation was managed and I soon began to know which songs Theo particularly liked. As the weeks went by, he gradually began giving me some eye-contact and a rapport began to grow between us. As a result he began to listen more and generally seemed calmer within the group. Theo's mother had a very good relationship with him and she clearly enjoyed the music, often commenting on how much he responded to the music. Without words Theo communicated his enjoyment through facial expressions, movement and eye-contact. In this scenario it is clear to see that, although this group was a community music session, I reacted and responded as a music therapist. The crossover between the two is blurred, as many of the interactions were similar to that which you might see in a music therapy session. Over the course of the year that Theo attended the group, his interactions with his mother, with me and with other children and parents increased. He gave more eye-contact and he responded to particular songs with movement and smiles although there was no verbal communication.

During this time I enquired through the centre as to whether Theo had been seen by a health visitor regarding his communication and interaction with others, as I noticed characteristics at this stage that were similar to children on the autistic spectrum. I also spoke to his mother at this time to see if Theo's behaviour was similar at home. She said that he did say some words at home and that he had so much energy all the time, right from the moment he woke up. She viewed a lot of his behaviour as naughty. Others working with Theo at this time had made similar observations and subsequently the wheels were put in motion, through a health visitor, to assess Theo at home and at the local child development centre. As a result Theo was diagnosed as being on the autistic spectrum. This diagnosis was made during the summer break after Theo had left the group (aged three) and as he began nursery at the centre.

This situation highlights the benefits of the varied role of the music therapist at this centre as my observations, along with those of others, led to an assessment of Theo. Also, as he began at nursery in the autumn term, I provided a link between the family and the staff. I talked with the staff about Theo's behaviour in the group and how he responded positively to music. After discussions with staff and his mother it was agreed that I would see Theo for individual music therapy. This way of working closely with families and young children has also been documented by other music therapists, in particular Drake, who writes about her work with families attending the Coram Centre in London (Drake 2008).

Music therapy sessions

Theo had some difficulty settling into the nursery so initially his mother came into the class each morning in order to help him to settle. Theo managed to stay for an hour in the first few weeks and over the course of the first term this increased to two hours and subsequently to the whole morning as he gradually became more familiar and comfortable with the place and the people. Theo seemed pleased to see me in the nursery, recognising me from the music group and reacting positively to seeing me in a different situation.

Indeed when he first saw me he took my hand and tried to lead me to the music room! I began seeing Theo with his teaching assistant within the first few weeks of the autumn term. He was happy to come to the room, explore it and all the instruments, looking to us both for reassurance and to show his pleasure. Although the room is set out slightly differently for music therapy sessions to the way it is for the community music group, there seemed to be recognition from Theo, along with possibly some confusion as to where everyone else was. After two assessment sessions, I set out the following aims for Theo:

1. to develop interaction through the music-making
2. to encourage vocalisation
3. to develop use of eye-contact.

The sessions went from strength to strength with Theo really using the space well. His teaching assistant continued to come to the sessions as we felt that he needed the support and it was also useful for her to see him interacting in such a positive and enthusiastic manner, as this was not always the case in the nursery. Indeed for much of the first term, Theo could become quite distressed in the nursery and it was difficult for the staff to find activities that he enjoyed. In the music therapy session, Theo was able to interact with us both and the sessions were often full of smiles and lots of positive interaction. Theo was able to communicate with us through the music and it was beneficial for his teaching assistant to see that and to be a part of it. As the weeks progressed Theo's interactive play increased and he began giving us more eye-contact and smiles. He began to notice if we responded to his playing, for example, by copying what he had played. He seemed pleased when contact was made between us, when there was some communication through the music. He particularly enjoyed playing the piano with me, responding positively when he heard a familiar song by playing alongside me. When we played music, Theo began to vocalise. We would usually echo this back to him, which he enjoyed and responded to positively with a smile or by vocalising more. As the term progressed he started to sing the last word of some lines in songs, such as 'Twinkle Twinkle Little Star', and began joining in with some actions, for example, clapping in 'Wind the Bobbin Up'. At times, he responded to one of us saying 'ready, steady...' and made a good attempt at saying 'go'. He enjoyed this activity, playing along when he said 'go' and stopping when I said 'stop'.

Theo has responded well to his music therapy sessions. We have gradually seen more interaction through the music and increased communication both in the music and through vocalising. He is clearly motivated by music and the therapy sessions have enabled him to develop his communication and interaction through a medium that is both fun and positive for him. Theo's mother commented on her experience of the music group and music therapy:

> The music group was helpful for Theo – it encouraged him to talk. It is amazing to see how children react to music therapy. He loves music and is always calm when he is around music. Music therapy has helped my son in many ways. He is saying a lot more words now and when he's upset, if I sing a song, he calms down straight away.

The setting provided the opportunity for this young child to express himself and to communicate with others through music. Initially the community music group enabled that to happen and later, the music therapy sessions. The flexibility of the role of the music therapist in this instance helped to identify needs early on. Theo consequently received more individual music therapy, which helped with his transition into nursery and facilitated his social development.

Staff views and reflections on music therapy

Thoughts and views expressed by learning support assistants, teachers and the head teacher from The Fields were collated by Emma and Clare using questionnaires and carrying out interviews in 2010 (see Appendix 3).

Learning support assistants who helped out in music therapy sessions seemed to be clear about their role in supporting children in sessions; one said that music therapy was 'very useful. It gives the child a chance to express themselves through music.' Additionally assistants felt that musical interaction had become an important part of the children's lives and expressed surprise about responses from children; one commented that 'Music therapy is such a good way to communicate and to get good eye-contact...and it is a great way to watch them share and take turns.'

One of the teaching staff filled out a detailed questionnaire about how her view of music therapy had changed since the provision had been established at the centre. Initially she was unsure of the benefits, even after sitting in on sessions, where she felt the main positive focus was the one-to-one attention the child was receiving. After Emma's workshop to staff, her understanding of music therapy completely transformed:

> I then had a totally different idea of what it was all about. I viewed it as a therapy and very much a means of communication between the child and therapist. I could see that the music was a means to communicate and the important thing was about communication and not the 'music learning'. I could see that it was a gradual progression built up over many sessions and it was more to do with personal, social and emotional development and communication...

This teacher also felt that the clear objectives for sessions fitted in extremely well with curriculum objectives at the nursery, such as social, emotional and linguistic development. When asked about the involvement of parents in sessions she agreed that this could potentially be very constructive, particularly 'if the parent had had an explanation of what their role should be in the music therapy session and how the therapist was working'.

The head teacher at the centre expressed her view that: 'The Fields supports vulnerable children – there are high levels of children with language delay and special needs, and addressing communication problems is a top priority to support children in order for them to develop and flourish. Music seems to be a key which unlocks – it is non-threatening and enables children to express themselves freely.'

Conclusion

In this chapter we have described the process of setting up a music therapy post within an early years setting and explored how it has developed over time to respond to the needs of young children, their families and people involved in their education. We have both learned much from the experience and hope that we have been able to share some of the challenges we have faced and describe the ways in which we were able to overcome them. The integration of music therapy and the importance and value of music into the whole centre's environment and approach has taken time and is now clearly valued by staff and parents alike. Being flexible and open to different ideas and ways of working has been vital in the continued success of the role of music therapy at the centre along with good communication with staff and parents.

The use of music in individual sessions, community group and singing sessions has proved to be beneficial for children, parents and staff in developing non-musical elements of a child's growth such as self-confidence and positive interaction. Sharing ideas and skills with staff, parents and carers has broadened our view of music therapy and we believe has provided greater long-term benefits of music therapy for the children. One of the most interesting aspects of the role has been to explore the ways in which music therapy can go beyond the therapy door and begin a musical journey for children and their carers which will hopefully continue long into their lives.

Chapter 2

Open Doors, Open Minds, Open Music!

The Development of Music Therapy Provision in an Assessment Nursery

Nicky O'Neill

Personal context

In 1997 I decided to make the move, for part of my working week, from adults with learning disabilities living in a countryside community to an assessment nursery for children with special needs. It was a move from the charity to the health sector – as huge a leap then as it is nowadays.

I had worked in this charity-funded community for the first seven years of my career. It had been the perfect learning ground for me, in that I had been able to focus purely on developing my craft, both alongside an experienced clinician and with a newly qualified peer. We listened assiduously to our tapes with the door shut, examining in detail every note of interaction and then assessing them with our Nordoff-Robbins rating scales. There were no demands from other agencies as there were minimal links and we worked very separately from class/college staff and other therapies such as physiotherapists and speech and language therapists.

The community included people with severe learning disabilities as well as far more able people who, these days, would no longer be placed in a residential community. They were people whose conversations, interactions and experiences, both musical and verbal, had a profound and forming effect on my personal and professional development. We ate, played and learned together and I felt part of their lives.

I have no doubt that good quality music therapy was practised but it started coming to a cyclical point where the same people kept being referred. I began to feel my own limitations and needed a change in direction and a new challenge. Furthermore, I needed accountability – there were minimal links or demands from other organisations and with that came minimal opportunities for learning about broader contexts, and other peoples' ideas and perspectives. I was ready for my next challenge – ready to open my mind and my musicality.

The move I made was to join the expanding paediatric music therapy service serving the London Borough of Greenwich. We were a National Health Service provision with a strong emphasis on developing external contracts, particularly with local schools.

History of music therapy in the London Borough of Greenwich

When I joined the Greenwich Music Therapy Service in 1997, it was situated in an expanding, creative and communicative paediatric health team. The music therapy service was based in a purpose-built bungalow in Eltham, sharing the building with the Early Intervention Centre. The service continues to provide individual and group music therapy within a clinic context for children referred by local agencies, namely the health team, education, and social services and voluntary sector. In addition, in 1997, there were contracts with four special schools and the Child Development Centre.

I had been aware of this service through its developing reputation within Nordoff-Robbins London, but it was on reading the job description that I realised it would be a whole cultural shift for me which would be both exciting and frightening. It seemed to be promising me the learning and development that I was craving. The job description was thorough, detailed and forward-looking and seemed embedded in a culture of development and strong knowledge base. Like the community I had just left, it was led by Nordoff-Robbins therapists, which I found so helpful in further developing my craft. We spoke the same language and yet I was now learning in more detail about the younger end of the disability spectrum. Although it was paediatric learning disabilities and autistic spectrum disorder in which I was originally trained, in this service the knowledge of the client group and then the adaptation of the Nordoff-Robbins approach had been taken far more in-depth than I had previously experienced – a whole new skill-set had been developed (Hadley 2000). Of course, in other venues as well, specialists in early intervention and assessment were developing their models of work (Oldfield 2006a). The Greenwich music therapy service was also strongly committed to multidisciplinary team working, with music therapists co-running a variety of joint group sessions with physiotherapists, occupational therapists and speech therapists.

Educational context

In 1997 the education inclusion agenda was in its infancy, consequently, there were many more special needs schools throughout the UK. In the London Borough of Greenwich there were originally six special schools and these were streamlined onto two sites, namely Willow Dene School (nursery and primary) and Charlton School (secondary). The assessment nursery at Willow Dene School, where I started working in 1997, assessed each child, provided short-term intervention and was sometimes able to feed children back into mainstream provision. If not, they remained in local special needs schools.

History of client group

The demography in the late 1990s was very different to the current time, with far fewer children with complex medical conditions. There were more children with moderate learning disabilities and emotional and behavioural difficulties being educated in specialist schools, due to the government's introduction of inclusion, sometimes alongside children with more severe learning disabilities. Consequently, the 'team around the child' looked very different.

As children with more complex medical conditions began to survive due to improved medical intervention (Joy 2005) and children with communication difficulties were diagnosed, the multidisciplinary team expanded accordingly to fulfil these increasingly severe needs, which could not be met by education alone.

Table 2.1 Employment at Willow Dene sites in 1997

1997	Assessment nursery	Moderate learning disability/ Severe learning disability school	Autistic spectrum disorder school
	(population: 40)	(population: 70)	(population: 50)
	Days per week:	Days per week:	Days per week:
Music therapy	0.5	0	1
Speech and language therapy	2 (therapist) 2 (assistant)	2	2
Physi- otherapy	Estimated: 1 (therapist) 0.5 (assistant)	Estimated: 2 (therapist) 1 (assistant)	0
Nursing	5, across all sites ⟶		

Willow Dene School

I am going to focus mainly on the development of the music therapy service in the assessment nursery for the London Borough of Greenwich. As previously mentioned with the changing demography within the specialist nursery, the children require a high level of therapy input. Having come from a community where joint work did not exist, it took me a while to establish my practice. It quickly became apparent that the children and I needed a familiar member of class staff in the room. This was essential, partly due to the young age of the children and their need for emotional security, and partly because of the staff's ability to physically handle the children.

Table 2.2 Employment at Willow Dene in 2010

2010	
Whole school (population 180)	
Music therapy	3.5 days / week
Speech and language therapy	2 x full-time posts plus a therapist working 1 day / wk and 1 full-time assistant
Physiotherapy	3.5 days / week (therapist) 3 days / week (physiotherapy technician)
Occupational therapy	3 days / week
Play therapy	1 day / week
Nursing	1 full-time nurse 3 full-time health care assistants Management time

Compared with the experience of working with my previous adult client group, I remember being bowled over by the immediacy and quickness of the children's musical responses, as well as by the overall feeling of enjoyment and often, I suspect, unconscious hope of the staff.

Rationale for music therapy intervention / integrating into nursery context

My brief, in just half a day, was to assess and provide short-term intervention (12 week blocks) for each of the 30 children during their stay in the nursery. Their stay would average one to two years. The task seemed overwhelming having come from a community which offered life-time care with little sense of urgency as no one was going anywhere or expected to move on. Here in the nursery, the input, the results, the reports and my professional opinion mattered and contributed toward the team's overall assessment of the child.

During the early years my focus was on working with the classroom staff team, rather than the rest of the small multidisciplinary team which surrounded me. I was not aware of how to use or work with my fellow therapists, compared to now, when joined-up working is essential due to the severity and complexity of the children's conditions.

To return to 1997 I will describe how I developed my clinical work and, through it, built relationships with the classroom staff team. Through my Nordoff-Robbins training, I had been taught to video/audio record every session, to analyse in detail what I was doing and then show the development of work with the use of the video edits. Toward the end of the first term, I asked the classroom staff team whether I could have some time in order to be able to feed back the work with the children and they readily gave me three weekly before school slots of 20 minutes each.

It was easy to explain music therapy and show what I was doing using musically descriptive language and paralleling it to the child's physical, cognitive, emotional and social difficulties. My aim when presenting and sharing work is to engage the audience and allow free and shared thinking and discussion to happen, thereby turning listeners from audience to participants. I have consistently found that if I accurately describe what the child and I are doing musically, then the paralleling part is easy for the staff themselves to articulate. Once the connection is made, I can then suggest possible reasons for certain behaviours and other ways of working with the child, or indeed some staff may make their own interpretations and suggestions.

This style of learning through dynamic engagement benefits both me and the team and ultimately the children. The aim is to deepen our shared understanding of the children's strengths and difficulties and the journey we are travelling together in terms of achieving the possible outcomes. After one of these early morning feedback sessions, a particularly scary and tough learning support assistant came up to me afterwards and said, 'I used to think music therapy was a load of xxxx, but now I think it's xxxxxx amazing.'

It takes a lot of extra time and effort to constantly video, analyse, edit and present, but I still notice, especially with a changing staff team, when I have not done enough feedback sessions. This lack of sharing can be demonstrated in staff attitude and interactions at various levels. This might present itself as the staff forgetting you are working that day, so taking the class out without telling you or having a new member of class staff in the sessions who is not attuned to what you are doing. I find it important to pay attention to these signs, no matter how busy I am, as it is essential that the staff and I work together with an ease of understanding in order to meet the children's needs. If, as a therapist, a class member is not with you then the energy between you can have a crippling impact on one's own ability to tune into the child. In fact, I find this energy can block or distort my connection with a child.

The following case study demonstrates how finely tuned, sensitive teamwork is a powerful way to meet the needs of a child with severely complex needs, allowing that child to access his music expression.

CASE STUDY 2.1: DANIEL

Daniel was three years old when I met him. He was blond, blue eyed, with a round beautiful face. He had a condition called lissencephaly, in which the brain is mostly smooth. For him, the resulting effects were regular fits, both major and less discernible, severe swallowing difficulties, learning difficulties and constant chest infections. He was not able to show facial or vocal expression.

I worked with Daniel for three years – much longer than was usually necessary within the nursery. Daniel was often asleep, in discomfort, unwell, fitting, his chest sounded, and indeed often was, full of fluid. For all these reasons, positioning, constant physical handling and attention to him was essential. Daniel continued to develop through the medium of music, which was particularly significant when other mediums were difficult for him to access. Music therapy therefore became a priority in his life.

Any movement, any communication for Daniel took a huge amount of energy. The people around Daniel, starting with his mother, realised that he had a subtle but definite ability to communicate, but you needed to be very attentive and focused in on his every move in order to be able to read him. The best way to connect with him was to hold him in your arms. However, in order for me to be able to communicate with him I needed access to instruments and I didn't know his body signals like the staff in his classroom did. For the first 18 months, Linda – the nursery nurse in class – became his regular support in the sessions. We developed an intimate musical dance in which each of the three parts was dependent on the other. The aim was his musical expression. Daniel's response to the music and the music's response to him was dependent on Linda feeling and facilitating his movement, which would start within his core and then as she felt his body begin to wake and move as much as it could, she would move her body to support him. My music would match his tempo, as much as I could feel it, and often bring in sequences to help him to organise his movements and be able to predict when he was going to make the mammoth effort to bring his arm up to play on the descending downbeat. Sometimes he could manage four piano clusters, which would be spaced and start off each new sequence. Occasionally these would be accompanied with an exclamatory vocal sound as he lifted his body with Linda's support to make the movement to depress the keys.

As the sessions progressed we developed a flexible structure with the choice of piano, wind-chimes and guitar, all of which offered him something different, yet known. This pattern, which would always start with the piano and then might stay with the piano or might move to either of the other instruments, began to be led by him. Each week, he made a definite choice which instrument to save his energy for. It was felt that Daniel's quality of life was enhanced by music therapy and that the treatment should continue. When he entered Key Stage 1, a new nursery nurse, Lyn, took over from Linda and our seamless dance continued. Daniel was sometimes asleep for 23 hours a day, so offering a timetable for him to fit into was not practical. We developed a team approach to enabling him to access his music therapy, which would start with his mother reminding him in the morning that it was music therapy today and then, when he arrived in school, Lyn would call me to alert me to his current state – if he was awake she would bring him straight over. If not she would call at any time throughout the day and I would adjust my timetable and fit him in. I thought of this approach as an example of implementing the true meaning of equal opportunities in terms of ensuring an equable access to music therapy. For Daniel to be on a level playing field with other children in the nursery my timetable had to respond flexibly to allow for the limitations and constraints placed on Daniel by his medical condition. This is now an approach which has informed the whole music therapy team's practice with other children.

Two years later Daniel was mostly at home and in and out of hospital due to a long and continuing period of illness. He was not expected to survive for very long. I happened to meet his mother, Constance, in a car park on Christmas Eve, where she invited me to come and say goodbye to him. Wendy Faulknall, then the head of the community children's nursing team, joined me for the visit and, ever hopeful, I put my instruments in the car. When I got there I was overwhelmed by the beauty and care of the scene – he was lying in the centre of the house on the hearth surrounded by coloured lights and toys, etc. – it was like a manger.

As music therapists, we are influenced partly by intuition and partly by the skills we are taught. My intuition strongly told me to get the keyboard and offer it to him – even though he seemed too sick to be able to play. His mother held him, commenting to both Daniel and me how unsure she was about what to do, as she had never been in his music therapy sessions. It didn't matter, as she was soon led by him, his energy and body responding to our familiar musical relationship, reaching out to play the piano in his usual style. The session – if that's what it was – was short but definite. One of those experiences which left us all stunned and moved and grateful to be part of a child's last creative and willful moments. He died two days later.

Daniel's music therapy both in school and in particular the experience at his home sowed the seeds for Wendy Faulknall (now Director of Care for Demelza Hospice in Kent and the new Demelza South East London) and myself to create a new music therapy post. This post would follow children across community settings and therefore be responsive to the complex health needs of the children in a way which was not possible with organisation-based services, i.e. when Daniel was not on school premises I was not able to provide therapy for him at home or in hospital. For children like Daniel the impact of music therapy on the child and family's quality of life was huge and therefore the lack of access to this therapy when the child was too ill to go to school was significant.

Demelza South East London has been open since June 2009. A music therapist works for them two days per week, embedded into the Greenwich Community Health Services Music Therapy Service, commissioned by Demelza, with a Jessie's Fund contribution. This is the first such collaborative post with the statutory sector for Demelza. Children from my caseload and other colleagues' are also seen at Demelza. Daniel opened a door for us and we have all followed the idea and have taken it forward. This is an exciting new service for Greenwich and its neighbouring boroughs. Although this service is in its infancy, Demelza Kent has a well-established music therapy post, which has flourished for many years. Daniel was a child who influenced the way I work and made me expand my thinking and my creativity to fit his needs. In these days of increasing government legislation and data inputting, we are even more challenged to keep our doors, minds and music open and creative.

2010 at Willow Dene

The multidisciplinary team is now huge – we have a therapy team of 24 catering for a growing population of both children with complex communication disorders (namely autism and severe learning disabilities) and those with severe medical complications. The level and importance of skill and knowledge required by education and health staff must not be underestimated. Staff are now required to undertake certain medical procedures for some children, such as giving rectal diazepam or suctioning. Music therapists are required to equip themselves with much more medical knowledge as well as learning how to use and understand the child's means of communication, for example: signing or using symbols for children with autism. The school operates a total communication environment and we must be part of it. Now, before I even meet a child I check with the speech and language therapists about the child's level of understanding and their communication system. I additionally liaise with physiotherapists where appropriate about positioning. Unless these core needs are understood, the child can be uncomfortable, in pain, or maybe have raised anxiety if I have not communicated with them in a way that they understand.

Figure 2.1 'Altogether now!' Group music therapy with children from Willow Dene

Full class groups and joined-up working

Until 2005 children were seen on an individual basis, mostly supported by class staff or in small groups, sometimes jointly run with class staff or with speech and language therapists, but with the music therapist taking the lead in the delivery of the group. The aims of the joint intervention were to capitalise on our joint knowledge and skills and learn from one another through transfer of skills both during the session and afterwards in the debriefing and joint record-keeping.

Figure 2.2 Singing to and with each other. Monitoring children to communicate through music

As the client group grew in numbers and complexity, it was even more important as music therapists to be more visible throughout the whole school, demonstrating what we could do, through group work, as well as being able to identify the children who needed to be seen individually. Therefore all three music therapists aim to work their way round all 18 classes in the whole school, by undertaking full class groups as well as identifying, along with the therapy and classroom staff team, the children who need smaller group or individual music therapy.

The advantage of being in a shared office is that ideas can emerge through informal discussions, often starting from a stance of peer support. One such discussion with a speech and language therapist concerned a group of seven-year-olds with severe learning disabilities and autism. She was struggling with how to encourage some cohesion and shared activity. This discussion led to a joint music therapy and speech group. We ran the group within the class with all the class staff, interspersed between the children. The speech and language therapist acted as co-therapist from the floor, whilst the music therapist jointly led the sections from the keyboard. This was a great learning experience for both of us: I realised how crucial my timing needed to be in relation to children with autism. For some, a one-beat turn-taking song was too quick for them to listen, process and react. However, a full group improvisation with everyone playing an instrument all at once was equally difficult, as the children were often not able to listen and process everyone else's lines and could then become absorbed in the mechanics of the instrument or become overwhelmed by the sound level, some adverse behaviours resulted. By contrast the speech and language therapists also learned that with the therapist's perseverance and the week-by-week familiarity, the children *could* listen, process and react when a groove could be found in the group improvisation. Those fleeting spontaneous responses, so difficult to elicit in children with autism, began to be more apparent and available to them.

From time to time, we shadow each other in the multidisciplinary team in order to better understand the others do and how to share ideas. On one such occasion, when I was shadowing the physiotherapist, she spoke about wanting to do a sitting group for a group of children for whom she was encouraging independent sitting. Each child's seat was different dependent on their need, such as a class chair, a bench, a ball, etc. On observation I deemed that we should use music to help the children forget about the new equipment they were seated on and thereby hope they would stop hopping off. Each of the above joint groups took place over a term and proved successful in their different ways. Since then further class groups have been run in the nursery over the past year. In one of them there were seven children with profound and multiple learning disabilities and each member of the multidisciplinary team was present on various weeks. For all of us it was a useful opportunity for assessment and a good way of demonstrating, to the class staff and each other, different ways of working with the children.

As a music therapist running class groups, I think of it as a method of triaging – I have the opportunity to assess who finds it difficult to function in a group and, at the same time, through joint debriefing with the multidisciplinary team, I can work out why. In the most recent group it was evident from his behaviour and background that one little boy needed some individual work. He was not able to access the music-making in the group, showing a high level of resistive behaviours, possibly due to lack of experience, low self-esteem and minimal previous peer contact. Through individual work my aim became to develop his confidence and enable him to access that spontaneous part of his responses which he kept blocking.

My day in the nursery is now very varied, moving from class group to training session, to supervising students, to individual work and last week to jointly leading a whole school INSET on joint working with the therapy team. The staff team totals about 100, with 24 therapists and students on placement.

The INSET day was preceded by an away-day for the multidisciplinary team the previous summer in which we had the opportunity, primarily, to reflect on our practice. During this day we considered a number of different factors which have impacted on our work:

- As a team we have expanded dramatically over the years.

- Our workload and skill level has had to increase in order to meet the needs of severe and complex cases.

- Our accountability has increased and a need for more joined-up agency working, partly stemming from a climate of serious case reviews.

We shared our knowledge and skills through presentations of our work on video and explaining the theory behind it. The deputy head joined us for the whole day and the head teacher for part of it. Afterwards they invited us to re-run the day to the whole school staff team, hence the whole school INSET day.

Rather than re-run the day, we decided to involve class staff in each presentation, showing examples of current joined-up practice, thereby achieving in the presentation what we were aiming to do in practice – namely joined-up working for the ultimate benefit of the children and their families. These two staff development days helped consolidate our joined-up health and education team approach and allowed the team to reflect on all the recent developments and value the work that is going on. Of course, time for reflective practice and for skills sharing is an eternal journey, which needs continuous work and investment from all involved in the children's care.

Both the music therapy service within Willow Dene and I, personally and professionally, have come a long way over the past 13 years, hopefully adapting to the ever-changing needs of the children through opening doors, minds and music.

Chapter 3

Nordoff-Robbins Music Therapy in a Nursery Setting

Supporting Music Therapy Students on Placement

Chris Achenbach

Introduction

In this chapter the author will present the development of a Nordoff-Robbins music therapy service at a Scottish Children and Families Centre, focusing particularly on the therapeutic use of music and song with children up to five years old. The service is also a first-year placement setting for students training in music therapy, and the chapter includes an examination of some of the core clinical/musical skills developed by students during placement.

Eskside Children and Families Centre

Eskside Children and Families Centre (not its real name) is a Scottish council service established under Section 27 of the Children (Scotland) Act. The centre provides support to vulnerable children from birth to five years of age, and assistance to their families. A service is also offered to children with additional or complex needs, or who are affected by issues of disability. Although formally part of the regional social work service grouping, the centre provides pre-school education in collaboration with the regional education department. Eskside is the only service of its kind in the council area.

In 2009 inspection by the Care Commission resulted in a grading at the highest level and the service was commended for its excellence. Many parents and visiting professionals have also praised its work.

At the time of writing, a music therapy service has been established at Eskside for just under four years. The service is funded within Eskside's own budget, as no NHS-based music therapy provision for children exists in the council area (in which several schools and other services also purchase music therapy directly from charitable agencies or self-employed practitioners). Music therapy is purchased for three hours on a midweek morning, allowing for approximately two hours' contact time during the session.

As with many other family-orientated services, the Eskside service has a considerable community presence, focusing on assessing the needs of children and families, and offering ongoing support to them. However, Eskside's day-care service is perhaps the most visible, and certainly the most intensively staffed, component of its work. Although the design of this service during the period of music therapy provision has varied according to the needs of the children and families that use it (not least by dividing attending children into age-related groupings), its consistent feature continues to be the provision of staffed playrooms within the building.

On the morning on which the music therapist attends, up to 17 children (more if additional staff support is arranged) aged up to five years may attend the two main playrooms, many with their parents or carers. For a number of these children where there is a history of parenting difficulties, the service is the setting for supervised contact with a parent, while other parents are simply welcome to spend time in the playroom with their child or children. A proportion of the children present with additional needs across a broad spectrum, including autistic spectrum disorders, cerebral palsy, developmental delay and problems arising from prematurity.

Eskside playroom staff are skilled in supporting children as they explore, and grow from, the experience of play. The Centre information booklet for professionals notes that it is by means of physical, social and cognitive play that 'children learn to master basic skills and to discover some pattern in the confusion of the world in which they find themselves'. Clearly the types of play mentioned here have their parallel in children's experience of music therapy, particularly in motor skills-based work with instruments and opportunities to share experience and enjoyment with peers. Music therapy work has taken place in a number of identified rooms within Eskside, all of which have been adjacent to the main playrooms. For obvious reasons, the most effective rooms have been those with reasonable sound insulation, and the present room has proved appropriate, being fairly small, relatively unencumbered with furniture or toys and reasonably distant from the playrooms.

I am a Nordoff-Robbins trained practitioner of nearly 25 years standing, and have been employed both in the NHS and voluntary sectors, and am now freelance. Paul Nordoff and Clive Robbins developed their distinctive approach to music therapy from 1959 onwards. Their early collaboration has been examined by Aigen (1998), and their development of clinical strategies and techniques of clinical improvisation is more fully described in Nordoff and Robbins (2007). The Nordoff-Robbins methodology is now employed by therapists across a broad range of clinical practice with both children and adults.

Music therapy at Eskside

The business of music therapy is to harness the potential of musical experience in ways which meet the individualised needs of each child, and to offer a physically and psychologically trustworthy structure within which this work can be effective. Assuming that the clinical application of improvised music and song is viewed as a central component of UK music therapy practice, it must particularly be in work with younger children that such a component is of vital importance. Music, and especially song, is a core component of early mother–infant relationships. For very young children it provides an enhanced medium for the development of language, interpersonal skills both in the context of parental and peer relationships, and skills of self-expression.

There is undoubtedly a widespread base of good practice in the therapeutic use of music, ranging from mother and toddler music and movement groups to nursery education, to help achieve the above aims. Many fellow professionals, particularly those advocating community music therapy, such as Pavlicevic and Ansdell (2004) and Stige et al. (2010), seek to locate music therapy practice within this spectrum of music work, and I have often found myself considering this too, not least when teaching strategies for therapeutic music-making which relate to aspects of music therapy practice.

In my opinion, music therapy is distinctive, however. As a therapeutic intervention, its nature is that of clinical focus, including assessment of client need, identification and employment of specific clinical strategies, continuous assessment of clinical work, and regular review of its effectiveness. The clinical relationship itself is uniquely distinctive in its combination of musical and psychological components. The nature of this relationship is contingent on the child's response in that musical activity is not imposed on the relationship, but grows within it; similarly, the aims of music therapy with a child, however carefully considered beforehand, essentially evolve from the experience (and analysis) of the work itself.

From the outset it has been clear that for most of the children and family members attending Eskside, group music therapy has been the best way of delivering a service within the limited time available. However, a small number of children have needed to be seen individually. It has usually been possible to arrange for up to three groups and two individual sessions on a weekly basis, thus ensuring that all attending children (if appropriate) receive music therapy.

For both group and individual work, instruments are provided by the therapist on a peripatetic basis. These include a digital piano, a selection of larger and smaller drums (including an ocean drum), up to two metallophones or glockenspiels, wind-chimes and bellsprays, and a selection of smaller (including shaken) instruments. Most sessions are audio recorded for subsequent analysis.

Group music therapy

The structure of group music therapy sessions at Eskside varies considerably according to the needs of the children concerned. Groups may consist of up to five children, but are usually smaller; three or sometimes four children normally attend. Parents and carers are welcome as participants, although some do not feel confident in this role and prefer to observe, and are still encouraged to sit in the group. Playroom staff members are also always welcome and regularly attend, often to supervise parental contact.

Group sessions typically last between 20 and 25 minutes, depending on the tolerance of the children concerned. Participants (children and adults) sit in a rough semi-circle starting clockwise from the treble end of the piano. If the therapist is working alone, he or she may sit at the piano or directly in front of the children. Children are normally encouraged to remain seated (on chairs, cushions or an adult's lap, according to particular needs) during the group, but may sometimes stand to play, walk across to the instruments to choose one, or hold an instrument for another child to play. The therapist usually takes care to remain seated to provide an appropriate model for the children.

Groups usually start and finish with simple hello and goodbye or thank you songs. Intermediate activities tend to have an instrumental focus. These are split broadly into activities using instruments which can be played simultaneously, two examples being bellsprays which can be individually held, and the large gathering drum which can be played in a circle by all the children, and those encouraging turn-taking and using a single instrument such as a drum. Some instruments, such as metallophone, may easily be shared by two children together.

Activity structures evolve according to the needs and responses of the children and normally incorporate a simple refrain song; this, however, will very often be improvised as part of the activity, or specific words or phrases like 'look' or 'listen' may be incorporated into an existing song. Songs include children's names and other key words wherever possible but wordless song (usually as support, but sometimes jointly with the children) is also employed during many activities. Some songs may be more complex, for example, to support several different ways of playing an instrument, such as hitting and stroking a drum.

Key components of instrumental activities include playing together, turn-taking at varying paces, opportunities to play individually for short or longer periods, choosing from a selection of instruments, choosing the next player and sharing single instruments, such as an ocean drum, between two or more children.

While the piano is available for use as instrumental support for activities, it is not always used. Song is by far the most important means of supporting the children's responses, reinforced when necessary by the use of piano or another instrument as appropriate. In general, older children (from two years upwards) seem to derive most benefit from being supported by means of accompanying instrumental music, whereas younger children often reach for the accompanying instrument instead of the one they are already playing.

Some movement and action songs may also be used, although in practice focusing on shared instrumental activity has proved the most useful strategy for this work.

While parents (usually mothers) often attend group sessions with their children, this experience can be difficult for some. This can be because some parents expect their children to behave or play nicely, but is more usually because the relationship between parent and child has been damaged or strained, for example, by the child's removal from the parental home. Parents who are receiving help with parenting skills, and/or who only see their children at the centre, may feel that they are under close scrutiny during the time they spend at Eskside. As a result, they may be highly attuned to what they perceive as negative behaviour on the part of the child, viewing this as a perceived failure on their own part, perhaps becoming upset or angry and even taking their children out of sessions. Children who only see their parents at Eskside often appear unusually unresponsive to them, or behave in manipulative or oppositional ways. Whatever the circumstances, music therapy can still offer an opportunity for parents and children to experience music play together.

CASE STUDY 3.1: GROUP MUSIC THERAPY FOR JILL

Jill was three when she first attended music therapy at Eskside. She presented with cerebral palsy with an associated learning disability and had no speech. During six initial group sessions (with up to four other children from her playroom) she consistently appeared anxious when other children were playing instruments or vocalising, particularly with unexpected or high levels of sound. She refused to remain in the room during two additional individual sessions, becoming upset and starting to cry immediately upon entering.

Group activities were planned to avoid use of especially large or loud instruments. Jill's anxiety appeared to lessen slightly when she held an instrument herself and this seemed to be because she could directly control the sound. She also seemed more settled in a group session attended by only two other children. She seemed particularly drawn to wind-chimes and bellsprays, and later ocean drum, in shared activity, but still became increasingly upset when other children were playing. It was clear that she was becoming anxious about simply entering the room at the start of sessions.

Due to her anxiety, Jill was given a break from music therapy for around seven months. When she attended once more, she sat on a staff member's lap during sessions, initially behind a low room divider close to, but separate from, the other children. She seemed comfortable with this arrangement and the divider was dispensed with after four sessions. Jill was subsequently able to take part in all activities without becoming upset by noise levels, and clearly grew to enjoy the liveliness and humour of group sessions. On the few occasions when she seemed concerned by loud or unexpected sounds, her response was limited to a fleeting change of expression. She was able to choose, play and share a wide variety of instruments, working hard to hold both instruments and beaters and often imitating others' playing styles during shared activity, including circle activities seated around a large gathering drum. She often vocalised when playing or waiting to play, used gesture to communicate and started to sign and vocalise single words and names.

Jill continued to attend and enjoy group music therapy sessions until leaving the Eskside service to commence school.

Individual music therapy

Reviewing the service, it is clear that there have been three broad reasons for children to be seen individually. A number of children with autistic spectrum disorders have found it difficult to function in a group setting. In general, group work has challenged their ability to share a setting with their peers and/or to share the attention of an adult while doing so. A second group of children are those who have been dealing with difficult life circumstances, which often include separation from their parent(s). They have often presented with significant emotional difficulties and frequently with challenging behaviours, particularly towards a parent who they have only been meeting for a short time each week at Eskside. A third group of children have received individual therapy due to their level of additional and sometimes complex needs.

As might be expected, the strong focus on improvised activity in group work is also found in individual music therapy with children at Eskside. In this work, the form of the session depends entirely on the needs and responses of the child concerned. Children may be encouraged to make music with the therapist, choosing, playing and/or sharing a number of instruments while doing so. Hello and goodbye or thank you songs tend to mark the start and finish of work, and songs with or without words are a characteristic component of the jointly created music, as well as of the therapist's supporting music. However, the child's responses completely determine the progress and content of each session and in this respect the created music is, like the therapeutic relationship, a seamless and continuous component of the work.

For children who have been damaged by life experience, it is essential that music therapy offers a robust and trustworthy setting in which their responses, behaviours and emotions can be contained and accepted. This is no less important for children with additional needs such as autism, even though the aims of the work may vary.

A child's responses in individual therapy may also include extra-musical play, such as disassembling a metallophone or building a structure out of several drums then knocking it down. Such play can be an explicit re-enactment of the child's experience of loss and violence.

CASE STUDY 3.2: INDIVIDUAL MUSIC THERAPY FOR SARAH

Sarah, whose family circumstances were difficult, was nearly three when she commenced music therapy sessions at Eskside. During initial group sessions her playing on instruments was loud and rather uncontrolled and she seemed intolerant of sharing activities with others. In subsequent individual sessions her playing was often gentle and responsive to accompanying music and song for short periods, but these qualities tended to be obscured during frequent episodes of behaviour with strongly compulsive features. At such times she treated instruments roughly, playing dramatic loud clusters on piano with fists and elbows, disassembling tuned percussion, throwing beaters away or trying to jump onto drums. She often seemed regretful of such behaviour immediately afterwards as if wary of a negative response from me.

While Sarah often verbally narrated aspects of activities as they progressed and often chanted words or phrases, she did not actually sing with me until her seventh session as we played drum together. Shared song, particularly singing 'goodbye' together, became a significant component of most subsequent sessions and she accepted my accompanying song during most activities.

Sarah increasingly spent time in non-musical play with groups of instruments. In her tenth session she created a family group of 'mummy, daddy and girl' with two different-sized drums and metallophone, saying that she 'needed the mummy drum [to] be happy next to the girl'. In the following session she placed the 'baby' ocean drum under the large 'daddy' drum then hid under the large drum herself, speaking in a 'baby' voice as she asked me to play it. In a subsequent session the metallophone in the 'family' grouping became a 'sad baby' which she knocked over and disassembled before reassembling it, accepting my help to do so. In her final individual sessions Sarah often returned to this family group, representing 'baby' with metallophone or rainstick, knocking the instrument over then setting it upright once more, clearly becoming more confident and less anxious about doing so. She also seemed more relaxed about sharing the piano keyboard with me, initiating territorial finger games from each end of the keyboard and playing exuberant runs of many notes up and down the keys.

After 16 individual sessions, Sarah briefly returned to group music therapy during which, while sometimes dominating the group by her behaviour, she seemed increasingly able to share a range of activities with other children.

Therapeutic song

It seems important to further describe some distinctive features of therapeutic song as used in work at Eskside. It will be clear from the above paragraphs that the most effective songs appear to be those which either evolve from improvised encounter or activity, or are chosen to enhance such activity. In either case, this does not necessarily mean that the song should be entirely original or new; rather, that the therapist should intuitively perceive a fit between it and its utilisation. Whether or not the song is pre-composed, it immediately becomes an evolutionary component of the current therapeutic encounter, itself subject to change and evolution. It will come as no surprise that fragments or phrases of song may well be just as significant as those songs perceived as complete. In addition, the pitches and pitch contours of sung melodies or melodic fragments, and the extent to which song or song fragments successfully mirror speech rhythms inherent in their lyrics (if any), are significantly important considerations. It is clear that the care and attention to such detail shown by music therapy practitioners in their utilisation of song is a distinctive and important feature of music therapy practice.

Liaison with Eskside staff

The therapist and students normally take part in the playroom music circle at the conclusion of the morning sessions, working with Eskside staff to support children as they choose and participate in a range of songs and activities.

It must be added that it has been vital to maintain good communication with Eskside staff at all times, not least because music therapy is physically separate from the playrooms. Written reports are made available on a regular basis and these have been the most effective means of contributing to review meetings, as these are usually held on days when the music therapist is not present. However, it does seem to be the practical day-to-day collaborative work with playroom staff that provides the strongest means of forging and sustaining positive relationships.

Eskside as a student placement

Since 2007 Eskside has been a first-year placement for students on the two-year music therapy (Nordoff-Robbins) Masters programme at Queen Margaret University, Edinburgh. The placement concerned lasts for 30 weeks between October and May, so each student (or student pair) has an opportunity to get to know the service well. An initial period of clinical observation between October and December is followed by the start of students' own practice, with responsibility each for work with an individual child and a group. Responsibility for clinical supervision is split between the placement supervisor who oversees the student in the placement setting and also has specific responsibility for supervising group work, and a supervisor tutor, based on campus, who supervises students' work with individual clients. The supervisor meets the students in small groups on a weekly basis.

Students are required to keep a contemporaneous placement log as well as a personal reflective diary. A mid-placement review helps in identifying both students' strengths and also areas for further development. A written comparative case study of two children receiving music therapy is submitted in January and a case study presentation of work with an individual client is made to course staff at the conclusion of the placement. The student's placement logs are also submitted at this time. In addition, the placement supervisor and supervisor tutor complete a final profile of professional competence for each student. The students must pass all sections of this profile which include clinical awareness, musical and therapeutic skills, interpersonal and intrapersonal skills, clinical management and supervision.

Placements are, by their nature, distinctively different from each other, not least in the approach taken by the placement supervisor in helping to shape each student's learning experience. The remainder of this chapter focuses on the placement experience at Eskside, and offers a personal view of some of the learning processes involved, both for the students and the music therapist.

For placement at Eskside, it is clear that the reality of clinical practice shapes student experience in a number of ways. These include the need to respond flexibly to children's varied attendance patterns which results in shifting membership of groups, and the need not just to accommodate, but to actively welcome, participation by parents and carers in sessions. In addition, the practical requirement for students to prepare for autonomous clinical responsibility in group work has resulted in their staged active involvement in group sessions well in advance of the formal start of their placement. This results in a blending of observation and clinical practice which helps to smooth the transition between the two, and significantly increases the time available for the students to gain confidence in hands-on work.

Much is asked of music therapy students on a first placement. While learning *how* to practise, they must also develop their understanding of *why*. This involves relating theory to practice by means of observation and analysis. They are simultaneously required to prepare for, then engage in, their own practice, planning for and delivering sessions, then analysing, documenting and ultimately presenting evidence of the observed progress and perceived experience of their clients. As psychological therapists they must also continuously reflect on their personal experience and process. They must demonstrate an ability to work effectively and courteously within the placement setting. Not least, they must develop their ability to become what might be termed clinical musicians. This last area of skills development is unique to music therapy, and the following paragraphs describe some of its features in relation to placement at Eskside.

Individual and group music therapy each require the employment of a number of core clinical musical skills: the first of these is the ability on the part of the practitioner to sustain an improvised musical encounter, attuning to what the child brings moment by moment, and responding appropriately.

In musical terms, what perhaps distinguishes supportive improvisation in music therapy from other interactive paradigms (e.g. jazz) may be the simple unpredictability of the child's response, ranging from no engagement at all to complete involvement in shared music-making, and including instrumental playing, vocalising and body movements. This challenges the therapist's ability to improvise both vocally and instrumentally in appropriate and effective ways.

In practical terms much depends on the student therapist's ability to harness their increasing improvisational resources working not just within their level of competence, but also by extending the application of those resources while continuously attuning to the child. In practice, this balance will sometimes be difficult to achieve. Personal music practice seems to help enormously, helping with the student's instrumental and vocal confidence during the sessions themselves. Campus-based teaching exposes students to an increasing range of improvisational musical resources as the placement progresses. These include such areas as modes and scales, including church and pentatonic modes, chord construction and the use of chord inversions which is a particular feature of a Nordoff-Robbins curriculum, and music from a range of cultures. If time is not taken by the individual student to become familiar with such material, it is not only difficult to access it in an instinctive way during sessional work, but the attempt to do so can have a negative effect on the amount of attention that can be given by the trainee therapist to what is actually happening in the moment.

In a sense the development of a trainee therapist's ability to improvise spontaneously may actually reflect the freedom that it is hoped the child can experience; to engage freely and expressively, share this experience in the moment of encounter, sustain it over the period of the session and develop and learn from it over a number of weeks and months. Both therapist and child have opportunities to grow.

In group activities a second core skill seems to be about maintaining a balance of attention between individual clients and the group as a whole. A basic example here might be facilitating an instrumental activity with a core 'refrain' song, offering children the experience of playing in turn for a shorter or longer time. A refrain may offer the opportunity to turn-take at a faster pace, before a single child, or several children, are invited to improvise with supportive vocal and/or instrumental support. In practice a student therapist may find it difficult to move between phases of this activity because they are unused to focusing on the many whilst being simultaneously attentive to individual children's responses and behaviour.

A third, related core skill seems to be that of adaptivity. As an example, an activity such as that described in the previous paragraph will nearly always require to be adapted in the moment. There are many possible scenarios here. A restless group's attention may usefully be refocused by incorporating more frequent episodes of fast turn-taking. Another group of children, more used to sharing activities with each other, may welcome longer opportunities to play in turn. Children may sing the refrain song in different ways; at different pitches, at a different pace, with a changed melody, or with different words, and so invite its transformation. Children with delayed physical response due to disability may transform the experience of brisk turn-taking to something more deliberate and purposeful. A group may evolve a particular response to an activity; for example, children may copy their peers by each hiding their faces behind a drum, or may conceal a beater behind their backs in turn, thus transforming the flow of an activity.

Any of this may challenge a therapist in training, particularly if a specific activity has been planned for a group session and not least if the facilitating roles have also been defined and rehearsed beforehand by two students. For this reason, students on placement at Eskside are encouraged to view group work activities as capable of being changed and even transformed, rather than as having fixed forms. This encouragement extends to those songs which they compose themselves for work in a session, all of which might well initially be viewed by the creators as finished and perhaps to be included in a portfolio of compositions. In the case of songs, pitches or keys may need to be changed; accompaniment if included may often be over-complex or too dense (and this is often the case with strummed guitar accompaniments), and in almost every case, the song will grow and change as it is used in work with a child or children.

Students differ as much as do the placements which they attend. It seems important to note that, whether or not a student views the process of training as the acquisition of a completely new skill set, it is also important that they may feel able to incorporate their existing skills into their professional development as music therapists. Many students with whom the writer has worked have already been skilled musicians, music teachers or facilitators. They might initially feel that the skills they have are irrelevant and all must be relearned. With support, and as they grow in confidence, these students can be encouraged to value and build on the skills they already have, while recognising that a very different approach is needed as a clinical music therapist.

Conclusion

I think the development of a music therapy service for children and families attending Eskside has been successful and provides further evidence of the appropriateness of this modality in such a setting. It is also clear that the first-year students placed at Eskside have benefited from the experience in a number of ways, not least by the opportunity to integrate their initial understanding of theory and practice into face-to-face work with the children and adults concerned.

Chapter 4

Multiple Views of
Music Therapy

Ann Bruce and Suzie High

Introduction

This chapter describes music therapy with Mia, a five-year-old girl with profound and multiple learning difficulties. Group music therapy is just one of many activities and therapies that Mia participates in during the week, as is commonly the case with children with severe disabilities: in addition to her curriculum-based education, Mia is also seen by a physiotherapist, occupational therapist and speech and language therapist. The aim in writing this chapter was to gather different people's perspectives of music therapy and to place music therapy in the wider context of Mia's life by bringing together the observations of her family and some of the other professionals who work with her. Although the music therapist has particular aims in mind when working with a child like Mia, and sees particular moments in each session as being especially significant, the authors (music therapist and teacher) wanted to see what other people thought. For example, might Mia's mother see music therapy as benefiting Mia in quite a different way to how the music therapist perceives it? What do other health professionals who work with Mia see when they watch music therapy? And how might what happens in music therapy relate to Mia's time in class?

To share information about music therapy and gather different perspectives about it, the authors videoed a music therapy session with Mia's group and selected three short extracts in which the focus had been on her. Copies of the extracts were given to Mia's speech and language therapist (Clare Myers), physiotherapist (Ida Creber) and occupational therapist (Rachel Doherty) and they were asked for their observations.

They were asked to comment on anything that they saw in the extracts, but in particular:

- How did what they saw in music therapy relate to their own work with Mia?

- What did they think that music therapy was providing that was *different* from other interventions that Mia received?

Mia's mother was invited to view the DVD with the authors and to talk about what she had seen and how she thought Mia's music therapy related to other aspects of her life. She was also given a copy of the DVD to take home so that the rest of the family could watch it. As well as the comments that she gave the authors in person, Mia's mother wrote a detailed letter on behalf of the family, giving their views on what they saw. This information is incorporated into the chapter.

The school context

Mia attends Sandside Lodge School in Ulverston, Cumbria, and this is where her music therapy takes place. Sandside Lodge is a school for pupils aged 2–19 with severe and profound learning difficulties. The school has a child-centred focus that respects the fact that each child will have his or her own unique life journey. The school aims to teach its youngest pupils fundamental learning skills. These vary from person to person and might include interaction skills and early National Curriculum skills. Older pupils develop independence, self-management, self-organisation and early vocational skills.

Supporting and encouraging total communication (communication through multiple means, including language, signing, symbols and pictures) underpins the work of each classroom. Teachers celebrate and develop the communication ability of the pupils, and so music therapy fits neatly into the total communication ethos of the school.

Music therapy was established at the school in 2007 with a grant from Jessie's Fund, a charity that supports music therapy for children with special needs. The music therapist works at the school for one day a week. Joint working between the music therapist and other health professionals in a school setting can be very productive both for the child and the professionals involved (Twyford 2008). However, direct joint working has not so far been possible in this school as the music therapist's day in school does not coincide with that of the physiotherapist, occupational therapist or speech and language therapist. This is not an uncommon situation where each professional works in a number of schools. The consistent link with the child's teacher becomes central in this instance, and it has been very useful that Mia's teacher has been willing and able to come to the music therapy group each week, not only supporting the work directly, but forming a bridge between music therapy and other aspects of Mia's education. Writing this chapter provided an opportunity for the authors to focus closely on one child and to invest more time than is usually possible in linking with other health professionals and the child's family.

Mia

Mia is in the Early Years class. Mia has an identical twin, and is diagnosed with twin-to-twin transfer syndrome, where an abnormality in a shared placenta causes an imbalanced flow of blood between identical twins during pregnancy. She has cerebral palsy, which particularly affects her right side. She is therefore very left-side dominant in both arm and leg movements. Mia has physiotherapy on a regular basis to build overall strength, and in particular to encourage more use of her right arm and hand, which are very tight and weak.

Mia has severe learning difficulties and does not use any language. However, since starting school full-time she has developed a good sense of cause and effect and now uses switches regularly to make something happen or to communicate intentionally. She enjoys using the large interactive whiteboard to cause a reaction. Mia is a very sociable child: she can spend many minutes watching and enjoying interaction between other people. She co-operates best when she has peers to work with. She finds humour in accidents and mishaps, and enjoys other children being told off.

The music therapy group

Mia attends a music therapy group with two of her peers (Jamie and Brandon), who also have severe learning difficulties. The group started at the beginning of the school year but the filming that was mentioned earlier occurred after the group had been running for four months. Sessions take place weekly and last around 35 minutes. The group is led by the music therapist, Ann, with the support of Suzie, Mia's teacher. The aim of the group is to enable the children to engage and interact as fully and as independently as possible using sounds and music as the main medium of interaction. The group starts and finishes with familiar greeting and goodbye songs which provide a frame to the session. Within the main part of the session there is no fixed structure. Instead, opportunities are provided for spontaneous interaction by offering choices of instruments and by following the children's lead whenever possible. Ware's description of a 'responsive environment' sits well with this approach: a responsive environment is one 'in which people get responses to their actions, get the opportunity to give responses to the actions of others, and have an opportunity to take the lead in interaction' (Ware 2003, p.1).

Individual aims for Mia in music therapy included encouraging her to use her voice communicatively, developing purposeful use of her hands and enabling her to initiate communication and interaction. As it happened, on the day of the filming, one of the other children was absent, so there were only two children in the group that day (Mia and Jamie).

Extract 1: Mia and the recorder
The music therapist describes the extract
I begin playing the treble recorder. At first I am facing Jamie. Mia smiles and pats her left hand on her right hand (a sign that Mum says means 'more'). She raises her right arm. Jamie vocalises loudly, and waves his arms. Mia is quiet, and her head is down. I am not sure whether she is watching and I move closer to her. Mia sits up, gives a big smile and reaches out to the recorder and pushes it away. I vocalise 'Uh oh!' This feels to me to be a moment of playful connection and control rather than a rejection. Mia turns to Suzie, who is sitting on her left hand side, and reaches out with her left hand. Suzie holds out her own hand, palm up, and Mia pats it rhythmically, whilst turning to Suzie and smiling. I play along on the recorder to Mia's patting, mirroring its tempo and firm character. This continues for around 15 seconds which is quite a sustained physical engagement for Mia. Jamie is quiet during this, but vocalises again when Mia stops patting. Mia reaches out with her left hand, and makes an excited-sounding, ascending vocal sound whilst pushing the recorder away with another big smile. Mia begins to 'dance' in her chair, bouncing her arms up and down vigorously. Again, I play in time with her bouncing. After a pause, Mia reaches out again, and once more pushes the recorder. My playing mirrors the sudden surge of this movement. Jamie begins to vocalise a kind of low hum. Mia vocalises a high 'ay' sound, turns briefly

to Suzie with a smile, and begins bouncing again. This continues on and off for around 30 seconds, sometimes accompanied by excited-sounding, squealy vocal sounds. I continue to respond to her bouncing with my playing, weaving responses to Jamie's vocal sounds into the music. Mia then turns and puts her left hand out to Suzie again, and begins patting again, faster than her arm-bouncing. I respond by accelerating my playing to match her speed.

Jamie vocalises more strongly and at a higher pitch and reaches out to hold the end of the recorder when I approach him. While I focus on Jamie, Mia is quieter for a few seconds, but then smiles and starts bouncing her arms and vocalising, in key with my playing. I wonder if she is calling me back to her. Suzie claps her hands, mirroring Mia's rhythm. For a few moments, Mia and Jamie seem equally engaged, both moving their arms and bodies in ways that seem to respond to and also direct the music. Then Jamie becomes more vocal, making long ascending and descending vocal sounds. Mia is again quieter. After a moment I turn to her, and play a short phrase on the recorder – an invitation to engage. She looks thoughtful, and taps her lips with her left index finger, which Suzie mirrors. Mia suddenly bursts into activity, bouncing her arms and vocalising strongly. Jamie also vocalises. Mia turns away for a moment and turns back with a wide open mouth. I wonder if she is yawning, but then she begins a long, high vocal sound. At first this seems a happy sound, but then changes to an 'ee ah' sound which, to me, sounds less comfortable. I wonder if she has had enough, and I turn back to Jamie. Mia's head is down and she has her left hand to her mouth. She begins to vocalise again, quietly, then gradually sits up in her chair and smiles. Jamie begins to vocalise once more and I reflect his sounds on the recorder. Mia begins to bounce her arms and she turns briefly to Jamie. Mia then pats her left hand on her arm, vocalising 'ah ah' in the same rhythm. This feels to me to be a very direct attempt to engage. I turn back to her, play a rhythmical answer and then pause. Mia immediately answers with more patting and rhythmical vocalising. When she stops, I turn back to Jamie and Mia waggles her arms again.

Observations from Mia's speech and language therapist

Mia appears really engaged in this extract: her main focus is on Ann, although she also watches the other child and looks at and engages with Suzie. This is in direct contrast to the high degree of 'nosiness' (interrupting what other children are doing when the focus is not on her)

Mia displays at other times. She watches and listens even when she is not the focus of attention herself and does not resort to some of the more disruptive behaviours she can exhibit elsewhere.

She pushed the recorder away, which could have been interpreted as rejection, but her behaviour during the rest of the session indicates that far from rejecting the recorder she actually thoroughly enjoys the activity. This is a useful observation which could influence both the way Mia is offered choices and adults' interpretations of her choice-making behaviours.

Mia interacted with Suzie, who was sitting beside her, and enjoyed the opportunity to clap hands following the tempo of the music. An increased tempo led to Mia using whole body movement to react and when the tempo and volume decreased she became still and calmer for a short while, then began moving and vocalising to indicate that she wanted the music to increase in tempo and volume. This was in addition to the left hand tapping on her right hand/arm which Mia uses for 'more' and 'I like this'.

At one point when Mia was not the focus of attention she began touching her lip, opening her mouth and looking at Ann playing the recorder – it would be interesting to see if this occurs again as it may be interpreted as an early message such as 'look!' or 'I want to do it'. Mia used vocalisation to great effect to tell the adult that she wanted to be included in the activity but she was not unreasonably demanding of attention and waited for the other child to have a turn.

Observations from Mia's physiotherapist and occupational therapist

It was an absolute joy to watch Mia in music therapy. She clearly enjoyed the session, which was demonstrated by her smiling, vocalisation, physical movement and the intensity with which she watched and participated.

From a therapeutic perspective, the session encouraged her to access a total communication approach. This was demonstrated by her engaging in eye-contact, turn-taking, vocalisation and physical movement. For example, at one point she batted out at the recorder. She used all of these above skills to indicate that she wanted more and her desire to take part in the activity. Mia demonstrated anticipation and was wonderful at turn-taking during the recorder extract. The music therapist was very good at giving her time to respond and to gauge the rhythm to stimulate a reaction in Mia. Mia used both arms together (bilateral) during this extract, and also unilaterally.

Mia clearly responded to the differing tone and tempo of the music, her body language and movement clearly demonstrating this. Mia was very animated, clapping both hands, again to the faster rhythm. She enjoyed being in a group and watching the others' reactions.

Figure 4.1 Mia interacting with the recorder

Extract 2: Mia at the piano
The music therapist describes the extract

Mia is sitting to my right at the digital piano. Suzie is with Jamie and has a selection of instruments to offer him. Mia turns to me, but is quiet. I sing 'Mia's gone quiet!' above a sustained chord, and Mia immediately bangs the keyboard strongly with her left hand twice. I begin a rhythmical nursery-rhyme style accompaniment, and Mia begins to play in a more sustained way, moving in and out of a steady pulse. When she slows for a moment I follow her new tempo. Jamie, who is exploring a drum with Suzie, begins to vocalise loudly. I sing an answer, and Mia turns to me and begins to play more vigorously with her left hand. I wonder whether she is responding to Jamie's vocalisation, or if she is calling me back to pay attention to her, or both. At the same time, she lifts her weaker right arm a little, and then lowers it so that her fingers are touching the edge of the piano keys. Mia plays in several short bursts with her left hand, sometimes playing more strongly immediately after Jamie has vocalised. After a few moments she stops, withdraws her hand and turns away, towards the camera. I am wondering if she has had enough for now. I play quietly, reflecting her stillness. Jamie is also quiet at this moment. Mia then turns back to me and plays another short burst with her left hand. It feels to me that she is taking the initiative in reconnecting. Mia raises her right hand and lowers it to the keyboard at the same time as bouncing on the keys with her left hand. Although she manages to make a sound only with her left hand, she seems to be working hard to bring her right hand into play as well. At one point Mia looks as if she is trying to push herself away from the keyboard with her left hand but then starts playing again and re-engages.

Observations from Mia's speech and language therapist

Although Mia appeared less engaged in this extract, and spent some time looking at the camera, there were some very good instances of eye-contact and joint attention during this segment. It was apparent that she was aware of cause and effect: in particular that her behaviour would have an immediate effect on Ann's responses. Mia banged the keyboard with increasing force when she wanted the volume or tempo to increase. She enjoyed being able to direct adult behaviour. At one point Mia seemed to disengage from the activity, but she engaged again with no coercion from the adults: it may be that she needed a short time-out occasionally and would then return to the task at hand with no adult interference. This may be worth bearing in mind at other times, as adults can often be too swift to judge either that a child has had enough and end an activity, or try to direct attention back to the task when the child just needs a little breathing space.

Observations from Mia's physiotherapist and occupational therapist

Mia was observed to change her sitting posture frequently and was working hard on head control. It was a joy to see how much Mia involved her right arm, independently of her left. These are all occupational therapy and physiotherapy targets.

From a physiotherapy point of view, it was pleasing to see moments when Mia was playing the piano with both hands involved. Her posture improved as she was more upright. She was excited and motivated especially with the faster and more rhythmical tones. She also initiated play, mirrored activity and anticipated her turn.

Figure 4.2 Mia playing the piano

Extract 3: 'Bye bye'
The music therapist describes the extract

We are all seated in a circle again. I say 'It's time to sing…' and pause. Mia waves with her left hand. She continues to wave during the goodbye song. After the first time we have sung it, Mia pats her left hand on her right hand (I wonder if she is requesting more?) and we sing the song again, with more waving from Mia. I pause before the last word of the song and Jamie adds a vocal sound. Mia adds a single short vocal sound too.

Comments from Mia's speech and language therapist

Mia very obviously anticipated the song and the end of the session, waving before the song had begun. She also began to sign for 'more' but it is unclear from viewing one session whether she was asking for the session to continue, a repetition of the song, or whether she was telling others that there was more of the song to come, i.e. it was sung more than once each time.

It is obvious from watching all three extracts that the aims for Mia have been met very clearly and successfully. She used arm movement ('more') with and without vocalising to indicate that she wanted something to happen, to continue or to be repeated. She used her voice to accompany the music as well as to request something. All too often therapy is therapist-led: music therapy, it would appear, is very much child-led, responding to the child's behaviours and reactions in a completely non-judgemental way: there is no right or wrong way for the child to behave. From a speech and language therapy perspective it is useful to have had this opportunity to see these extracts of Mia in order to develop her communication skills further.

Comments from Mia's family

The whole family – including Mia – have watched the DVD of Mia having music therapy. We had to watch it over and over at Mia's insistence. Her enjoyment of the sessions is evident immediately. We all found the footage mesmerising because we had never seen Mia so involved with something before.

The first clip with Ann playing the treble recorder sees Mia becoming very excited when the session starts and then waiting patiently for her turn, watching with intense concentration whilst the focus is on another group member. Her pleasure is evident when it is her turn with her clapping and dancing and using her voice to ensure the session continues. It is fantastic to see Mia so animated. Normally Mia is a people-watcher so participation to this extent is amazing to witness. Music has always been an important part of Mia's life. She has many musical toys – pianos, guitars, drums – which she enjoys playing. This is because it is something she can do and it provides a reaction from others which she likes. Music therapy differs because here she is drawn into an activity that someone else is doing, gives a reaction that gets a reaction, and this two-way event is obviously giving her confidence to voice what she wants: a fantastic achievement from someone who is non-verbal and usually unable to voice anything. It is the first time we have ever seen Mia so totally involved with something as an equal. That she drums her hand onto Suzie's hand in excitement and with rhythm on one or two occasions is also an indication of how confident and happy she is.

At the piano, Mia is very comfortable and happy to let Ann know what she wants. As you would expect, Mia does reach out to the keyboard with her left hand but, unexpectedly, she also attempts to reach out with her right hand and arm which is a fantastic effort on Mia's part. Usually, such intense effort would cause her arm to retract into her body due to spasticity so she has to be incredibly relaxed to achieve these movements. We have used musical instruments at home to help to exercise her right hand and arm in the past but we have always needed to encourage the movement. That we see her doing this voluntarily for herself is no mean feat.

It is interesting to see Mia's reaction at the start of the clip of the goodbye song. She is correctly pre-empting what is coming and is waving goodbye, but she is happy with it. At home, she does this when she knows a favourite TV programme is ending. She always used to get upset at home at this point. It may just be coincidence but we have found she has not been upset for the last few months. Seeing her reaction during this clip makes us wonder if this is helping her to understand that saying 'goodbye' is not a bad thing and it doesn't have to be for ever, and is helping to mature her ability to say goodbye without becoming upset.

Every family member feels very positive towards music therapy for Mia. Without exception this is due to seeing Mia so happily joining in and using her voice and body so easily. We see a big difference in Mia's participation with us at home, particularly where music is concerned. She enjoys singing to us and dancing and enjoys the reaction she gets from us when she does these things. We are sure her personality is being allowed to shine through and it is making us realise there is a person inside with a huge voice and capabilities. We look forward to seeing how she develops in the future with the help of these sessions.

Reflections from Suzie High, Mia's teacher

From my perspective, music therapy has been about the self-agency of the children in the group. By this, I mean enabling them to become aware that they can influence their environment, and take positive control of things themselves. Music therapy gives Mia the chance to be her own person. She has been able to influence and direct and be active in her decision making. She is understood, heard and recognised as a person to be listened to – her participation in the music is valued. As an educator, I am always looking for creative ways to deliver the Early Years Foundation

Figure 4.3 Mia waves bye bye

Stage curriculum. Music therapy links well with the four Foundation Stage principles (Department for Children, Schools and Families 2008), which are:

> *a unique child*: enabling each child to be resilient, capable, confident and self assured
>
> *positive relationships*: building strong relationships which enable a child to develop strength and independence
>
> *enabling environments*: creating positive environments for learning
>
> *development*: acknowledging that children learn in different ways, and responding to each child's learning style.

In contrast to a traditional educational approach, music therapy offers a different way of being with the children: it contributes to their education from a new perspective and can give wider insights into the child. In music therapy I experience Mia in a way that informs me of her true capabilities and motivations. There is a loosening of educational targets during music therapy sessions: it feels as if the group is in a therapy bubble where educational targets do not come in and everyone can just be. During music therapy, we can be creative in the moment, and spontaneous with the sounds and relationships around us.

The music therapy approach has permeated into the class environment and the sessions have influenced my relationship-building with all the pupils in the music therapy group. I am able to take direction from the children and how they communicate, and allow myself to follow the lead of the child. I now watch for smaller signs of communication and have become more intuitive. I draw upon my skill and knowledge base as a teacher as well as listening to my instinct to work sensitively with the children. My awareness of the client-centred approach of music therapy – those principles of meeting Mia and responding to her – filters into my relationship with her in the classroom.

The music therapy is refreshing and gives me a sense of agency. It centres me and gets me in touch with my relationships with the children. It provides a place of spiritual stillness. It is possible to feel real and in touch with my pupils as individual people: meeting them where they are rather than handing out instructions and delivering demands.

Reflections from Ann Bruce, Mia's music therapist

The comments from the other health professionals show that, although they each see music therapy from their own professional perspective, there is much in common between us: a recurring theme was the child-led nature of music therapy, which allows Mia to have some control over her environment, and the multifaceted nature of communication in the session (sound, gesture and movement). The speech and language therapist notes how observations of what a child does spontaneously in music therapy (such as tapping her lip or re-engaging after a pause) can contribute to a fuller assessment of a child's communication.

The observations from health professionals also highlight the potential for music therapy to address multi-professional aims. For example, whilst in a music therapy session the music therapist's main focus might be on enabling the child to play an active role in communication, the child's physical posture is simultaneously improved as a result of his or her intense engagement in a motivating activity. This is very much the case with someone like Mia who works best whilst in the company of others. In music therapy, elements of her physiotherapy (such as maintaining head control and using her right arm) can happen naturally through

Mia's engagement with the music, even though this may not be the music therapist's primary aim.

The experience of music therapy allows Mia's teacher to reflect on her own practice, to experience the children in new ways and to develop her own relationships with them. It has been of great benefit, both to the music therapy group itself, and to the children in their class setting, that the same person has been able to attend the group alongside the music therapist each week. Sometimes there are staffing issues in schools that make this difficult, and sometimes staff ask if they can take it in turns to come to groups so that they can all experience what music therapy is like. Perhaps there are settings in which that might be feasible, but our experience from the work with Mia's group is that the consistency of staffing is very important, as well as the choice of who that person will be.

For the family, in this instance, the benefits of music therapy are primarily around enjoyment, engagement and the spontaneous expression of a personality. They value the opportunity that music therapy provides for Mia to have control over her environment, and they clearly perceive that what happens in a weekly music therapy group can, and does, have an effect on Mia's life in general.

A happy by-product of writing this chapter has been the opportunity to spend much more time than is normally available for us, the authors, to reflect on the work together, and also to collaborate (albeit in an indirect way) with other professionals. As a team we are now considering how we can work together in more efficient and effective ways, which will be beneficial for the children with whom we work, but also refreshing for us: how to gain the benefits of co-working without necessarily working in school on the same days.

The last word goes to Mia's family:

> Music therapy is giving Mia a voice. She's being a part of something and she's being an equal in something, and you're reacting to what she wants. It's like she's telling you and you're doing it straight away. She's got control – that's why she likes it.

Chapter 5

The School Challenge

Combining the Roles of Music Therapist and Music Teacher

Jan Hall

Introduction

My joint music therapy and teaching career has presented many interesting challenges. However, it is through combining these two roles that I have discovered over the years some very effective ways to meet children's needs. I have often wondered about my dual roles as music therapist and music teacher in the same school and suspected that many would ask how I could fulfil them. I would argue, however, that it has enabled me to effect more change with more children than I may have done if I was only working within one role.

My background

I have been a music therapist for 27 years. Before that I worked as a music teacher and was head of music for four years in two secondary schools. As a music therapist I have worked in six special schools and an assessment centre. I had not considered being a music therapist and teacher in the same school but, in order to gain enough employment within the areas where I lived, I had to accept the fact that my work would only be funded if I took up the position of music teacher and worked concurrently as a therapist. At first I felt that this situation was far from ideal and felt awkward about working in this way but, as I will describe, I have gradually seen the benefits, and many of the disadvantages, that I used to worry about, have become positives.

The overlaps of therapy and teaching

Music therapy and music teaching are two very distinct professions. They require different training, objectives and expectations, as well as unique record-keeping and support networks. Each has different things to offer but there are major overlaps as well. In the most basic sense, this might be evident through some of the activities used by both therapist and teacher to reach their respective goals, when the same activity may be used but the rationale for choosing that activity is completely different. It is often only when this overlap is identified and acted upon that it is possible to support children with a wide range of difficulties and needs. Indeed, I feel that it is essential to develop an awareness of these overlaps across all areas of a child's school experience. It is sometimes pointed out in evaluative literature, such as that of Adam Ockelford (2008), that elements of some music therapy sessions appear to indicate that music education is occurring. This is sometimes stated in a derogatory way as if one negates the other.

However, it could be argued that if communication within the therapy session occurs through the use of music the fact that the child is at the same time acquiring music skills is not in any way detrimental to the communication process. Might this not be as ridiculous as deriding a verbally conducted therapy session because, by trying to put feelings into words, clients might have extended their vocabulary or verbal communication skills? Musical skills may indeed be acquired in the course of a music therapy session but this would not necessarily be the aim of the session. When the argument is used the other way round, however, and music teaching is viewed as music therapy, it may be talked about differently. In fact, in some establishments any music with children with special needs may be called music therapy. I have often heard staff or parents saying things such as, 'He loves his music, he finds it really relaxing,' or 'She was a lot less angry after singing today so I did a bit of therapy with her.'

As someone who is passionate about music I am always pleased to hear about any positive responses and would not deny that any musical experience can be therapeutic. However, I am concerned that any situation when music calms or entertains is viewed by some as music therapy. Music teachers essentially have music skills foremost in their minds when planning but any skills achieved musically within a therapy session usually happen as other changes occur.

My role as music teacher

I am the only music teacher at the special school where I work and, in this role, see all of the children for group music lessons in blocks of terms. I lead a singing club, plan, implement and support art weeks and develop, rehearse and play for school shows. I take the school choir to perform at festivals and concerts with mainstream primary schools and the school is very involved in music events in the local community. This is similar to the models which are described by Wood, Verney and Atkinson (2004).

My role as music therapist

As a music therapist, children can be referred to me for individual sessions, having been assessed for need against agreed criteria, which I discuss later in this chapter. I also run a block of music therapy sessions for the nurture group, which takes children from the local primary school. The nurture group is a friendly, structured environment where children who are finding life at school difficult can develop important social and emotional skills. These are the areas that we work on in the group music therapy sessions.

I supervise music therapy students and support the art and drama therapists employed as part of our Change School project, which addresses the emotional well-being of all the school's pupils and staff. This project aims to support staff through training sessions, therapy workshops and a drop-in breakfast, where they can discuss issues which come about from such challenging work.

Dual roles

I have found that it is essential to ensure that boundaries are clear from the outset as they are different for therapy sessions and music lessons. I also use different objects of reference, or symbols, for each. If difficulties with boundaries arise, or are anticipated by myself or by colleagues, we arrange it so that the child only attends one or the other, i.e. either the group music lessons or individual therapy sessions or, indeed, changes to a different form of therapy.

When I first took up the challenge of the dual roles, I was concerned that the overlap might be problematic for the children. Over the years, this issue has not arisen as often as one might expect. One helpful spin-off is that as the children see me around school daily in my role as a teacher most tend to show less anxiety coming to a therapy session for the first time. This is especially true for the very young children.

Children who are capable of speech often talk about both the group and therapy sessions with me and in many cases, although they are young, are aware of the differences between the sessions and quickly show an understanding of what is taking place.

Working with staff

Most support staff that I have worked with in sessions have been very supportive and can see the benefits of therapy. There have been times, however, when staff have found it difficult to relax and realise that the playing of music does not always have to be a performance. This can be linked to the way that many adults learned music at school. The message then seemed to be that there were people who were musical and others who were not. This is, of course, nonsense but this mindset does restrict the ability of many adults to relax into improvisation or allow children time before they respond through music. I have often had to remind staff not to 'do the playing' for the child. In observing and reading about musical activities for children with physical difficulties it often seems that much of their musical participation is done for them. For example, in the Equals Schemes of Work (Music PMLD 1999) and Planning, Teaching and Assessing the Curriculum for Pupils with Learning Difficulties (QCA 2009) there seems to be a lot of emphasis on co-active work. This often leads to children being helped to play whilst listening to different types of music instead of being actively involved and having some control over their environment. 'You'll have to help him: he can't do it himself,' is heard less now within the school as staff, who support in sessions, have a greater understanding of music therapy and accept that children can make choices and may take time to respond and communicate through music.

I am sure that many staff over the years have winced at times when seemingly erratic and unbridled noise is coming from my room during therapy sessions. It is therefore an advantage to be the music teacher as well so that staff can see and hear me working in a traditional way too.

There are some exceptional county music services in the UK but not all of these are geared to children with special needs. There can be an assumption that anyone can teach music to a child with learning difficulties as they do not really need to have good musical skills themselves. Although there are many aspects of music that can be developed by non-musicians with children with special needs, such as singing action songs and music and movement activities, some aspects of teaching music do require the skills of a qualified teacher. For example, making carefully judged choices of the music used, based on a broad musical vocabulary and identifying what is needed musically to help the child develop.

Benefits of dual roles

Can I successfully fulfil both roles? I hope so! Supervising music therapy students ensures that I constantly question my practice and I have often considered whether I should work as a music therapist in one school and a music teacher in another, if it became possible. This would certainly make boundaries clearer. However, I cannot say that carrying out both has proved detrimental to either aspect of my work. I enjoy the way I work, although more time and another therapist on board would help more children to access music therapy.

Since training as a music therapist at Roehampton in the 1980s I find that, even when I am wearing my music teacher hat, I approach my lessons as a therapist – in both planning and execution. An awareness of difficulties emerging in individual therapy sessions can also be transferred into group lessons. I am happy to say that this was picked up in one of my Ofsted inspections: 'The teacher's therapy skills are utilised to the full in lessons and this enhances the learning significantly,' and 'The influence of music therapy is seen very clearly in the way pupils listen to one another, take turns, and value their contributions. As a result, pupils are confident to take part and perform solo or in a group' (Ofsted 2000 p.40).

I find that, because I see the children in lots of different situations, I am well informed about all aspects of the child's school life. This, coupled with my observations within group music lessons of the whole child's response rather than just musical ability, often enables me to identify a child who would benefit from individual therapy quicker and more rigorously than through the usual route of referral.

VIGNETTE 5.1

I work with a child whose speech is always unclear, which proves very frustrating for her. In one session she appeared to want to use sticks to play the drums but the drumsticks weren't right. It was only when I remembered the Indian dancers who had visited the school the previous day that I suggested some similar sticks which they had used and they were just what she wanted. The rest of the session was full of dancing together and creating rhythmic improvisations on the sticks.

VIGNETTE 5.2

One child was unpredictable, violent and frequently destroyed equipment and threw objects. He became increasingly isolated as staff attempted to protect other vulnerable children. Many staff, myself included, were at times wary or frightened of his erratic and aggressive behaviour. There were concerns over his mental health in addition to his learning, speech and language difficulties. When he was referred for music therapy I initially tried working in the classroom that was used just by him but, although very brief interactions occurred, it was difficult for him to cope with me entering his space. My relationship with the head teacher and other staff enabled me to act quickly and proactively in a way that might have proved a lot more difficult as a visiting music therapist. A previously communal area was identified, cleared and adapted with the agreement of staff. Together we set up a secure room, containing just the piano (with the lid fixed back for my safety) and a heavy-duty box that held secured instruments and was surrounded by cushions on the floor. There were no objects to throw or to use as weapons. He could have picked up the box but this didn't happen. He was free to move around the room and make choices. Working with his feelings in the sessions, I saw a different side to him – he was a gentle, very sad child wanting to interact and express himself. As the sessions developed we took turns vocally and played the box of tethered instruments. An intense closeness emerged through the music, something he had seemed unable to experience outside the sessions. My notes, reports and video enabled staff to gain new insights into him and informed future interactions with him throughout the school.

In some individual sessions children like to sing songs from familiar films and if we have sung these previously at other school occasions, I am able to find them quickly and in the key that the child is familiar with. In most cases this enables the child to relax. Due to the freedom of expression and child-led nature of therapy sessions, it has also been easier for me to identify children who have been particularly gifted in music. One child, for example, could play any song by ear on the piano and was keen to learn more. When therapy sessions ended, I set up individual instrumental lessons, albeit not in the traditional way. I taught piano skills through improvisation and games with moments of gentle direction. Oldfield (2006b) when writing about therapeutic music teaching says: 'Unlike many piano teachers who develop systems of teaching, my teaching method will be very flexible and be completely modified and adapted to the learning strengths and choices of each individual child.' I feel that, as a music therapist, I am often able to work in this way, adapting my teaching to meet the child's needs. This approach is also used by Cobbett (2006).

Referrals

The art, drama and music referral forms are sent to me. Through discussions with school staff including the senior team, nurses, other professionals involved and all the arts therapists, a decision is made regarding priority and which therapy should be offered for the initial assessment. The child may already have shown a positive response to a particular arts activity or shown expression through a particular medium and this would need developing. Discussions about how the sessions are progressing and any other change in circumstances are ongoing, to ensure that the needs of the children are being met.

The school's music therapy referral form identifies the child's degree of emotional, behavioural, social, communication difficulties, lack of developmental and educational progress, and evaluates the cause for concern on a scale of one to ten. Children are then prioritised by their score and the findings of multidisciplinary team discussions before being offered music therapy for a block of sessions, such as a half-term's assessment (six weeks), a school year, or for longer.

Due to the close working relationship of the entire staff team, children may often be referred as urgent cases. For example, one child found out at the age of 11 that he had been adopted and found it very difficult to cope with this news but was not able to verbalise how he felt. Experiences such as these often lead to the child exhibiting behaviours and emotions that are almost impossible to deal with in a normal class setting and putting additional one-to-one support in place is vital.

Self-referral has played an increasing part in my work, as have these crisis intervention sessions. Children who are having a very difficult time may themselves ask if they can come for some music therapy. After playing music together, they may talk about what has happened to them and I give them the space and time they need. Sometimes we improvise together as the child's feelings may be too difficult or painful to verbalise but, through the music, feelings can be shared. Music therapy provides a safe environment in which children can work through issues and, as their therapist, I contain their often very difficult, sometimes overwhelming feelings.

CASE STUDY 5.1: JACK

When Jack started school, he responded to the new structure and environment with increasingly challenging and violent behaviour. He only attended this school for half days at first but his escalating behaviour difficulties led to him being permanently excluded from school after just one term. He then attended a nurture group for children with emotional and behavioural difficulties for two days a week for a couple of terms. Jack was diagnosed with autistic spectrum disorder when he was five. He eventually moved to another infant school where the dedicated staff developed a close and trusting working relationship with his parents. After several further assessments, it became apparent that the usual approach for children with autism was not working effectively. Jack's needs were reassessed and further investigation suggested that some of Jack's behaviour was indicative of Pathological Demand Avoidance Syndrome and strategies for dealing with this particular syndrome proved really effective and positive.

At the end of his time at the infant school it was difficult to identify the next appropriate placement for Jack. Due to his violent outbursts and difficulties following usual classroom rules and routines, Jack spent a year in his own individual classroom at another mainstream school. In his classroom, he was supported by two key-workers from the special school near by, and he joined in occasionally with some activities at the special school. Later, a base was created within the special school and he was able to move in full time.

He attended group music lessons when he moved to the special school. At first he tended to sit near the door but not join in with the group at all. I fear that this would still be the case if I had not been in my dual role and managed to find a suitable slot for him so that we could also start individual music therapy. Since he began music therapy, Jack has become more relaxed and has moved further into the music group. He is now joining in more and will sit with his peers and not just with his key-worker.

Jack's music therapy sessions have varied each week. He often wanted to explore how the instruments worked and experimented with sounds, by creating them in very different and often unusual ways. In the early days communication with me was very much a means to an end – a way of getting what he wanted – but over time we have built a good relationship. I have also been able to support Jack as he develops increased empathy with those around him and this has been particularly rewarding.

In one session, for example, I had a mat, the Soundbeam and switches in the corner ready for the next session. Jack asked what they were for and when I told him (in a non-specific and general way) that they were for a child who had to lie on the floor and could not use the usual instruments, he said that he wanted to try them out and set the room up ready for the other child. I was astounded how he could change the sounds on the computer for the Soundbeam, his problem-solving ability and his knowledge and interest in switches and sounds. He wanted to know how everything worked and tried out all the different instruments and switches before deciding which was best and he could tell me why. He then placed switches carefully and thoughtfully so that the child would be able to create more than one sound. I felt that Jack was very aware that he was being kind and helping somebody with more physical difficulties than himself, before carrying on with his own musical improvisations and taking turns to lead. I told his teacher about his information communication technology skills so that they could be extended further in lessons.

Over time, Jack became more involved in the many different music lesson activities. On one occasion, when the group was quite small he joined in with group music-making and played a solo on the drum-kit. This would have been unthinkable just a few months before. In another lesson he even commented very accurately on the music we had played together, which was wonderful as he is usually very reluctant to speak out in the group. Jack's new ability to be part of a group is, without doubt, due to the work of the whole team around him but I also feel that the individual music therapy work has enabled him to feel more relaxed and trust me, the same person in both the individual and group sessions, in a way that he may not have done with different people for each. With all the strategies that have been developed by the staff working with him from when he joined the school, he has made incredible progress. Jack is now fully integrated and, with support, is coping extremely well.

CASE STUDY 5.2: THOMAS

Thomas always connected with music. This was evident when we met as he first started school. Initially music therapy helped him settle into a school environment and cope with being parted from his mother, who brought him to school. He usually did not want to stay and could become quite upset. Although he had a severe physical disability (very low muscle tone and inability to sit unaided) and no speech, Thomas showed his personality through music-making in our individual sessions. He had a great sense of humour and a good level of understanding, shown immediately in the way he improvised and through his enjoyment of musical jokes.

Thomas's physical skills deteriorated over time but certainly not his love of music. Through the use of existing and home-made technology and switches, he was able to access a wide range of sounds – even when he had to lie on the floor to be comfortable. He used whichever part of his body he could move to create his own music, giving him an essential means of self-expression. Thomas often became a one man band by operating many switches at once. In some sessions he would dance, moving to the music as he turned himself over to the side and rocked back, playing the switches. Throughout all of our sessions, I could feel Thomas's intense concentration. He chose which sounds he wanted and was very specific about what he wished to play. He gave very definite yes and no responses with his eyes and it was very clear what he wanted. Thomas loved singing and vocal improvisations became a large part of our sessions. His singing was related in pitch to the music. He vocalised to complete the Hello and Goodbye songs as well as when he played. Thomas always let me know when he did not want to finish the sessions by arching his back so it was very difficult to get him back into the portable bed in which he would be taken safely back to class.

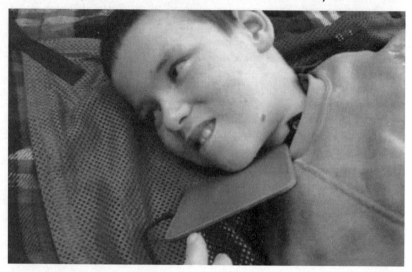

Figure 5.1 Thomas using his chin to access sounds with a Pal Pad switch and an automated drumstick to play a range of instruments

As his confidence increased and I found more and more ways to use switches and technology to help him (developed through my attempts to aid his communication during therapy sessions), Thomas thoroughly enjoyed being able to participate in school shows and concerts. He was often lying down at the front surrounded by his drum-kit of switches. As Thomas's condition developed he had many periods in hospital and long periods away from school, which frequently happens with many of the children I work with. Because of the lack of funding for music therapy there was no way of providing this service at home or in the hospital. Thomas died from his condition, at the age of ten, sadly before any music therapy at home service was put in place. In desperation and sick of waiting for funding, Lucy (Thomas' mother) and I set up Thomas's Fund in 2007. This is a charity that provides music therapy at home for children and young people who have life-limiting illnesses (that is, they are unlikely to reach adulthood) or who, for medical reasons, have to spend long periods away from school. Pre-school children are also assessed on an individual basis. The fund has gradually developed and there is a team of therapists on board. This is very similar to the service offered in the outreach work of some children's hospices, but there is no children's hospice in Northamptonshire.

CASE STUDY 5.3: HARRY

Thomas's brother, Harry, was four years younger. He displayed the same symptoms as Thomas and could not sit unaided or speak but, like Thomas, loved vocalising to songs. Although originally Thomas was thought to have cerebral palsy, it was later discovered that both brothers had an unknown neuro-degenerative condition, which has no name or cure. Harry began music therapy when he started school at the age of three and he too responded immediately to the music. Despite his physical needs, he was able to access a range of traditional instruments. When he played the drum, transferring a drumstick between his hands, his playing was strong and forceful. Harry's sense of humour emerged in the sessions in the playful interactions initiated by him. He enjoyed trying to pull over some instruments or hitting his glasses with a drumstick. He found it liberating and fun to be naughty and initiated many playful games. Dialogues developed using voice and on a range of instruments and it soon became apparent that music was vital for Harry to be able to express himself. This was particularly important for him to help him work through some difficult feelings when Thomas died.

Figure 5.2 An early session with Harry

As Harry's physical condition deteriorated and playing traditional instruments started to become more difficult for him, he still tried very hard to play forcefully. To continue helping him to express himself through music, we introduced the Soundbeam with switches, a Beatmaster (a switch-operated drumstick), keyboard, drum machines, switch-operated bells and wind-chimes. While still able to sit upright in supported seating, Harry used a head-switch. He lifted his head up and played forcefully, enjoying being able to control my responses. He laughed immediately if a silly sound was set up on his switch or if we were playing together and he could catch me out. Harry loved music and any opportunity to play or sing (vocalising to a song or completing the phrase of a melody) in class, to the school or in a performance was taken on enthusiastically by the school team. Everyone became aware of, and increasingly sensitive to, the need to wait for his response. He had a wicked sense of humour and enjoyed the anticipation of making everyone wait! He loved his solo spot in concerts and loved vocalising into the microphone. Harry continued to receive music therapy at home through Thomas's Fund until he died.

Figure 5.3 Harry creating music using Pal Pad switches to operate a range of sounds using technology

I firmly believe that it is my dual role of therapist and teacher that enabled me to work with children such as Thomas and Harry in this way. Thomas and Harry both enjoyed taking the lead in the group lessons and interacting with the other children vocally and on instruments, often interrupting with a vocal or instrumental sound while I was waiting for someone else to respond. The relationship that is built up in therapy enables children to have greater confidence to play and sing in the same way in other contexts, such as a music lesson or school performance. Children trust that my responses to them will remain consistent, that I will match their tempo and wait for them.

Conclusion

It is indeed challenging to take on a dual role within a school, and it may not be for everyone. However, I have found it to be very effective and rewarding and am thrilled when I receive positive feedback about the benefits to the school:

> The professionalism and dual role of music therapist and teacher has... enhanced the music provision within the school, supporting both staff and children to develop and move on in their understanding of music as well as emotionally. Working in this dual role has brought to the school the opportunity to introduce other therapies... (Assistant head teacher)

Finally, I hope that my role within the school staff team provides a therapist's and a teacher's viewpoint, support for staff and training opportunities on tap for the entire school family. This seems to be much appreciated, as one teacher stated:

> Having a specialist (teacher and therapist) on site is brilliant. For me it means I can ask her expert advice to improve my confidence and improve my lessons... For our most troubled children it means we can speak to her and prepare her about the children. It also means we receive feedback which can help integration back into the lesson. She is on hand to discuss problems and often offers support with extra or more targeted sessions.

Chapter 6

Music Therapy and the Expression of Anger and Aggression

Working with Aggressive Behaviour in Children Aged Five to Nine Who Risk Mainstream School Exclusion

Jane Brackley

the fascination with anger has led to many myths and fantasies developing around it. There is, for example, a myth that it is dangerous to suppress anger... There are also myths about expressing anger. There has been a pervasive idea that anger must be acted out. The analogies used are those of dams holding back floods, or volcanoes waiting to explode. This sort of analogy is inaccurate. Expressing anger makes us more angry. Violence breeds violence. (Cairns 2002, pp.82–83)

Rationale for this chapter

In my work as a music therapist with primary school-aged children I have frequently found myself citing 'self-expression' as a clinical aim. This has sometimes led to an assumption, or acceptance of the myth, that, in the name of self-expression, anger and aggression must be acted out in music therapy. With this in mind, the idea that expressing anger makes us more angry has resonated with questions and doubts that have arisen in the course of my clinical work with children aged five to nine who risk exclusion from mainstream school. In particular, it has led me to consider whether responses in music therapy that promote the expression of anger and aggression may, in certain circumstances, or with certain children, do little more than collude with and even reinforce children's destructive and antisocial patterns of behaviour. In other words, it has raised the question: *How far is it therapeutic to encourage and support children to express their aggressive impulses in music therapy?* This and associated questions form the basis of a current PhD research study in which I seek to explore issues around effective music therapy practice when working with children's aggressive behaviour. For the purposes of this chapter, I will link some of these questions to case study examples and thoughts arising from my clinical work with children whose social, emotional and behavioural problems place them at risk of school exclusion. By way of introduction, I will begin by outlining the setting in which my work has taken place, before defining aggression and considering briefly what, if any, viable function it may serve.

Introduction: the setting/context

In this chapter I will focus on music therapy which has taken place within the context of a county music therapy team. In doing so I will draw on experience gained over two years working on a behaviour support programme and pupil referral unit for five to nine-year-olds who risk school exclusion. Music therapy has since moved from the site of the pupil referral unit to a local child development centre where I have continued working with this population for a further two years. During this time I have adopted a child-centred music therapy approach grounded in psychoanalytic theory and theories of child development. The thoughts presented, and questions raised in this chapter follow my study for a Master of Arts degree (Brackley 2007), which found that certain common maladaptive behaviours could be seen in children of primary school-age who risked mainstream school exclusion. On the basis of data collated from referrals to the behaviour support programme, these behaviours were broadly categorised as poor self-regulation, disruptive behaviour, difficulties in play with peers and aggressive behaviour. Amongst these, the issue of children's aggressive behaviour was frequently cited by teaching staff as particularly problematic and a major factor contributing to pupils' school exclusion. This is borne out in Cairns' statement that 'carers and schools often put aggression and violence at the top of the list of challenging behaviours they find most difficult to cope with' (2002, p.119).

Definition and functions of aggression

Introducing her book *Aggression and Destructiveness*, Celia Harding (2006) refers to the negative connotations of the term 'aggression' in today's society. She cites, by way of example, the Collins Concise Dictionary definition of aggression as 'an attack, a harmful action, an offensive activity, a hostile or destructive mental attitude' (p.3). According to Harding, 'in everyday parlance also, aggression usually refers to its destructive aspect, overlooking its necessary and positive functions'(2006, p.3).

It is beyond the scope of this chapter to examine in detail perceived functions and underlying *causes* of children's aggressive behaviour. Suffice to say that psychoanalysis has offered an alternative view of aggression as an intrinsic, necessary and potentially creative part of our psychic make-up. Most notably, Freud recognised the need for healthy aggression to help us to 'grasp life, pursue it, master it, create it, live it' (quoted in Harding 2006, p.5). Freud's successors drew on his insights to develop a range of theories emphasising different aspects and functions of aggression. In particular, these were 'aggression in the service of individuation and development, self-preservation and as an inevitable part of the ambivalence we feel towards our objects' (Harding 2006, p.5).

What constitutes aggressive behaviour in music therapy?

For the purposes of this chapter, I do not intend to address more overt forms of physical aggression towards the therapist, occurrences of which, in my experience, have in any event been rare in music therapy with the client population in question. Instead, seeking first to define 'what constitutes children's aggressive behaviour in music therapy?' i.e. what does it 'look' or 'sound' like? I will focus on issues associated with what seem to me to be three main areas of aggressive presentation of children in music therapy:

- loud, forceful and aggressive playing on musical instruments
- an aggressive, controlling manner towards the therapist
- aggressive play or role-play.

By looking at these areas in relation to clinical case studies, I hope to consider the effectiveness of music therapy approaches in working with the aggressive behaviour of primary school-aged children who risk mainstream school exclusion.

Loud, forceful and aggressive playing on musical instruments

CASE STUDY 6.1: JAMIE

In his early sessions, Jamie is keen to play on the drum-kit. His playing is typically very loud and physically energetic. He seems to look for ever more forceful ways to play on the musical instruments, for example, jumping up and down with both feet on the bass-drum pedal, using the largest available beater (a tam-tam beater) to play the hi-hat, screaming and shouting whilst stamping on the hi-hat pedal and sitting on the piano keys. He says that he is very angry and looks around for other ways to find release of his aggressive feelings. He hits a beanbag in the room and uses all his strength to strike a cymbal. When I try to play music with Jamie, or to match the volume and force of his playing on the instruments, he either demands that I 'stop playing' or seems so self-absorbed, with the volume of his playing so loud, that I am unable to hear my own music and wonder why I continue to play. Finally, Jamie finds some photographs of children's different facial expressions and places one on the table drum. He 'smashes' it with a beater and says that he wants to 'fight and kill' the boy in the photo.

Jamie was aged six when he was referred to the behaviour support team on the grounds that he risked exclusion from mainstream school. He lived with his grandparents, having been removed from the care of his mother in early infancy following some suspected and some known abuse and neglect. Jamie was said to have been an unwanted child, with the situation exacerbated by the evident preferential treatment of a younger sibling. His behaviour was reported to include inappropriate touching, physical and verbal aggression towards peers and adults (including threatening language, shouting, kicking, punching and biting), non-compliance and attention-seeking behaviour. In addition, Jamie was said to display low levels of interest and motivation, a fragile sense of self-worth and a negative self-image, together with a tendency to flit between hitting out at and hugging teaching staff.

Reflections on Jamie's music therapy

Jamie was referred to music therapy by staff from the behaviour support team. He attended term-time sessions over a period of one year and ten months. There was frequently a disturbing feel to Jamie's early sessions and I wondered how far it was useful for him to express his levels of anger and aggression in ways such as those described. Outlining the attribute of loudness as a basic element of sound, Bunt (1994) draws attention to the young infant's lack of inhibition about making himself heard and making an immediate impact on his environment. Bunt suggests that ongoing freedom to be loud affords the child important opportunities 'to make inner connections with troublesome areas of...life and to begin to explore ways of integrating and balancing such aspects of [the] personality' (1994, p.53).

In Jamie's case, his loud and forceful playing on the instruments clearly allowed a degree of release of physical and emotional tension, which could itself be seen as therapeutic. It also offered a means to express his ambivalent feelings about our relationship. In the long term, it was possible that such playing could offer a way of making inner connections or integrating his personality. At the same time, however, without the capacity to stop and think about his feelings and actions it began to feel as though expressing his anger was only making Jamie angrier. I began to wonder whether, in my attempts to match the quality of Jamie's playing, I was in danger of colluding with patterns of evacuation and catharsis that were less a potential means to healthy development, than to the ongoing destructive use of force and volume to powerfully obliterate my music and presence. Perhaps what Jamie actually needed was help to find an alternative, more constructive and relational way of expressing and thinking about his anger.

In addition, whilst I felt that my role was to bear witness to and contain Jamie's feelings, so as to demonstrate to him that they were manageable, I questioned how far he was able to experience my musical presence as containing if he was unable to hear it. It seemed to me that to feel contained, he surely first needed to be aware of my presence as a supportive and containing adult figure. That being the case, the question arose: if I could not be heard, was Jamie afforded the positive experience that I had survived his aggression or rather that I could be, and had been, effectively obliterated? This question led to discussions in clinical supervision as to whether there were circumstances in which it was inappropriate and perhaps untherapeutic to support or collude with a child's expression of anger and aggression. As a direct outcome of this, my supervisor and I agreed that I needed to intervene rather than to continue to support Jamie's expression of destructive impulses.

In future sessions when Jamie began to play the drum-kit loudly and forcefully, rather than try to match and support his music, I therefore sat and waited for him to become aware of my presence and non-participation. On one occasion, this included sitting within Jamie's line of vision and beginning to draw a picture. Gradually, he became curious, saying aloud, 'What's she doing?' before finally approaching me. I showed Jamie my drawing, which was of a wall with him on one side and me on the other. I said that I felt that he was making a 'wall of sound' between us. Jamie's response was to add to my drawing to make the wall higher, leading to a conversation about his experience of 'the wall'. Thereafter, drawing became a useful means to capture symbolically in image form our experiences within Jamie's music therapy, including his fears and anxieties about forming an attachment. This, in turn, offered opportunities for dialogue and reflection. Returning to music, initially as a means to express feelings represented in our drawings, Jamie continued to demonstrate his ambivalent feelings towards me in our shared improvising. It was, however, significant that he was now able to begin to recognise and express his anger in more pro-social ways, either through song or verbally, i.e. he seemed to be developing the capacity to think about his angry, aggressive feelings.

An aggressive, controlling manner towards the therapist

CASE STUDY 6.2: CONNOR

Connor's punitive and dictatorial attitude in sessions is striking. When asked in an early session if there is anything he wants to tell me about himself, Connor states authoritatively: 'You must do as you are told and put your hand up.' Connor is easily upset by his own perceived mistakes and frequently berates himself as 'rubbish', 'useless' or 'stupid'. As I play the musical instruments, he invariably shouts disparaging comments such as, 'Not like that!' or 'You've got to get it right!' He spends a good deal of time demonstrating my 'incorrect' way as compared to the 'correct' way of playing the instruments. To my confusion, there is frequently little apparent difference between these 'right' and 'wrong' ways of playing. Attending music therapy after an exclusion from school, Connor attributes his exclusion to his inability to 'defeat' another pupil. He suggests that we set up a music shop in sessions, before introducing into this play an element of danger in the form of burglars and imposters. At his direction we play music to capture the drama and emotion of scenarios during which his role switches from threatening robber to my protector and ally. On one occasion, Connor pretends to be a wild animal, crawling on all fours, snarling and roaring. When I comment that I think the wild animal in the shop is trying to scare me, Connor replies that he is 'getting his own back' because I scared him once when he arrived for a session and thought that I was not there.

Connor was aged seven when he attended the behaviour support programme for a half-term period. He lived with his parents and two older brothers and had a history of antisocial behaviour dating back to an initial exclusion from nursery. When Connor started primary school, staff described a pupil who for periods of weeks seemed 'too polite'. After a few months, however, his disruptive behaviour became more prevalent and, by the time Connor had attended school for a year, almost daily incidents of antisocial behaviour were reported. These included hitting, shouting, biting, screaming and aggression towards peers. In addition, Connor showed signs of feral behaviour, where he would crawl on all fours making growling sounds, snarling or baring his teeth. Areas of concern cited on Connor's behaviour support programme referral included disruptive behaviour, difficulties with peers, non-compliance and verbal and physical aggression. Connor found it difficult to cope upon his return to mainstream school and was permanently excluded within a short period of time.

Reflections on Connor's music therapy

Connor was referred to music therapy by teaching staff on the behaviour support programme. He attended weekly individual sessions during term-times over a two-year period. In music therapy, Connor's verbal communication and manner towards me were sufficiently contemptuous and derogatory to lead to powerful counter-transference feelings on my part of being bullied and abused. I understood Connor's punitive and dictatorial manner as indicative of his need to control our musical and verbal interactions, to undermine my efforts and to project outwards, so as to rid himself of, unbearable feelings of inadequacy and self-loathing. In addition, Connor's behaviour seemed to be his response to a perception of the world in terms of winners and losers. This stance pervaded sessions, leading to tension-fraught battles for dominance on Connor's part. Any challenge to Connor's behaviour seemed only to reinforce his need to assert himself. My response at this early stage of therapy was therefore to allow Connor the experience of power and control. At the same time, I tried to promote conditions for Connor's increased flexibility, creativity and acceptance (of self and others) via an emphasis on 'different' as opposed to 'right' and 'wrong' ways of doing things such as playing the instruments.

Having initiated the playing of shops in sessions, Connor found in role-play a means to express his ambivalent feelings towards me as he switched roles from my oppressor to my protector in the face of newly introduced robbers, imposters and ghosts. Connor's feral behaviour in music therapy coincided with incidences of similar behaviour in the classroom. According to Connor, one such episode at school had been prompted by a pupil suggesting that Connor was scared. In music therapy, Connor had always been quick to distance himself from feelings of fear, saying that he had 'never in his life' felt frightened. When I commented now that I thought the wild animal in the shop was trying to scare me, Connor's admission that he had been scared when he thought I was absent one day felt a significant breakthrough: it suggested that he felt sufficiently secure and trusting of our relationship to own and express his real anxieties, to acknowledge the significance of our relationship and so allow himself to be vulnerable in my presence.

Connor seemed subsequently to find in shared musical improvisation a means to symbolically face his anxieties as at his instigation we played music to 'make the ghosts go away'. At the same time, he continued to revert to dictatorial, controlling behaviour, for example, asserting that his was the 'right' way and that he was 'the master'. Tyler (2003, p.4) describes her comparable experience of music therapy with Beverley, a troubled eight-year-old, whose 'lack of containment was apparent, as was her need to control…interactions and the environment'. Tyler continues, 'it was important that I could withstand these attacks and not retaliate, nor make myself into a victim' (p.45). As time passed with Connor, I became concerned that we risked settling into a relational pattern whereby he felt that his aggressive behaviour was accepted and acceptable and I routinely felt bullied and abused. In other words, withstanding his attacks and maintaining a non-retaliatory stance, I was in danger of becoming an apparently willing victim.

My increasingly unbearable counter-transference feelings led to discussions in clinical supervision as to how I might now respond to Connor. Insofar as the therapeutic relationship felt sufficiently established to begin to challenge his aggressive and controlling behaviour, and to avoid doing so risked collusion, I began to both verbalise my feelings of being with Connor and to adapt less exactly to his needs. I adopted an approach whereby, when Connor began to shout or speak to me in a derogatory manner, I remained seated and still until he became curious and asked why I was no longer playing with him. I responded by highlighting

Connor's manner towards me at which point, on one occasion, he lay under the keyboard, using a glove puppet to demonstrate that he was worried that I would not play with him and sad that I 'might not do music therapy with him again'. Whilst I was able to reassure Connor otherwise, it felt significant and necessary to have reached a position where he was able to begin to acknowledge his aggression, to develop an awareness of its impact on others and to work together to find more constructive terms for its expression. This included the capacity to voice, channel musically and so begin to think about his feelings, for example, using instruments, such as the thunder tube, to express feelings of frustration and aggression when I did not do as he wished.

Aggressive play or role-play

CASE STUDY 6.3: BILLY

Billy enters the music therapy room. Following a greeting song he is keen to play with the soft toys. He immediately begins to enact scenes of fighting, using one soft toy, as aggressor, to kick and punch another before throwing it to the floor. Billy's movements are sudden and unpredictable. He says that the toys are biting each other and then that one has bitten him. In play, his vocal tone is aggressive: he shouts and screams on behalf of, or at, the toys, frequently calling them 'bad' and 'naughty.' At other times his vocalisations include crying sounds. This type of play has become a pattern for our weekly sessions. Billy seems both excited and terrified by it and laughs a little hysterically as he enacts scenes of violence. Occasionally, Billy shouts at the toys, 'Stop that fighting!' He finds a glove puppet with different facial expressions on the fingers and plays with it on the table drum, saying that he is 'Mr Angry'. He asks me to put on the glove puppet, to be 'Mr Angry' and to try to catch him. He voices his fear of a large gong in the room, which he refers to as a monster. When I strike the gong, he asks, 'Did you punch it?' Having summoned up the courage to strike it himself, Billy seems fearful of the loud noise that it makes. He responds by telling me not to worry and that I will be alright.

Billy was aged five when he was referred for music therapy. An only child, he was reported to have enjoyed the company of other children at nursery. Concerns arose when, at the age of three, he began to have temper tantrums and to show aggression towards other children. In school, Billy's behaviour was described as oppositional and immature. His parents had separated a year earlier following alleged domestic violence, during which time Billy had lived with his mother and grandparents. His behaviour was said to have deteriorated, becoming more aggressive since the family break-up, to the extent that Billy was described by teaching staff as wild. His solitary play was observed to be violent and disturbing. Other behaviours reported included a resistance to follow adult instruction, violent tantrums, repetitive comments, emotional volatility, low frustration levels and a low threshold for perceived criticism. In addition, Billy was reported to have special educational needs in the form of cognitive delay, speech and language delay and poor gross and fine motor skills.

Reflections on Billy's music therapy

Billy was referred for music therapy by his head teacher at the time. He attended weekly individual sessions over a period of one year and nine months. Billy's play with puppets and soft toys was violent and aggressive from the outset. He quickly assigned different roles to the soft toys. His erratic movements, volatile behaviour, sudden changes in vocal dynamic and attribution of violent intent to physical actions (e.g. asking had I punched the gong) were both striking and disturbing. I understood his behaviour to be communicative of overwhelming emotion and confusion associated with traumatic scenes that he had experienced. At this early stage in Billy's therapy, I felt that my role was to bear witness to the replay of these events, whilst supporting and acknowledging musically and verbally the dynamic intensity of Billy's expressive shouting, screaming and crying vocal sounds. Insofar as Billy presented as quite immature in his behaviour, thinking and speech relative to his chronological age, it seemed that acting out or evacuation represented the only means then at his disposal to express his destructive impulses. As Harding states:

> Without the psychic means to contain overwhelming states of mind, the self becomes overwhelmed by pain, loss or terror, the capacity to mentalise feelings collapses and the person becomes liable to resort to action as a concrete form of containment. Destructiveness that cannot be processed mentally has to be evacuated and/or enacted. (2006, p.14)

Difficulties arose for me when Billy began to ask me to enact the role of aggressor during our play (e.g. in the form of a character he had named 'Mr Angry'). On the one hand, I wondered whether Billy required me to fulfil this role in order that we might explore his feelings towards his aggressor and as a suspected witness or victim of domestic violence; on the other hand, I instinctively felt uncomfortable that, were I to fulfil Billy's request, I risked becoming in his eyes less the means to a safe therapeutic encounter than a threatening adult figure closely identified with his projected aggressor. Insofar as my overriding instinct was that I needed to afford Billy the experience of a benign relationship with an adult, I decided that it was inappropriate to engage directly in this role-play. I therefore responded to Billy's request by saying that I did not wish to be 'Mr Angry', even in play, as I had no wish to frighten or hurt Billy.

As time passed and Billy's highly aggressive play continued to dominate our sessions, I began to question how far it remained therapeutic for him to re-create such scenes of violence. In particular, I wondered whether Billy's ongoing play still offered a useful means of healing or whether there was now a danger that, keeping his traumatic experiences alive in the present, he was actually reinforcing them. Perhaps he also risked becoming habituated to feelings of anger and aggression as a learned pattern of emotional response. Cairns states in this regard:

> Anger is the feeling associated with a particular set of physiological changes. Like all such change sets it can become addictive. The body and mind can become habituated to the experience... People can become addicted to being angry. When this is part of the problem, children who are being helped to manage anger will also need help to accept a different version of how it feels to be normal. (2002, p.94)

Whilst in Billy's case his destructive play was the evident result of his traumatic experiences, perhaps what he now needed was help to find a different way of being and playing. A significant breakthrough seemed to occur when, on the basis of counter-transference feelings that we were becoming stuck in sessions, I spontaneously challenged the abusive soft toy in Billy's aggressive role-play. Addressing this toy calmly, but firmly, I simply stated that it was time to stop, that we had had enough of this toy being angry, shouting and hurting the other toys. Billy's delight and disbelief at this challenge were clearly evident. He appeared both excited and relieved, asking me to repeat my words in this and subsequent sessions. Whilst other factors no doubt contributed, this challenge seemed to mark a turning point in sessions, following which Billy began to show a more regressed and vulnerable side to his character, for example, lying on the floor with the soft toys and requesting that I play and sing nursery rhymes or lullabies. At the same time, Billy seemed to find in musical copying activity on the drum and cymbal a means to not only express, but also to begin to organise and channel his aggressive impulses. My ensuing experience was gradually of Billy's greater resilience, more integrated, robust personality and even his more mature and age-appropriate behaviour and speech.

Summary

I began this chapter with a quote from Cairns (2002, p.83) which challenged the idea that anger must be acted out and warned rather of the risk that 'expressing anger makes us more angry'. In summarising this chapter, I wish to revisit Cairns, who goes on to say: 'Pretending that we do not feel angry is also inappropriate. The effective approach is to find some prosocial way of saying who we are and how we are and what that might mean for other people' (2002, p.83).

In the same way, my intention in this chapter has not been to advocate an approach whereby there is no place for aggressive behaviour in music therapy. (Clearly, this would also be untherapeutic, echoing the purported societal view of aggression as a predominantly destructive force and giving the message that aggression, despite being a part of every child's make-up and heightened by some children's traumatic experiences, is unacceptable even in therapy). Rather, my aim has been to begin to explore what constitutes effective practice in working with children's aggressive behaviour. In this chapter, this has involved looking at questions that have arisen through personal experience of working clinically with aggressive behaviour in children aged five to nine who risk mainstream school exclusion. In particular, three forms of aggressive behaviour in music therapy have been considered in relation to case studies:

- To recap the case of *Jamie*, one could argue that his *loud, forceful and aggressive playing on the musical instruments,* as recourse to the physical release of tension, was in itself therapeutic. For myself, however, I did not feel that it was constructive to try to continue to meet Jamie's loud playing so long as he was unable to hear my presence. Rather, I felt that it was only when I ceased colluding with his destructive patterns of behaviour and found other ways to try to engage him that we were able to *think* together about his aggression and to find more pro-social ways for him to express his feelings.

- In the case of *Connor*, having afforded him the initial experience of control and mastery, a purely child-centred therapeutic approach carried the risk of ongoing collusion with his *aggressive, controlling manner*. This, in turn, could have communicated to him that it was acceptable to objectify others and to adopt an abusive, bullying stance towards them. It was only when he began to recognise the impact of his behaviour on others that Connor was able to reflect on his patterns of response and to begin to find more constructive and pro-social ways of expressing his aggressive impulses.

- Finally, *Billy* clearly required a forum at the start of music therapy for the release of traumatic memories and associated destructive urges. As time passed, however, the question arose as to whether Billy's ongoing re-enactment of scenes of violence through *aggressive play and role-play* might actually be serving to reinforce the original experience of trauma. For Billy, his continued expression of anger and aggression also risked becoming a habitual, learned pattern of behavioural response. With this in mind, perhaps my symbolic challenge to his aggressor modelled a position of strength and resilience as a healthier, more robust alternative to the polarised, fragmented positions of aggressor or victim.

Conclusion

According to Cairns, for children who are learning to manage their anger, 'the first step is always to enable the child to identify their own inner experience... Next, children need also to become aware that others have needs and feelings' (2002, p.95). This seems to have been true of all three case examples presented, although it was arguably first necessary to witness, or be subject to, the child's loud, forceful playing on instruments, controlling and abusive manner or violent role-play, in order to then find more pro-social means for pupils to express their aggression. In addition, in all three cases, counter-transference responses ultimately provided some measure of when, in the therapeutic process and relationship, to begin to challenge pupils' behaviour. Tyler points to this essential function of counter-transference as she writes of her work with Beverley:

> I would...monitor my counter-transference response to her frequent commands for me to 'stand up,' 'sit down,' or 'go in the corner.' If I began to feel despised or abused by Beverley I would reply firmly that

I would stay on my chair and allow her to experience the frustration of not being able to control me. (2003, p.42)

In concluding, I wish to acknowledge the significant role of clinical supervision in thinking about effective ways of working with aggressive behaviour in five to nine-year-olds who risk mainstream school exclusion. Above all, discussions with my supervisor highlighted for me the fine line between acceptance and acknowledgement of pupils' expressed aggression and collusion with the ongoing cathartic, evacuative, *unthinking* discharge of it. To say that anger must be acted out in therapy is evidently too simplistic; to say that anger must be suppressed would clearly be untherapeutic. To end with the words of Cairns:

Managing anger is not about never feeling angry, nor is it about pretending to feel something else; it is about recognising the inhibited impulse to destroy and transforming the energy to other uses. (2002, p.93)

Chapter 7

Music Therapy in a Special School

Investigating the Role of Imitation and Reflection in the Interaction between Music Therapist and Child

Jo Tomlinson

For the last 15 years I have worked in special needs and mainstream schools in Cambridgeshire, UK, employed by Cambridgeshire Music, the local peripatetic music service. (See Appendix 1 for information on how the music therapy service was established). I currently work two days a week; one day at a special needs school and one day at a mainstream nursery. I shall discuss the work at the special needs school, which caters for children with a broad spectrum of disabilities from the age of 3 up to 19.

History of the school

To put this work into context I shall reflect on the history of the school and the role of music therapy within this. In Cambridgeshire there were four special needs schools that were closed down in 2006 and replaced by two larger ones. This was a complicated and traumatic process for all the staff and children involved. The old schools were very well established and part of their local community. The amalgamation of staff and replacement of management teams created a great deal of tension. The children, many of whom were autistic and craved predictable and familiar structures and places, were extremely unsettled for a while. However, after five years, it feels as if the atmosphere has calmed, and staff now work very well together as an efficient and caring team.

Music therapy at the old school was well valued and I had built the post up from one day a week to a full-time post over a period of five years. This post was shared between three music therapists. There was also an art therapist and a speech and language therapist at the school whom I met on a regular basis, and sometimes ran sessions with.

During the change-over process we were promised additional funding and two music therapy rooms to accommodate music therapists working at the same time, with larger numbers of pupils. Due to a tighter budget than first thought this did not happen. Art therapy provision was completely cut. Initially there was provision for one full-time music therapy post. However, after three years this was reduced to two and a half days, which makes it very difficult for us to meet the needs of the 150 pupils on roll.

Although this paints a gloomy picture, I feel very optimistic about building the post up to full-time again. It took time to establish music therapy at the old school, and it may be possible to develop the post on a similar scale in the new setting. The reduction of music therapy hours has meant that the other music therapist and I have met more frequently with the head and deputy head of the school to create a fair system of referrals. Meeting with the management team has provided us with support in making decisions over which children should have music therapy, and for how long, and has also helped us to feel more established within the staff team. Due to the large number of children and staff at the school the other music therapist and I decided that it would be simpler if one of us worked with the primary department and one worked with secondary, so that we each had fewer staff to liaise with. This has worked well in this particular context.

Imitative and reflective responses from the therapist during musical exchanges

Over the time that I have been practising as a music therapist I have become fascinated by the regularity of imitative and reflective responses that occur in my music therapy sessions. I have often been struck by the quality and intensity of interaction that can be achieved through this type of exchange. When this is enhanced by a musical framework the results can be extremely rewarding and therapeutically constructive.

I shall begin by exploring corresponding psychoanalytic and music therapy literature and then move on to my own case studies. Within the case studies I shall examine my responses as a music therapist and consider the impact of these on the child, in terms of both therapeutic objectives for sessions and my relationship with the child.

Imitation can be defined as 'following the example of, mimicking or making a copy of', and reflection suggests 'throwing back, showing an image of, or corresponding in appearance' (Oxford English Reference Dictionary 1996). Many music therapists have written about imitative and reflective exchanges within musical interaction (Alvin 1966; Muller and Warwick 1993; Oldfield 2006a, Oldfield and Flower 2008; Pavlicevic 1997; Robarts 1996; Wigram 2004). Juliette Alvin (1966) stated that 'Imitation and repetition are two processes through which man learns, develops and creates. They apply to sound when it becomes a verbal or musical language' (p.79). Alvin goes on to quote Aristotle, 'And further when we listen to imitations we all acquire a sympathy with the feelings imitated even apart from actual rhythms and melodies' (p.79).

In his psychoanalytic work, Donald Winnicott (1991) debates the significance of the mother's mirroring role in relation to the child's changing moods. He considers the potentially detrimental impact of the mother's inability to reflect back the child's mood state if she is too preoccupied with her own emotional condition. To Winnicott the mother's face needs to be the child's first mirror.

Music therapists (Ansdell 1995; Bunt 1994; Oldfield 2006a; Pavlicevic 1997; Robarts 1996; Wigram 2004; Wigram 2002 et al.) have drawn parallels in their work to the developmental and analytical perspectives of the psychoanalytic theorist Daniel Stern. Stern (1985) describes early mother–infant interaction and the role of the mother in constantly imitating the child's behaviour. The essential element of this, however, is that the imitation develops and evolves into something else, so the child's interest and focus is retained: 'the dialogue does not remain a stereotypic boring sequence of repeats, back and forth, because the mother is constantly introducing modifying imitations or providing a theme-and-variation format with slight changes in her contribution at each dialogic turn' (p.139).

Stern elaborates into his theory of 'affect attunement' in which the 'feeling states' of the infant are monitored and reflected. He differentiates between an obvious mimicking of behaviour and an attunement which encapsulates the infant's emotional state. He claims that the mother demonstrates an understanding of the infant's emotional or psychological condition through physical and behavioural imitation and then makes musical parallels within the affect attunement and refers to elements of the exchanges. These consist of levels of intensity, temporal beats, rhythm, duration and shape. These elements are obviously highly relevant to interactive musical exchanges in the music therapy context.

Child psychologist Colwyn Trevarthen (1996) considers the impact of a lack of ability to imitate and engage on a basic level with others: 'autistic children's varied impairment in imitation, which correlates with the degree of impairment in social relating, is part of a fundamental inter-subjective deficit, an aspect of an overall impairment in reciprocal communication' (p.55).

Leslie Bunt (1994) discusses imitation in his work with children and suggests that imitative play can be crucial in the process of establishing contact with a child at the start of music therapy work. Bunt also writes about the research of developmental psychologist Susan Pawlby: 'Early in infancy a mother tends to imitate the child more frequently, with the child imitating the mother as age increases. The kinds of behaviour Pawlby observed being imitated are interesting: vowel-like sounds, bangs and consonant sounds were the three most frequently imitated behaviours in her sample of mother–child pairs' (p.92).

Music therapist Hanne Kortegaard discusses mirroring in relation to music therapy work with schizophrenic patients. He claims that 'By mirroring the patient's music in her own sound language, the music therapist's integrated self may serve a reverie function in relation to the anxiety which the patient expresses in the music' (1993, p.62).

The use of imitative techniques is present in other types of therapies – Linnet McMahon (1992), in her book on play therapy discusses the play therapist Virginia Axline's technique of 'reflective listening'. This involves the recognition of the emotional state of the child through play and discussion, and then reflecting the feelings back, enabling the child to gain insight into their behaviour. Dance movement therapist Hilda Wengrower (2010) writes about the use of 'mirroring and empathic reflection' in work with children with autism, which facilitates the development of a constructive therapeutic relationship and enhanced communication.

Figure 7.1 Imitative exchanges in a music therapy group enhance communication and develop basic social skills

CASE STUDY 7.1: ELIZA

An example of my direct vocal imitation of a child within her music therapy session comes from my work with a girl called Eliza. Eliza has a diagnosis of Down syndrome and is seven years old. I worked with her for three years.

Eliza is very controlling in the way that she relates to other people and prefers to initiate interactive exchanges rather than listening or responding to others. She has a tendency to be very emotionally reactive and finds it hard to cope if she does not feel in control of situations. She resists close physical proximity with other people and moves away from me if I approach her or attempt to join her in shared instrumental playing. Eliza has a great sense of humour and can often be drawn into interactive exchanges that are pleasurable and engaging. Once she is focused on shared playing Eliza is able to explore her voice freely in imitative vocalising with me.

Eliza often brings some sort of transitional object with her to sessions and this is frequently her doll, Rosie. Eliza uses the doll for projecting both her aggressive and loving feelings onto, and generally alternates between hitting Rosie on the head and then cradling her and saying 'Poor Rosie'. She also uses Rosie as an intermediary between herself and me, finding communication via the doll less threatening to her sense of control.

Over the time that I have worked with Eliza her capacity to explore vocalisation has developed enormously. She has been encouraged by my vocal imitation and musical support, and has become increasingly adventurous and creative in the use of her voice. Eliza often focuses on her doll for security and attracts my attention both through making the doll dance around and accompanying the dancing with vocalising.

I shall now describe some video excerpts that I analysed in order to explore our relationship and the way we were interacting in sessions.

Vocal exchanges supported by a rhythmical piano framework

Initially Eliza makes her doll dance around in the air, at the same time as deliberately attracting my attention. She is not facing me and prefers to keep her distance, attempting to maintain her sense of control. Her main focus is on Rosie the doll, but she is also aware of my rhythmical piano accompaniment and moves in time to the music. Eliza then gasps to openly attract my attention and increases her vocalisation. I begin to imitate Eliza vocally and this encourages her to develop and extend her vocalisation. She moves closer to me. The rhythmic piano accompaniment appears to soothe Eliza and it provides a secure, predictable framework within which she can explore imitative exchanges.

The piano accompaniment I use is based around a 12-bar blues structure and is an accompaniment which I find particularly useful in supporting vocal imitation and exploration. The blues chord progression has a relaxed rhythmical feel to it which can contain tension and anticipation without unnecessary pressure and expectation. If a child feels like vocalising in response to the therapist the structure provides support, but if the child does not respond vocally the therapist can continue without a break in the music. In addition the blues have the advantage of being less childish in character than some other predictable chord progressions.

Within this musical framework I continue in my vocal exploration with Eliza. We allow moments of silence, sometimes followed by sudden vocal sounds from me which re-engage Eliza in our exchange. Towards the end of the extract Eliza moves away from me but is vocally more engaged than ever. Her focus and eye-contact remain fixed on Rosie, but vocally she explores my capacity to attune with her. She then experiments with a range of vocal sounds with varied intensity and pitch.

During this interaction a number of factors enable Eliza to take a more relaxed and sustained approach to shared exchange. Eliza needs to retain her sense of personal space but at the same time is testing out my capacity to reflect and respond to her vocal contributions. My reflection with musical and vocal embellishment leads to a sustained and exciting interchange.

This type of communicative progression is described earlier in the quote by Stern (1977) as the way in which mother–infant dialogue develops. The music therapist has the advantage of having the unique medium of musical improvisation with which to augment and intensify this interactive process.

I shall describe two more excerpts from Eliza's sessions, both of which demonstrate my reflective instrumental playing. In this next extract Eliza is manipulating a response from me on the flute. She is controlling my behaviour through her shaker playing; I become 'her reflection' both physically and musically and she makes definite responses to this.

Reflective musical support

Eliza explores 'shaky' playing on the egg shaker and I respond to this by playing a trill on the flute and copying her physical movements. Eye-contact between us at this point is intense and sustained. Eliza then slows down the shaking to observe whether I will meet or attune with her in this behaviour. The quality and intensity of the playing is extremely variable and she makes it quite difficult for me to follow her. Every time it feels like her rhythmic pulse will settle she dramatically increases or decreases the tempo.

Silences within the playing exchanges allow us to have eye-contact and smile at each other. These silent moments create tension and anticipation during the musical dialogue. Eliza begins to thoroughly enjoy her control over me and this establishes enhanced security and balance within our relationship. Humour lightens the intensity of the interaction and makes shared contact more enjoyable and less threatening. During this musical exchange I reproduce both Eliza's physical and emotional state, which again reiterates Stern's concept of attunement.

Reflective play is illustrated again in this next extract where Eliza and I play the xylophones together. Eliza can clearly dictate and predict my responses to her playing. She requires an accurate reflective reaction from me and the intensity of the dialogue is maintained through this expectation and anticipation of my response. Eliza seems particularly aware of her need for me to imitate her playing and to attune in this way.

Imitative support establishes interactive contact

Eliza and I sit opposite each other with two xylophones between us. She is initially prepared to play the xylophone in a conventional way. We both focus on our own musical instrument. Eliza explores glissandi looking up to examine my response and to see if I will copy her, which I do. Eliza quickly becomes bored of playing like this and wants to embellish her approach to the instrument. Again she is constantly assessing whether I am in tune with her movements. She begins to explore bouncing the beater up and down on the carpet. I attempt to draw her back into the playing but quickly realise that I need to directly reflect her movements if we are to retain our sense of dialogue.

Eliza explores playing the beater on the floor the wrong way up. It takes me a while to copy this exactly and it is not until I do that she re-engages in playing the xylophone. We then continue with reflective xylophone playing together and I introduce vocalising and singing, which Eliza joins in with. Had I purely mimicked Eliza's beater investigation on the carpet she might have become fixated with this behaviour. Instead I directly imitate for a brief moment to meet her within this investigation, and then move the exploration on to further instrumental playing. In this way there is a forward flow of interactive ideas, rather than an obsessive or repetitive pattern of communication.

My role of imitator and reflector in my work with Eliza has been of paramount importance to the development of our relationship and in the achievement of therapeutic objectives. This has been primarily due to the fact that Eliza needs to control dialogue with other people. By allowing her to retain this sense of control, she has been able to engage in shared, co-operative interaction. Eliza does not like to conform socially in the conventional sense, but can be enticed into enjoyable reciprocal exchanges that evolve into Stern's 'theme-and-variation' format of communication. Eliza's amusement and involvement in this process then allow her to relax and loosen her control over the interplay.

In the next two casework examples I shall demonstrate the use of instrumental rhythmical reflection, where the focus for the playing is based around song structures.

CASE STUDY 7.2: DANIEL

I have worked with Daniel for two years. He was eight years old when I started working with him. He is quite severely autistic although relatively sociable. Daniel can be obsessive and repetitive in his communicative patterns, and is demanding and attention-seeking in the classroom setting. Daniel is exceptionally motivated by music and I rarely see the more difficult aspects of his behaviour in the music therapy context as he is generally focused on singing and playing.

Daniel is primarily motivated by singing activities in his music therapy sessions, and for the first year of his music therapy was totally disinterested in the musical instruments. However, he has gradually begun to explore expressive playing on the complete range of instruments available. The development of his playing over the last two years has reflected his overall social and emotional development. Whereas initially he could only focus in a very fragmented way on social exchanges, he has become more consistently engaged and his playing is increasingly rhythmical and sustained.

The following two descriptions of video excerpts of music therapy sessions demonstrate Daniel's ability to connect musically and socially with me whilst involved in song-related playing. In the first extract Daniel has suggested one of his favourite songs, which I play on the piano. I attempt to support rhythmically and follow his somewhat fragmented drumming, at the same time as keeping the basic structure of the song coherent. Daniel joins in with occasional words to the song. This extends and reinforces his use of verbal communication.

Musical support and reflective rhythmical responses

Daniel has requested his favourite song 'The Inchworm'. He launches into a spontaneous drumming accompaniment in reaction to my piano playing. Daniel's playing begins rhythmically and enthusiastically but the rhythmic consistency gradually diminishes. I reflect this evolving rhythmic progression on the piano. Daniel is so fixated with the words and melody of the tune that he finds it hard to keep focused on the drumming. He periodically sings out the last word to each phrase. He glances up at me regularly and is totally engaged in the song and the shared experience of playing and singing.

Daniel appreciates the control he has over me in dictating which song we select and my rhythmic following of his playing. However, he is extremely flexible in comparison with earlier sessions, where he could not focus on an individual song all the way through before demanding another. In a similar way to the exchanges with Eliza, there are periods of silence which add to the intensity of the interaction.

A combination of factors enables Daniel to remain focused on co-operative play. The structure of the song provides security and predictability which seems so helpful for children with autism. This enables Daniel to take control and lead from the drum, and I can then reflect his playing in a rhythmical sense from the piano. The excitement and anticipation of singing the words to songs promotes Daniel's language development.

In a similar way in the next extract Daniel has selected a song for me to play on the flute, which he chooses to accompany on the tambourine. Again I attempt to follow the faltering rhythm that he establishes on the tambourine. Through this rhythmic following Daniel makes intense contact with me and this provokes him to offer me the tambourine to contribute to the playing on this instrument. Without this rhythmic engagement and extreme musical motivation Daniel would find it hard to share interactively on this level, without some type of obsessive or attention-seeking behaviour taking over.

Figure 7.2 Shared imitative drumming can promote the use of eye-contact and develop turn-taking skills

Rhythmical reflection leading to structured turn-taking

In this excerpt Daniel leads both in his instrumental playing on the tambourine and in his choice of song, 'Never smile at a crocodile', which I play on the flute. I reflect back his rhythmically faltering tambourine playing on the flute. There is sustained eye-contact between us; he is focusing on the tambourine playing but is also very aware of me and is predicting my playing.

Daniel spontaneously expresses an interest in more structured turn-taking on the tambourine and holds out the instrument for me to play. He then shouts out 'Jo play the tambourine' and shows some confusion in the fact that I am playing the flute. This interest in turn-taking exchanges is something which has developed over time and demonstrates his increased flexibility in relation to communicative interaction.

It would feel inappropriate for me to engage in direct imitative vocalising with Daniel, primarily because of his verbal abilities and his capacity to focus on singing. I find that direct vocal imitation is generally constructive with children who are pre-verbal, and particularly in the initial stages of language development. Obviously this is not age-dependent but developmentally related.

Daniel's interest in structured turn-taking activities is an element of our music therapy sessions that has developed over the last couple of years.

Initially Daniel needed to have absolute control over the singing in sessions and could not explore the instruments, either musically or mechanically. He gradually began to explore the percussion instruments and was able to engage in expressive playing within the predictable framework of turn-taking. In this extract Daniel holds out the tambourine because he wants more of a physical and obvious exchange between us, in addition to the musical dialogue. As with Eliza, my reflective musical responses to Daniel's singing and playing have enhanced his capacity to connect and relax into communicative play.

CASE STUDY 7.3: SAM

My final case work example is of a 19-year-old boy with a diagnosis of Down syndrome. I have worked with Sam for three years, primarily in a small group, and then individually as I felt that he needed the space to express himself freely in a one-to-one context. Sam is very lively and humorous in his response to social activities but can also be extremely stubborn and controlling. Within school he has limited opportunities to express the more boisterous elements of his personality, which are sometimes perceived by staff to be tiresome. He is generally very popular amongst his peers and with staff, but in the further education unit has little time to express himself either vocally or musically. As he has very limited verbal communication Sam needs a space for spontaneous and humorous expression that is not perceived as 'attention-seeking' or 'demanding'.

In this extract I follow Sam's drumming on the piano and we engage in imitative vocalising. Here there is a combination of rhythmical and harmonic support from the piano, which provides the basis for vocal imitative exchanges and again I use the 12-bar blues structure to support the interaction.

Vocal and instrumental dialogue based on imitative exchange

Sam begins his playing with a few definite beats on the drum which I reflect back on the piano. He looks up in recognition of the interaction and establishes eye-contact. Sam then experiments with a few lighter taps on the drum and grins when I reflect this back musically. Sam's playing becomes more rhythmically complex and he begins to vocalise. The interaction becomes increasingly communicative.

Sam explores a range of vocal sounds which are contrastingly low and high-pitched and is delighted by my imitation of these. He incorporates explosive and infectious laughter into our exchange. He begins to develop different rhythmic styles and body movements and seems quite liberated by both the musical and vocal support. The speed and intensity of the drumming builds up and Sam continues to engage in boisterous vocalising.

For Sam the music therapy space allows him to express the lively elements of his personality in a constructive and socially acceptable manner. Sam is extremely motivated by music and sound, and often becomes immersed in what Daniel Stern describes as a 'positive feedback spiral'. This occurs as Sam offers a musical contribution, I respond, he then vocalises, I imitate and the interactive intensity escalates. Sam's enjoyment of musical interchange has provided an incentive for him to co-operate with me in sessions and to take an increasingly flexible approach to shared playing. He has also been able to explore both the expressive and communicative elements of vocalising and verbal interaction.

Conclusion

Imitative and reflective responses within a musical framework are integral to my work with children with special needs. As a music therapist I am essentially emulating the maternal role by responding in this way, both vocally and musically. This enhances and nurtures the relationship I have with the child, and facilitates more fluid and connected interactive exchange.

Figure 7.3 Shared imitative responses to songs can promote a more flexible approach to interactive play

Imitative responses from an adult can enable a child to feel heard, and this reinforces the child's sense of identity and individuality. When this evolves into reciprocal attunement, a previously isolated child can be drawn into increased social involvement. Additionally, imitative exchanges can enable the child to take control of the dialogue. This can enhance self-esteem and give the child a much-needed sense of control.

Humour as part of this process can be a very useful tool (Haire and Oldfield 2009). I am often amazed how much fun it can be to engage with a child through imitative exchange, particularly if they have previously been difficult to connect with. Using humour within imitative exchange can subtly diminish social defences and promote more flexible, freer shared interaction. In turn this can lead the child into more extended periods of expressive play.

At times imitation is used as an attempt to reinforce existing behaviour, at other times it can be used to promote change. Imitation and reflection used within a therapeutic context can be powerful and valuable tools when used with care and sensitivity in relation to the needs of the child.

Chapter 8

'Music, My Voice' Projects for Children

The Development of One Aspect of a Community-based Music Therapy Service in York and North Yorkshire

Angela Harrison

Introduction

This chapter will describe the means by which a small team of therapists have introduced music therapy into special and mainstream schools. The North Yorkshire Music Therapy Centre is a registered charity which provides a music therapy service for people of all ages. With music therapy not being a statutory provision in the region, other sources of funding have been found to sustain an area of service specifically for families with children with special needs. The chapter will focus on the development of projects funded by 'Music, My Voice', a restricted fund into which schools, charitable trusts, fundraisers and donors contribute.

To set the scene we will look at the background to the charity, the ethos and founding characters, then move on to the development of a well-respected service for children and adults of all ages in York and North Yorkshire. I will describe the early establishment of a mobile unit, a van in which music therapy could take place, and following this the integration of music therapy into special and mainstream schools by a small therapy team working in a largely rural community. The crucial aspect of funding will be examined, particularly the creation of the 'Music, My Voice' fund, which since 2000 has provided full or subsidised funding for therapy for children. The many and varied sources for this fund will be described and the implications of this system of supporting music therapy explored.

Having looked at the establishment of a variety of 'Music, My Voice' projects we will examine in detail the development of a style of working to meet the needs of children and young people with a range of difficulties as they develop and move up through one particular special school. Finally, I will draw together the threads which, in combination, produce an intricate, effective pattern for service provision in a challenging economic climate.

Background to the charity

To explain the background to the charity, we have to go back to 1984, when music therapy was virtually unknown in North Yorkshire. At that time Mary and Raymond Abbotson set up a music therapy practice, working at their home near the North Yorkshire Moors. Mary had trained as a music therapist in the 1970s at the Nordoff-Robbins course in London, and Raymond had been a head teacher of a special school in Liverpool.

As their practice became established, Mary and Raymond were concerned by the long distances that families were having to travel in order to access music therapy and so, in 1988, they fulfilled their vision of delivering therapy in a mobile unit, designed by Raymond, to house a keyboard, computer and space for instruments to be transported.

The Abbotsons worked hard to set up the infrastructure for an organisation with charitable status, registering the North Yorkshire Music Therapy Centre with the Charity Commission in 1990. The ethos of the charity was based on Quaker principles and the approach of Nordoff and Robbins. The main considerations were:

- Every person has a right to be creative, regardless of illness or disability.

- Care can best be provided in a holistic way, considering all areas of a person's life.

Mary and Raymond made applications to a number of charitable trusts and gathered up sufficient funds to commission a purpose-built van to be created by a coach maker in Scarborough. The mobile unit was lined with carpet, had steps for access and provision for heating, lighting, running water and video recording. An electronic keyboard was installed as well as a computer and space for acoustic instruments. Working with specialists at the York Electronics Centre and the Department of Electronics, University of York they equipped the van to the highest specification, allowing for a variety of MIDI-based technologies to be used.

The mobile unit was conspicuous on the roads of North Yorkshire from 1992–98, providing a workspace and acting as an excellent promotional tool with its prominent livery.

Mary's style laid emphasis on co-working, client-led therapy and analysis of sessions through videotaped and/or sound-recorded evidence. She and her husband were dedicated to making music therapy available across a wide geographical area and also, through the use of technology, appealing and accessible to a range of young people.

The van made it possible to combine the Abbotsons' music therapy practice

Figure 8.1 Striking livery kept our service in the public eye

with the use of technology, another passion of this extraordinary couple. A built-in cupboard housed a computer which allowed clients to compose and create their own music through electronic means. Other innovative gadgetry included an ingenious microphone which enables the user to convert their vocal sound into a chosen MIDI sound on the keyboard. This has since proved invaluable in encouraging shy youngsters to use their voice, helping those with limited range of pitch in their spoken voice to experiment and those who cannot speak to develop their vocalisations into more recognisable sounds as their confidence grows.

I helped to provide the mobile service when I was working as an assistant to the therapist and later during my music therapy training. My job involved driving the van, supporting children in sessions and contributing to feedback for school staff and for session records. We travelled in all weathers, risking snow and ice to take the service to those who needed it. The van simply required an electrical connection to our place of work and we then had lighting, heating, video provision and a compact, but entirely adequate therapy area in which we could keep a consistent layout. Disadvantages related to the potential hazard of working in a confined

Figure 8.2 A compact, versatile, light and airy workspace

space away from the main body of the school and also the access to the van, which was without an electronic hoist. Driving along narrow country roads proved a challenge for myself and others after me but the great thing was that we were self-contained. All our instruments were stored in the van, we had music technology for use in the sessions and we were not making demands on schools for therapy space, a subject often fraught with difficulty. It is rare to find a room in a school which is large enough, in a location where the therapy will neither disrupt nor be disrupted by class work and where it is not necessary to rearrange the room and carry out a risk assessment for every visit. The van meant that we could work with children with a minimum of alteration to their routine and it also meant that children who were being taken out of school for their music therapy could be brought to a central point, wherever the van was parked, so saving parents hours of travelling time each week.

Nevertheless, the disadvantages finally outweighed the advantages and the van fell out of use in 1998, replaced by a commitment from schools and other workplaces to provide suitable therapy space and to begin to integrate music therapy into the overall provision.

The precedent of this mobile service should not be underestimated and music therapists similarly faced with serving a widely spread, sparsely populated community might well consider establishing such a vehicle, with better access and some form of ready communication with the 'outside world'.

There is likely to be an increase in the use of music technology in therapy and with the challenge for our profession to undertake more robust research, it is a real strength to have a regulated environment where equipment can be set up and readily available for use.

Development of the service

Moving on from the days of travelling with the mobile unit, the charity has developed a broad-reaching service to meet the needs of children and adults in a range of settings. We provide weekly therapy in respite care and family centres, care homes, hospitals and where a medical condition makes it difficult for a family to travel we will visit a client in their own home. Some school-aged children are brought out of school to community-based clinics or are seen at home, after school. We have developed good relationships with other providers of children's services and so our work continues through the school holidays in the form of workshops and individual sessions. Our provision in mainstream and special schools is made up of a combination of time-limited work and ongoing weekly input. The decisions as to how and where therapy might be provided are made on the basis of the needs of the child, suitability of therapy space, preference of families/staff and the availability of a therapist.

During the period 2000–09, our team expanded at one point to four therapists and we introduced music therapy into 26 schools in the region.

At the beginning of 2010 our team working with children had reduced to two therapists, but we were still visiting four special and five mainstream schools each week, in some cases offering a full day's provision and in others working with just one child.

Many of our schools are in small villages scattered across the countryside so when we plan our work schedules we have to take into consideration travelling time, particularly in winter. Our geographical remit is based on the City of York and North Yorkshire, the largest county in the UK. With limited resources we need to restrict our activities to York, the surrounding area, and a relatively confined area to the east of the county. This is difficult to explain when enquiries come in from further afield as there are few, if any, music therapists to whom we can refer on when a child needs, or a school requests, therapy.

The development of the North Yorkshire Music Therapy Centre's service for children in schools has largely been through word of mouth. Parents may contact the office of the charity to say that they have heard that the therapy can be helpful, or teachers will get in touch having been told of the benefits when networking with staff from other schools. A number of children have been referred for therapy by NHS professionals including consultant community paediatricians and clinical psychologists. These referrals are made on the understanding that funding will come from private or charitable sources.

Whilst the majority of the children and young people we work with in schools have a statement of special needs, music therapy has yet to be added to the statement of any child in York or North Yorkshire as a statutory provision. This puts the onus on individual schools who may choose to fund or part-fund a period of therapy or, in the case of looked-after children who have been referred to address problems relating to attachment and/or emotional and behavioural issues, short-term therapy may be funded by Social Services. Otherwise, there is an expectation that parents will purchase sessions by private arrangement (this will be discussed in the next section).

The exclusion of music therapy from the package of educational, social and healthcare support offered to a child by the statutory authorities means that we have to work very closely with the schools we visit to ensure that our input is integrated as far as possible into existing systems. This can be an extremely fruitful process and a learning experience for ourselves as therapists to find out more about the overall support available for each child. It can additionally enhance the capacity of the school team to think about the relevance of music therapy in supporting the emotional well-being and education of their students.

Long-term, consistent therapeutic input into a school has a cumulative effect. Active participation in music-making comes to be understood as a crucial factor in the development of the minds of young people. With this established, the specific use of music therapy can be separated out as an intervention applicable for benefiting certain children. Over time, the kinds of difficulties that can be addressed by music therapy become evident and also whether individual or group sessions are going to be most effective.

I think few things emphasise the value of music therapy more than when teenagers are flourishing, having had music therapy in their formative years and are seen alongside the younger children in school who are providing week-by-week evidence of the impact of the therapy. It is this situation which has prompted me to reflect upon the development of my style of working in one particular school and to consider the need for flexibility in the therapy to engage young people at different stages of their development. This will be described in detail later, but first we move to the thorny issue of funding.

Sourcing funds

Limitation on statutory funding for our service for children has acted as a catalyst for a number of imaginative initiatives and widespread community involvement. Funding for the North Yorkshire Music Therapy Centre's work with children is drawn from a variety of sources. These include contributions from schools, grants from charitable trusts or local councils, fees paid by statutory bodies, subsidised fees paid by parents and money raised by our trustees and numerous other supporters. We have actively sought additional support from a wide range of areas resulting in one-off donations, regular monthly giving, excellent media coverage and awards.

Parents have organised concerts, jumped from an aeroplane (with a parachute!), held coffee mornings and other fundraisers and sent individual donations. Local groups have invited us to present the charity's profile and engage them in musical improvisation and have responded with donations for our charitable work and for the purchase of musical instruments.

Other equipment has been funded by grants from trusts and businesses and we have been able to equip our therapists with the latest audio and video technology of the highest quality to record work, subject to permission. This has provided compelling evidence to support funding applications to schools and charitable bodies.

Our president and five patrons, all of international standing in the world of the arts, have generously contributed to raising our profile and attracting funds. They have each played an active role in the North Yorkshire Music Therapy Centre programme of events which has served to enrich the culture of the local community and to raise awareness of the existence and potential benefits of music therapy. This has enabled local people to contribute towards the well-being of some of the most vulnerable children by donating time, energy and money.

To evaluate the quality of our organisation, we have applied for a number of awards over the years. We have twice been shortlisted for the prestigious National Community Health IMPACT Awards, a partnership initiative by The King's Fund and SmithKline Beecham and have received two awards from HRH The Duke of York's Community Initiative panel.

The requirement to constantly find funds has put pressure on the organisation. Back in 1999, we were in a position where our resources were seriously stretched and this was threatening to exclude families from being able to access music therapy. Following two unsuccessful applications to major funders, the trustees of the North Yorkshire Music Therapy Centre had to make a radical decision or face the possibility of closure. A series of meetings with an external advisor laid the foundations for a new business plan and a strategy was devised to lead the charity into a more secure future. In 2000 the trustees decided to establish 'Music, My Voice', a restricted fund to support our work with children. This was designed to consist of a number of clearly defined individual projects as well as a general fund to be allocated to sessions as and when needed. In the first ten years, appeals for 'Music, My Voice' projects raised over £200,000 to help us to provide music therapy for children and young people.

Grants have come from charitable trusts situated in all parts of the country, each providing essential and much appreciated support. One trust passed on to us an investment portfolio which provides income to cover our support costs, many have given one-off grants and others generously provide us with sustained support, for which we are particularly grateful.

To have such a mixed source of funding provides us with an element of financial security, flexibility in the way that we are able to work and gives us the potential to respond quickly to new demand for our service. It does, however, create a great deal of work behind the scenes.

There is a wealth of administrative tasks required in order to secure grant aid in this way:

- Developing new projects in liaison with associated agencies.

- Researching sources of funding – establishing criteria, format of application, etc.

- Producing evidence of need and financial information to support an application.

- Completing project evaluation reports if request is for continuation of funding.

- Planning budget, timescale and sustainability of each project.

- Ensuring the availability of a therapist to do the work.

Once a grant has been received, the work continues and includes:

- Adding the project to a running spreadsheet to meticulously track the cash flow.

- Adjusting either the length of project or the weekly allocation of subsidy in cases where the amount requested has not been fully met.

- Working with therapists to write information leaflets, questionnaires/evaluation forms.

- Ensuring that permission has been given for photographic/video records.

- Publicising the grant aid where appropriate in the media and in the charity's website, quarterly newsletter and annual report and accounts.

- Delivering and monitoring the project.

- Preparing video footage, whilst preserving anonymity.

- Preparing a detailed report, with evidence on completion of the project.

- Circulating this to the funder, host school and individual reports to parents.

These lists highlight the multiplicity of skills that have to be developed if a team of therapists is going to provide a service in the way that we do. With little scope for paying an administrative team to undertake the work, there is reliance on the contribution of skilled volunteers and on versatility, combined with long hours, on the part of the therapists.

It is extremely rewarding when a school recognises that we have worked hard to raise funds over a number of years in order to provide music therapy and contributes at a level which begins to make the project sustainable. This level of commitment tends to be reflected in the extent to which music therapy is integrated into the curriculum and into the ethos of the school.

It is my work in one such special school which I will now describe.

Case work

Rather than choosing individual case work, I would like to present the method of music therapy which I have developed during eight years of working in this school one day a week. Music therapy has impacted on the lives of children from nursery up to secondary ages and I think it will be valuable to look at the changing needs which are being met at the various stages of development.

This particular school caters for children with communication, interaction and sensory difficulties, many diagnosed as on the autistic spectrum or with specific conditions which affect their development. Children are not grouped specifically by age, but move through the school in the most effective way to meet their learning styles and changing needs. They will be placed within a suitable peer group for each year and even this is flexible, for if it is found that a child is not settled or learning at the optimum level, they will be moved to a more appropriate class. These decisions are made with care and in consultation with families.

In discussion with the communication and interaction co-ordinator, also the head of primary, I have decided to describe the music therapy process through numbered categories, these relating more to levels of engagement than to age groups or strictly defined key stages.

Some children are referred for individual therapy, but for this analysis I will describe therapy in groups.

1. **Here we see a small group of children with significant developmental and language delay. They may not yet be diagnosed with a specific condition but all have a statement of special needs**

Music therapy brings an approach tailored to the needs of the individual child, within a group setting. I have developed a method which is held within a loose structure as follows:

- 'Hello' song.

- Offer the guitar to each child, allowing them to respond at their own pace and as they reach out to strum the strings, I sing about what they are doing, using their name.

- Show the children two instruments and ask them to indicate which one they would like to play. This may be indicated verbally, by pointing or by looking at the preferred instrument.

- Improvise a song with keyboard accompaniment which will resonate with the sounds of the instruments chosen and will include sections which highlight the playing of the individual children.

- Sing together a song with actions where the staff members present can support the children and encourage them to use their hands to join in with the gestures.

- 'Goodbye' song.

Working in this way requires the children to exercise the following skills:

- Responding to their name, either with a verbal response or with eye-contact/smile.

- Listening.

- Using physical dexterity to strum the strings of the guitar with a regular rhythm. This is encouraged by the singing of a song about their actions – a song inspired by the rhythm, energy level and engagement with which they play.

- Making a choice and communicating this to another.

- Playing an instrument, with or without assistance.

- Rehearsing actions to songs, watching and imitating.

Most of these skills are required in order to access learning of any kind. Without the ability to listen, communicate a choice, imitate and develop fine and gross motor skills, children will be disadvantaged.

For children at this stage I believe it is even more important that the process of self-awareness can be significantly assisted by the experience of playing or moving while the therapist synchronises a song with the child's rhythm, style and energy levels. This is a 'meeting' at a deep level and will lay the foundations for future development as the child moves up through the school system.

There may not be a great sense of group process within this class as each child is still absorbed by his or her needs and contribution. Evident awareness of others comes a little later.

2. **Here, the children have moved into a more focused learning environment, with some emphasis on shared activity. Each child is encouraged to develop in their own way, with respect and recognition of the presence of others, the staff team and their classmates**

Music therapy here follows a similar structure to the previous group, but with important differences which reflect the developmental stage of the children.

After the 'hello' song, again the guitar is offered to each child. This time there is encouragement to experiment with a range of styles, using a combination of plucking and strumming, and the song I sing while they are playing draws attention to the imaginative ways in which they are playing.

Language is likely to be further developed in the children here, so I can ask a child what song he would like, or in the case of a familiar nursery rhyme, each child can contribute with words and choices expressed verbally. Now, I am encouraging the children to develop their dexterity further, so I may offer, for example, a buffalo drum and demonstrate a sequence of hand movements for each child to copy. Options might be:

- using a fist, then open hand and back to fist to hit the drum
- playing repeatedly whilst counting
- drawing a geometric shape on the drum
- beating a short rhythm
- drumming individual fingers on the skin whilst vocalising.

In a situation where there may be anxiety or uncertainty about what is expected, I will take a more structured approach and explain to the group before we start exactly what is likely to happen and in what sequence. This can be very reassuring and may enable a child to stay for the duration of the group and tolerate waiting, listening, letting go of favoured instruments and allowing others to make choices and take their turn.

For these children, my input into the school week is informed by current topics, so I may introduce songs about animals, textures, foods, etc. if these are things which are being discussed in class.

3. The children at this stage are beginning to use their imagination and can bring their new-found literacy and numeracy skills to enrich the music therapy process

To meet the developmental needs of these children, I vary the structure of the group activities to allow for greater use of imagination. The children may invent their own songs, play tuned instruments and respond to verbal cues relating to colour, letter or number. More complex rhythms may be imitated and there will be a far greater sense of shared creativity with each child taking the initiative and being rewarded by a meaningful musical experience.

Alongside this, there may still be a need for the structure of the session to be explained at the beginning, in order to soothe anxiety and allow for praise and encouragement on the achievement of each element of the process.

4. By this stage, as the young people are gaining independence, greater demands can be made on their initiative, imagination, confident participation and courage to experiment

The sessions now bring together the opportunity to freely improvise, to discuss thoughts and feelings relating to the music and to take a position of responsibility. This may involve leading the music on a particular instrument, or conducting the group members to indicate, by non-verbal communication, variations in volume, style and tempo.

Drums are used to conduct conversations, allowing the young people to listen, to make eye-contact with one another and to take note of non-verbal cues. Messages are sent round the group using rhythm, and images are evoked by using instruments such as a tambourine, pretending that it is 'heavy', 'hot', 'sticky', 'noisy' or 'silent'. This requires imagination, self-control and a sense of drama. Over a period of time, the young people become confident and capable in such skills.

At this stage, there is more chance to contribute verbally and those young people who have difficulties with language can use a combination of signing, assisted communication, singing and words.

5. The young people have developed further and those who are referred for music therapy may be quite able in many respects, but still find social interaction challenging

Now the therapy has the potential to incorporate some quite sophisticated musical processes. Discussion is stimulated by familiar music, either from films or television and a combination of singing and playing relaxes the group members and helps them to contribute in a fluid and confident way. Supported by a member of staff, the young people participate by playing guitar and developing their own style, by choosing music to play or sing or by leading the group's music from the keyboard, deciding on sounds and rhythms to support their playing. Each group member is encouraged to talk about his or her interests and to share something of their knowledge. My role is to provide a catalyst for interaction, using my experience as a viola player to metaphorically weave a melody between group members, stimulating conversation and creating shared points of reference.

Improvisation is flexible and images are discussed as the music produces evocative sounds. Discussions are stimulating, drawing out information from each person which might otherwise not be forthcoming. There is opportunity for taking the lead, making choices for the group and relating to one another through verbal, non-verbal and musical means.

These are the teenagers referred to earlier in the chapter, who came into school and entered this therapeutic process as young children and who have been able, over a number of years, to draw from music therapy those things they have needed in order to flourish.

The head teacher of the school writes:

> Music therapy is highly valued by the children, staff, families and governing body. When music therapy was first introduced into the school, it was available to only a lucky few. We now consider music therapy to be an essential and integral part of the curriculum for the many students at the school who have significant communication difficulties and or autism. We budget for this each year.
>
> Through ensuring music therapy is included in the learning for these pupils we have seen very clear and improved progress. This progress is reported on at annual review. The therapist is often involved in our

training days and music therapy is included in our open evenings. Parents tell us they are very impressed with the therapy received by their children.

The greatest impact is demonstrated through the children's improved listening, independence, choice making, two-way interaction, turn-taking and concentration. The sessions also have a significant impact on alleviating symptoms for those pupils who suffer very high anxiety levels. In addition, all involved in the sessions feel a sense of achievement and enjoyment.

As well as the wonderful benefits for the students, teachers and teaching assistants have also benefited. We have been involved in teaching sessions and participated in training workshops with the therapist. Through these experiences we have gained a greater understanding of music therapy and have as a result reflected on all aspects of communication and interaction. This has improved our understanding and practice.

Conclusion

The value of music therapy as an intervention for school-aged children is gradually becoming established and recognised in York and North Yorkshire. For 20 years the North Yorkshire Music Therapy Centre has employed music therapists to work in special and mainstream schools to help children to develop and learn. These children and young people have a range of difficulties relating to communication, interaction, sensory input, emotional or behavioural problems, physical disabilities or attention deficits.

This provision has been made possible by the generosity of those who are convinced by the effectiveness of music therapy to change lives. Support has been given by people from all walks of life who have contributed time, energy and money to help to bring therapy to those children who need it.

Music therapy is such a flexible intervention that it can continue to meet the needs of young people at different stages of their development, as seen in the example of work in one special school in Yorkshire.

Finally, we see the model of working at the North Yorkshire Music Therapy Centre as a means by which members of a rural community can support music therapists in their work. By this they help disadvantaged children and young people to reach their potential and participate fully in the life of that community.

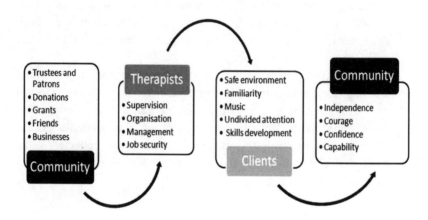

Figure 8.3 Serving, enriching and supported by our community

Chapter 9

Music Therapy in Interface Schools in Belfast

A Creative Response to Cumulative Trauma

Karen Diamond

Introduction

This chapter describes the CODA music therapy service being delivered to primary school children aged between 4 and 11 living in Interface areas in Belfast. The service is provided by the Northern Ireland Music Therapy Trust (NIMTT) and is funded through a programme for victims and survivors of the Troubles established by the first devolved Northern Ireland Assembly. My role in this service is to identify potential schools and to explore with them how a music therapy service could be established. I then monitor the service through visits and service evaluations as well as directly supervising the music therapists carrying out the clinical service delivery.

The Oxford English Dictionary describes a coda as something which 'forms a more definite and satisfactory conclusion', but which is independent of all that has gone before. CODA therefore seems an appropriate title for a service which aimed to use music therapeutically to help victims and survivors reflect upon their experiences, to confront issues which continue to affect their daily living and to achieve catharsis, which enables them to look forward.

When the CODA music therapy service was in the planning stages in 2002/03 it was not anticipated that the generation born after the Good Friday Agreement in 1998 would present with issues associated with being a victim or a survivor. However, in a needs-based assessment of groups and organisations working in the Victims and Survivors sector commissioned by the Northern Ireland Music Therapy Trust and carried out by the charity Save the Children in 2003, over 50 per cent of the 98 victims groups who responded indicated a significant deficit in provision for 5 to 11-year-olds. More recent research indicates that since the ceasefires young people continue to be at risk of violence, including punishment beatings and exiling from within their own communities (Radford 2010).

To understand why children living in Interface areas are impacted by the past it is necessary to understand how the Troubles contribute to their current experiences and difficulties by creating a segregated living environment and education system.

The Troubles

The Troubles relates here to the period from July 1969 until December 1998. According to the Conflict Archive on the Internet, during this time 36,923 shootings and an estimated 16,209 bombings occurred (CAIN 2010); there were 3,725 recorded deaths (McKittrick *et al.* 2007) and police statistics show that over 47,541 people were physically injured. The Cost of the Troubles (COTT) Study (Fay, Morrissey and Smyth 1999) revealed that the civilian population was severely impacted by the violence, experiencing 54 per cent of the deaths and 68 per cent of the injuries. Their study also indicated that the six NI postal areas where the CODA music therapy service is delivered (North and West Belfast and Derry City) accounted for 33.5 per cent of all deaths under the age of 25 (Fay *et al.* 1999).

Hillyard, Rolston and Tomlinson writing in 2005 found that 54,000 households had been forced to move from one area to another as a result of attack, intimidation and harassment.

This movement of people was most strongly experienced in the urban areas of Belfast and Derry/Londonderry where, in an effort to quell the sectarian violence between the two communities, the British army erected a number of brick and metal walls described as peace lines in the 1970s. These physical boundaries created what are known as Interface areas and although the Troubles are now officially over, these areas continue to exist.

Figure 9.1 A 'peace line' wall dividing the two communities

What is an Interface area in 2010?

An Interface area is a small geographical single identity area populated for the most part by people who are perceived to come from either the Roman Catholic/nationalist or the Protestant/unionist community. The residents are surrounded by the physical reminders of segregation and difference. This is visible in terms of the physical walls which separate their communities, heavily fortified police stations, walls adorned with murals and flags espousing one tradition or the other flying from lamp-posts. Another synonymous feature are gates which can only be passed through at certain times of the day and which will be shut if there is any community tension or rioting, severely impeding freedom of movement.

Living in an Interface area impacts on how residents go about daily activities such as shopping, visiting their GP, consulting the library or using the leisure centre. Evidence from studies into the lives of people living in violent Interface areas reveals that people are reluctant to access services and facilities which are perceived to be situated in the 'other' community (DHSSPS 2004). As a direct result the duplication of many services such as schools, health facilities and housing is evident. Segregated areas such as these present a significant challenge in terms of access to and the delivery of statutory services.

Paramilitary organisations on both sides of the divide have strong influences in the management of their areas as they police the informal criminal justice system in their areas with political and, in most cases, legal impunity (Knox 2002). The children of members of paramilitary organisations/ex-combatants in these areas experienced emotional and psychological stress during the Troubles and subsequently as their parents adjust to a post-conflict society (Jamieson and Grounds 2002; Leonard 2004). In such small communities everyone knows who the leaders and their associates are and the fear of getting on the wrong side of the paramilitaries is very much in evidence.

Interface areas witnessed some of the highest levels of violence and trauma during the Troubles and continue to be severely impacted by the legacy. The continuing consequences of conflict-related injury or trauma, the re-emergence of paramilitary activity from dissident republican groups and loyalist groups, contentious marching issues, the continuing impact of sectarianism and segregation and the effects of social and economic deprivation are acutely experienced in Interface areas.

The decades of intense violence severely undermined economic investment and development leading to high levels of deprivation which Horgan found 'exacerbated child poverty and impaired employment opportunities' (2005, p.13) leading to third and fourth generation unemployment. As a result educational underachievement, little engagement with education services, high levels of alcohol abuse and the use/abuse of both prescribed and non-prescribed medication are also features in many Interface areas today.

Figure 9.2 A gate allowing pedestrian access only, which is closed at dusk each night and all day when there is community tension

Education

The provision of education in Northern Ireland is also segregated, as children from Catholic and Protestant backgrounds do not generally attend school together, therefore significantly lessening their exposure to those from different backgrounds. Since the Good Friday Agreement in 1998 there has been a slight increase in integrated education, however, in 2009 the Department of Education in Northern Ireland found that approximately 93 per cent of children and young people attend schools which are either in the Protestant Controlled or Catholic Maintained sector. As Fraser and Morgan (1999) observed:

> The dual education system was one major element in a segregated social system which produced Protestants and Catholics with few contacts outside their own section of the community. Children and young people grew up attending separate schools and forming friendships almost exclusively with co-religionists.

For children living in Interface areas the segregated education system and the physical locations 'illustrate the durability of sectarianism and the consolidation of physical boundaries marked by continuing hostility' (Leonard 2004, p.106).

Defining trauma in this context – can we?

In the wake of such long-term political conflict the outcome in Northern Ireland 'does not conform to the *Diagnostic Statistical Manual* (DSM) definition of Post Traumatic Stress Disorder, as affected individuals are likely to have been traumatised numerous times' (Muldoon 2007, p.14). Gibson commented the consequences of the conflict 'are not adequately represented through reference to psychiatric symptomatology' as the events did not occur 'against the background of an otherwise harmonious existence' (Gibson 2001, p.70).

The Caring Through the Troubles Report (CTTR) observed that the 'residential segregation (particularly in cities) and cycles of intimidation accompanied by population movement cannot be without their health effects' (Smyth, Morrissey and Hamilton 2001, p.6). The traumatic reaction to the Troubles appears to permeate many levels of functioning, and the Northern Ireland Social Services Inspectorate report in 1998 spoke of 'an ever-widening circle of individuals affected, socially, psychologically and economically' (p.4).

'Northern Ireland is a small island community where people know each other intimately. In this context this is an overwhelming amount of trauma, often very violent in circumstance, for such a small community to absorb' (Schlindwein 2002, p.5). Nowhere is this more evident than in Interface communities where 'physical survival rather than psychological well-being is often the priority in situations of ongoing violence' (Smyth 2002, p.71).

Unravelling the threads of the past

'It is only since the situation here started to improve that people have had the confidence to speak about the things that they've been through' (Healy 2007, p.3). In addition to the number of people willing to 'come forward to seek help with troubles-related issues' (North & West Belfast Trust 2001, p.12) there is a growing realisation and understanding in Northern Ireland of the trans-generational impact of trauma experienced and its effects on the next generation. As Leitch observed 'We will carry the past with us into the future. Hurt and angry children without attention and respect, grow up into embittered adults' (Leitch 2000, p.45). The prevalence of 'anxiety, depression, deliberate self-harm and escalating suicide rates among young people' was noted in one Interface area by Kilkelly *et al.* in 2004, p.112.

The challenge to meet the many and varied needs appropriately, requires a multi-faceted approach (Schlindwein 2002) which acknowledges that relationships between people have been severely impacted upon, creating a degree of mistrust, acute feelings of fear and helplessness, a lack of openness, a shattered belief system and a sense of not feeling safe. For everyone in society, and in particular those living in the Interface areas as they continue to deal with the consequences of trauma, this has meant beginning to accept and trust people to share their experiences with, and trusting outsiders to come in and work within their communities. Anyone setting out to provide interventions needs to be very aware of this and deal sensitively with the specific needs of the people. This has certainly been my experience during the pilot phase of the CODA Interface Schools Music Therapy service in Belfast and the extension of the service to Derry/Londonderry three years later.

Establishing the music therapy service

The Northern Ireland Music Therapy Trust carried out an initial evaluated pilot project involving nine primary schools in Belfast to ascertain the needs of the pupils and to assess the potential role of music therapy. A total of 50 children were seen in individual and group music therapy during the pilot phase, which ran from April 2004 to March 2005.

Some of the initial issues which arose during the pilot and the later extension of the service related to:

- information required on the referral forms

- describing the service

- the perceived impact of the Troubles.

What information to include in the referral forms?

The funding received for this service came from a programme to support victims and survivors and as such it was essential that anyone who received the service could be defined as being in this category. For this reason referral criteria had to be drafted to ensure that this could be demonstrated to funders and to give the therapist as much background information as possible.

In addition to the standard demographic information regarding date of birth, age, etc. referrers were asked to indicate if the individual had experienced a single traumatic event or were experiencing ongoing trauma due to living in an Interface area or for any other reason. Referrers were also asked to indicate what level they believed the trauma had impacted or was impacting on the individual and to indicate if this was on one or more of the following levels:

- on a personal level

- on a family level

- on an intergenerational level

- on a community level.

The referrer could also indicate how the individual's exposure to trauma was impacting on their performance and learning in school in terms of their:

- behavioural presentation, i.e. ability to engage appropriately and attend

- cognitive presentation, i.e. ability to concentrate and self-esteem

- Physical presentation, i.e. levels of alertness or relaxation

- emotional state, i.e. angry, happy, trusting.

Initially some of the schools were anxious about including any information on a referral which they felt the parents might have issues around outsiders knowing about their family. This was a difficult situation which had to be sensitively and effectively dealt with, not least because without comprehensive background referral information the music therapist would be less well equipped when assessing the children. There was also the issue that the majority of mainstream teachers were less familiar with referring children on to other services; this was generally the role of the Special Educational Needs Officer.

When the schools were assured that any information received would be securely kept and not disclosed to anyone else, the teachers gradually grew in confidence about the information they provided in referrals. This was a very different experience for us from that in the special school settings where we work, where as members of the multidisciplinary team we have access to pupil records and there are no difficulties relating to the clinical, medical or social information given in referrals.

Referrals to the service indicated the wide range of issues impacting on the children and their communities. A high number indicated exposure to ongoing trauma and highlighted the difficulties of ongoing paramilitary activity in the communities and the inability of people to function freely.

CASE STUDY 9.1

Two siblings, a boy aged six and a girl aged eight, were referred to music therapy by their class teachers as their behaviour in class had altered significantly in recent months. The boy's behaviour in class had deteriorated, resulting in aggressive behaviour towards other pupils and verbally challenging the class teacher. He appeared to have great difficulty expressing himself or explaining why he engaged in such behaviour. His sister had become socially withdrawn and was often quite tearful during class and appeared reluctant to engage with anyone. Prior to this time both children had been very keen learners who were always fully engaged in class and small group activities.

The pre-disposing factor was considered to be that their father, with whom they had a very close relationship, had been ordered to leave Northern Ireland by local paramilitaries because of an internal group feud. Having been exiled, for the safety of himself and his family he could not return home at any time as exiles generally face paramilitary death threats on their return home. Contact with the children had therefore been dramatically reduced as the family could not afford to travel to see the father. Referral information indicated that not only were the children experiencing ongoing trauma but so too were their older siblings and their mother, who was now the sole carer.

Because the children lived in a small tight-knit community their teachers were aware that other pupils knew of their circumstances and teaching staff felt it would have been uncomfortable and distressing for the children to discuss any issues during lessons. Teaching staff hoped that music therapy would offer them a safe space where they could explore (non-verbally and verbally) the many issues they were experiencing as their whole family structure had been dramatically altered with no resolution in sight.

Describing the service

The terminology specifically employed to describe the service in letters to parents was for a 'creative music programme where children could work individually or in small groups using music for self-expression and to develop new skills'. Given the historic failure in Interface areas to engage with traditional medical and clinical services the word therapy was not used. Another reason was that some schools felt parents might be concerned about the negative connotation of what requiring therapy might imply about their child. The parents were invited to contact me if they had any concerns or queries which they would like to have addressed. The importance placed on confidentiality was also important as we were aware that they might be concerned about what a child might say or disclose in the sessions, as these were communities where keeping quiet and not speaking 'out' was a central component of survival. The letters also assured parents that they could meet with the therapist in the school at anytime to discuss the programme. We felt it was critical that we were as open and accessible to them at all times in the process if trust was to be established and maintained.

Perception of the impact of the Troubles

During the establishment phase of this service a very small number of schools were reluctant to be involved because of their view that the Troubles have had no impact on their community. As someone who grew up during the Troubles and who was aware of the conflict from an early age I was quite surprised that other adults of a similar age, teaching in areas which had and continued to experience sectarian issues such as rioting, punishment beatings and shootings, could hold this view. An example is one school, which having expressed interest in the service, saw the attempted murder of a member of the security forces at the school gates the week before I visited it. When the referral criteria for the service was outlined they indicated that their school had experienced no Troubles-related trauma and they could not envisage their pupils requiring the service.

On one level this can be understood, as often a school maintains a fragile link with the parents and the community and perhaps does not want to appear to imply that the children, families and community are not coping. It also indicates that not every community is at the same stage in their post-conflict journey and, as therapists, we must continue to be aware of this and remember to work at their speed and not where we feel they should be.

The CODA Service

Following the pilot phase in Belfast, five schools received a service of a half day or a whole day per week during the academic year 2005/06. Figure 9.3 shows the breakdown in terms of trauma level experienced, recorded in the 80 referrals received.

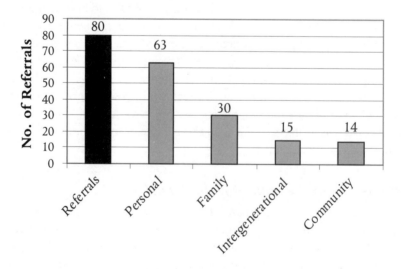

Figure 9.3 Type of trauma experienced by the children

Out of the 80 referrals, 63 children experienced personal trauma, 30 experienced family trauma, 15 experienced intergenerational trauma and 14 community trauma. The total number does not equal 80 because a number of children experienced several types of trauma.

Interestingly of the 80 referrals initially received 70 were for males in comparison to 10 females. This figure corresponds to the finding that boys will have had more exposure to community conflict, as McCallum argues, '11 and 12-year-olds are now routinely engaged in interface conflict within and between communities' (McCallum 2007). His findings also indicated that boys of this age will also have more difficulties expressing themselves; as a result of this there is a clear need to give them alternative methods for self-expression such as music which 'provides an accessible language and safe containing space where feelings, which may not otherwise be named, can be explored, expressed and contained safely' (Murray unpublished).

What are the main presenting features in the music therapy sessions?

The majority of the children have been seen on an individual basis and groups often include only one or two clients because of their difficulties in trusting others with sensitive or painful personal information. It is essential that children feel safe before being able to share difficult stories and for changes to occur because 'the restoration of a sense of safety is usually thought of as one of the fundamental requirements for healing' (Gibson 2001, p.75). In terms of the impact trauma was having on their performance and learning in school, Figure 9.4 shows the data for the 80 pupils referred.

This figure shows that out of the 80 referrals 51 children's behaviour was affected, 46 children's cognitive ability was affected, 18 children's physical abilities were affected and 13 children's emotional abilities were affected. As in the previous table the total number does not equal 80 as several children were affected in different ways.

The children referred to the service included a high number of siblings or children who were either related to one another or who lived in close proximity to one another. The backgrounds of their families included experience of multiple traumatic events including the murder of more than one relative, injury of a relative, intimidation, imprisoned parents, paramilitary involvement and fathers displaced by internal paramilitary disagreements. As one principal observed during the service establishment phase, 'almost every family has been directly affected by paramilitarism and the daily oppression it has exerted. Consequently we have children who are withdrawn, troubled or ill at ease with the world.'

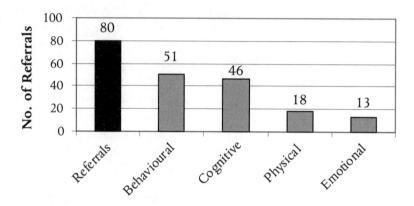

Figure 9.4 Impact on different areas of children's performance

CASE STUDY 9.2

This was clearly illustrated in the sessions with the two siblings described earlier who were both 'withdrawn, troubled (and) ill at ease with the world' dealing with the many emotions experienced as a result of their father's absence. They were both fully aware of the impact on their mother and their siblings which was a tremendous mental and emotional burden for such young children to endure.

Because of the issues of trusting others from outside their family they came to music therapy sessions together and were able to explore and express some of their fears and anxieties. They drew strength from one another as they realised they weren't experiencing things in isolation. Gradually as they began to feel safe with the music therapist, they formed their own community and created music and songs which reflected not only their anxieties but which spoke of their hopes for the future. An important aspect of this work is about enabling the clients to think beyond the current difficulties they are experiencing, letting them be children with the same hopes, dreams and aspirations as their peers.

'Is my music your music?'

An interesting aspect of the early work in all of the schools has been the need to find out who the therapist is, i.e. if they are 'one of us' or 'one of them'. During the initial sessions as part of the 'getting to know you' process the children were asked to share what music they liked and if they would like to sing or play some of that music with the therapist. It was really intriguing to see how many children suggested songs, music or instruments which could be associated with either the Loyalist or Republican traditions. This could be seen as a test for the therapist – if they know 'my' music they are 'alright and can be trusted' and if not the question is 'Can they be trusted?' For the therapist, refusing to acknowledge their music may potentially mean the child may not engage, while singing or playing this music only encourages a rigid pattern of functioning.

CASE STUDY 9.3

One nine-year-old boy in a Catholic/nationalist Interface school during the assessment sessions was reluctant to play any of the instruments available in the music therapy room because he associated the drums available with the Protestant/loyalist community and therefore associated the music therapist with that community. This was a potentially difficult situation for the music therapist to deal with and it was important to consider:

- the historical background and context of this perception
- the potential negative effect resulting from the client's perception that the music therapist was an outsider not to be trusted
- the need to maintain boundaries with regard to the disclosure of personal information which has no relevance in the therapy space.

A way around these difficulties was for the music therapist to offer to listen to music which the children brought to the session, emphasising that this music was their own and giving them a space to share. Another approach was to suggest that the instruments we use are world music instruments. This helps the children to gradually begin to accept that no instrument belongs to just one group or culture and highlights how a lack of awareness of the musical apartheid synonymous with Northern Ireland could be a minefield for the music therapists hoping to work effectively with the children from these areas.

Improvisation

Improvisation was not an aspect in early sessions as many clients found vocal or instrumental improvisation challenging. They found it difficult to initiate sufficiently to choose an instrument, begin playing independently when given the space to do so or determine when to stop.

As Allen observed, 'some clients were observed to be nervous and indecisive, while the more aggressive clients could only play in one way, music which was loud and drowned out any other person's music'. She went on to say that there appeared to be a 'fear of letting go and therefore losing control', it was difficult for the children to be spontaneous (Allen 2007, p.20). And as Austen observed, 'Play evokes spontaneity and spontaneity becomes associated with the fear of loss of control and judgement' (2006, p.138).

CASE STUDY 9.4

A nine-year-old girl was referred to music therapy. She lived with her maternal grandmother whose husband and brother had died in an explosion in the 1990s. Their deaths had not only impacted on the grandmother but also on the clients' mother who had issues with drugs and alcohol. The teacher indicated that the client had:

- very low self-esteem and had great difficulty concentrating in class
- expressive language difficulties which presented in a reluctance to speak or read aloud in class and in her use of written language.

In the early sessions the client found improvising especially difficult as she sat beside the therapist at the piano avoiding eye-contact and shaking her head in the negative when asked if she would like to sing or play anything. She would only agree to play with the therapist when the therapist offered to play the same instrument with her. Her playing was very quiet and she never altered the rhythm, playing the same rhythm over and over. It appeared that she found some comfort in the rigidity of the rhythm and could exercise some control of what was happening, perhaps afraid of what might emerge if she was to relax.

This clearly reflects their communities, where containing things has been the norm for so long that doing anything different is frightening. Improvisation, because of the freedom it offers, was too difficult and it was safer to stay within the rigid confines of pre-composed music. This typifies what Eli found was an evident sign of post-traumatic play in that it is a 'stylised form of play – repetitive, literal and rigid with a notable lack of spontaneity' (in Carey 2006, p.17).

Structured activities

In the early sessions the therapists found that it was easier for the children to engage and develop their social skills such as turn-taking, waiting and interaction skills through structured musical activities. These activities were time-limited to each session so that their particular needs on that day could be met and included a wide variety of approaches such as:

- Playing in a band – agreeing on who should play which instrument, when they should play, etc. This gave the opportunity to observe their interaction skills and to develop improved turn-taking skills especially valuable for those who found this a challenge.

- Music and drawing – to pre-composed music or music improvised by the therapist and afterwards talking about 'what the music made me feel like drawing'. This was generally used as a relaxing technique as it gave the children the chance to relax and work quietly, a particularly valuable activity for the reserved and withdrawn children as it removed any pressure from the situation.

- Creating musical stories and characters – again this work involved drawing or using photographs to create montages. The stories could be about real events in their lives or imaginary characters who were good or bad, scary or nice. This activity provided an excellent opportunity to create music to reflect each character, laying the foundations for improvisation in a structured manner.

As Allen observed 'the balance between the structured weekly activity and the freedom within that activity allowed the clients the opportunity to begin to initiate, express themselves and build up self-esteem' (Allen 2007, p.19). The children engaged with these structured activities and gradually began to share more of themselves in sessions, indicating their trust in the therapist and an increase in their self-confidence.

Because the client described earlier (Case study 9.4) appeared to have a preference and a need for structure the music therapist decided to use a visual session chart where the activities were established each week at the beginning of the session. This assured her that there would be no surprises and offered her the opportunity to indicate if there was something she would prefer not to do.

The structure for each session generally followed the following format:

- hello at the piano
- emotions chart – where the client pointed to an emotion to indicate how she felt that day: these included happy, sad, angry, scared

- drumming in pairs or turn-taking copying games where she was gently encouraged to introduce new rhythms for the therapist to follow
- song parody
- goodbye at the piano.

The client gradually began to engage more in the sessions and she contributed to the theme and lyrics of the song parody in particular. The songs used were designed to work on speech patterns and were quite repetitive to build up confidence and to reduce the need to recall too many lyrics. She initially sang a word or two in each line but was encouraged to perform more and more of the songs herself which she successfully managed.

Following sessions the class teacher observed how the client actively anticipated the sessions and how completely absorbed she was during them. She observed that the client had become much more confident in class in that she began to volunteer to go up to the blackboard and chatted to her peers more often. Her writing had also improved significantly in that the sentence structure, sequencing and the imaginative content used were more clearly reflective of her age.

Song parody and song writing

As the children relaxed and became more open to trying new things in the sessions they began to explore creating their own songs. Initially this was through song parody, where the melody of a song they recognised and felt familiar with was used and they created their own lyrics to fit with the melody. The themes in these songs included day-to-day activities such as getting ready for school, what they would like to have for lunch, where they would like to go for their holidays and who was going with them. These themes offered security as they were about familiar things but they also offered insight into their daily life and who was important to them.

When creating a song about 'what I'd like to be when I grow up', few children mentioned conventional jobs such as being a teacher, fireman or a doctor. The lack of educational aspiration, which is a feature of their communities, appeared to influence their choices, with the majority of girls saying they would like to have babies and the majority of the boys just shrugging their shoulders unable to think of anything and, when encouraged, saying they would like to sell papers on the street or work in a bar. This is in marked contrast to many other 6 to 11-year-olds whose career aspirations are indicative of a high degree of self-belief and their exposure to a wide range of positive career role models.

Gradually a number of the clients attending sessions over a longer period began to create songs which were much more autobiographical. The lyrics and the subjects covered in many of the songs related to very difficult and painful issues including abuse, attachment issues relating in particular to feelings of abandonment, fear of attack, feelings of powerlessness, anxiety about parents and many other aspects. That children so young should express such anxieties is evidence that music therapy provides a safe space and a vehicle in which to explore these concerns. As one child commented in a service user questionnaire, 'It's easier to talk about hard things in music.'

Feedback from the schools

I visit the schools twice in each academic year to meet with the music therapy co-ordinator and the principal to monitor the service. In advance of the meeting they will have been sent a service evaluation for their staff team to complete and the discussion revolves around their comments. The schools greatly value the service now and have gradually come to find that music therapy contributes a great deal to meeting the emotional and behavioural needs of their pupils.

It has been interesting to observe the change in attitude towards music therapy where, as one principal said, his school had moved from a 'we'll tolerate this idea' to the belief that music therapy is 'a very valuable tool in addressing the most needy in our school. The Troubles have left scars and the future presents many hurdles and obstacles but music therapy can give them a chance they wouldn't otherwise have had.'

As the service has become more embedded in each school the teachers greatly value what music therapy offers their pupils in a number of ways. School A observed:

> For our class teacher to address and devote meaningful time to these problems in our children is extremely difficult and practically impossible given their proliferation, nature and complexity. Yet these problems have huge impacts not only on the child's ability to learn but also affect those around him.

Many of the schools are finding that the children are more relaxed after sessions and are able to cope better in the learning environment of the classroom. School B indicated, 'We see the immediate benefit after every session and now we see longer term benefits of smiling faces where once there was obvious discomfort and fathomless anxiety.' School C felt that, 'When the children are able to deal with issues which affect them, or unburden themselves of worries they become more willing learners.'

The schools also find that parents are more accepting of music therapy and they 'now accept the process as a help to us all where once they were distrustful and suspicious'. This has largely been because of the immediate developments in sessions and what they can observe at home but also, as School D indicated, because 'the CODA programme has a good working knowledge of the school and local community profile which ensures that the provision is fit for purpose within this context'. The fact that our therapists understand the background and the unique features of each of the Interface areas means that we are able to use music flexibly to meet these needs.

'There is absolutely no doubt that the therapy they received, at crucial times in their lives, rescued them from potential pain.' This comment makes the sometimes stressful and slow process of establishing and maintaining this service worthwhile and highlights the role of music therapy to create a better future for the next generation. If we are to draw a line and consign the traumatic memories of previous generations to history, I and an increasing number of schools firmly believe music therapy has a significant contribution to make.

Conclusion

I hope this chapter provides insight on establishing music therapy in communities where there is a high level of fear and mistrust. It has connotations, I believe, for those who work in the mainstream setting in areas where gang and gun culture is on the increase, and where communities turn in on themselves. The increasing number of asylum seekers and refugees escaping conflict in their own countries will bring their own traumatic experiences and stories. The challenge for us is to offer the opportunity and the space to engage, using music in whatever manner works best for them.

Chapter 10

Music Therapy in a Special School for Children with Autistic Spectrum Disorder, Focusing Particularly on the Use of the Double Bass

Ian S. McTier

Introduction

I came to music through watching my father playing in orchestras and listening to him practising the violin and viola at home and, as a child, he started me on the violin. At the same time, I was singing in choirs, progressively lower parts as my voice broke. Once I reached the bottom register, there was something about singing the bass-line that felt very satisfying in the way it seemed to hold the music together. A chance opportunity to learn double bass at school got me started on my bass career, and when I homed in on music therapy as my eventual direction in music, it seemed natural to me to explore the therapeutic potential of the bass, which I duly did in my diploma research (McTier 2003). This convinced me of its value in music therapy, and the first part of this chapter is devoted to this aspect of my work – unusual in music therapy.

Oaklands, a special school that had had a brief history of music therapy (and there was little evidence that it had formed part of the core activities), was one of a number I approached after qualifying. Eventually, after a presentation I made to the staff, I started working there two days per week.

Initially in a rather small room I worked primarily with piano, voice and violin. Although I was keen to use the double bass, I had to wait until funds could be found to provide a modern robust instrument, as my own rather fragile (and somewhat more valuable!) instruments were too vulnerable to bring into the school. A suitable instrument was eventually bought, and has now survived for five years despite some rough treatment. Crucially it relieves me of any anxiety about possible damage to my own instrument, which clearly would have impeded my therapeutic effectiveness.

Later on in this chapter I talk a little more about the school, its ethos, and how my practice fits into it. I end with one or two case vignettes.

The use of double bass in music therapy

Why do human beings generally find the sound of bass instruments so easy to get on with? The roots of this affinity may be directly traceable to the womb, where the regular pulsations of the mother's heartbeat provide a constant rhythm against which plays the 'melody' of sounds external to the mother's body. These sounds are attenuated by the mother's body tissues, in such a way that it is predominately the bass notes which arrive at the foetal ears. By the time the infant is born, it has never known other than a backdrop of regular rhythm and low frequency notes which, through familiarity, are apprehended as safe and comforting. Low frequencies have been found (Wigram, Pederson and Bonde 2002) to have much more pleasant associations than high frequencies for crying infants.

Throughout life, these two – rhythm and bass – will continue to be an organising force: rhythm in holding us together in ritual, recreational and work pursuits (Bunt 1994; Gaston 1968), and bass frequencies acting as an underpinning to our world of sound, and providing the root – the bass line – of our music. The natural role of the double bass in music is to supply precisely this rhythm and this bass line.

The double bass produces a wide range of sound qualities and timbres. First, long sustained notes, melodic lines, and gentle, rhythmic pizzicato can often feel and sound distinctly maternal, warming, tender, nurturing, reflecting the instrument's own female shape, with its graceful sloping shoulders and hourglass figure. On the other hand, deeply ponderous or heavily accented bass might be felt to relate to masculine power, or authority, standing for the father figure, with its impressive size and ability to dominate physically. This symbolic use of the double bass as either masculine or feminine can be very significant in judging how we can use it in music therapy.

Considered in its female manifestation, the double bass can promote several of the more maternally-based underpinnings of psychotherapy:

Containment

In music therapy the double bass, with its versatility of sustained pedal notes and combination of rhythm and bass when gently played pizzicato, is an ideal *container* (Bion 1967) in the way it can frame a client's music. The timid or self-conscious client, the client whose feelings are difficult or unmanageable can be supported by the maternal warmth of the sound of the double bass, and their music sustained, whilst they further explore the experience.

The 'good enough mother' and 'continuity of being'

Winnicott (1990, p.54) suggested that successful maternal care establishes a *continuity of being*, the basis of ego strength. He further considered the mother's task as one of enabling the baby to establish its own identity, through *good enough* mothering (pp.145–146), and hence to enable it ultimately to separate confidently from her.

A nurturing backdrop of sustained sound from the double bass, sometimes felt rather than heard, parallels the all-embracing maternal care that supports the development of ego strength. Thus enveloped, the client may achieve a level of self-confidence that allows him or her to risk exploring his or her creativity, breaking away from tentative playing on the beat into more expansive improvisation.

Play and affect attunement

Winnicott's concept of play (1991) is a crucial one, in the sense that play underpins creativity, and creativity underpins the discovery of the self. Furthermore play is where the child learns interaction with others, and is where the therapy takes place. Creating a psychological space for play is therefore of special importance for clients who are cut off from themselves or others. Capitalising on the impact and the size of the double bass, the following are playful approaches one can take:

- playing 'peek-a-boo', by hiding behind the double bass and maintaining a musical rhythm by reaching from behind to pluck the open strings

- spinning or rocking it from side to side

- using the wooden body percussively

- general use of animation and exaggeration of body movements – as the instrument engages the whole body, these can be particularly striking

- using the instrument as a dramatic prop.

Like the human voice, stringed instruments can create a wide range of vitality affects (Stern 1985) through which a music therapist can reinforce or reflect aspects of a client's playing or of their emotional state:

- sound quality, tone and timbre – a huge range, whether pizzicato or bowed

- phrasing – fine tuning of volume profiles through phrases, with variable attack and flexible drawing out or tailing off, use of accents and a wide range of volumes.

The male or paternal role – discovery of the world, boundaries

The double bass or its player can, equally, represent the father, who supports the mother, on the one hand (George 1998), or draws the child away from her, on the other. As the child begins to separate from mother and start on their journey towards independent adulthood, 'the world in all its amazing variety is discovered "out there", and "the father therein" (Wright 1991, p.126). It is no coincidence that the prime use of a strong and defining pizzicato bassline, often heavily syncopated, is to be found in jazz, the music *par excellence* of aspiration towards independence and freedom, and played predominantly by men. Exaggerated and insistent bass is also traditionally the music that inspires warriors, and is a feature of much of today's popular music used, for example, in clubbing, where it stimulates disinhibitory behaviour (McCown *et al.* 1997).

The double bass, however, also invokes boundaries (George 1998) when played with a rhythmic, starker sound, fixed in form and creating a rugged, authoritarian framework for the music (good examples are the symphonies of Beethoven and Bruckner, where the double bass lines have a rhythmic intensity and insistence which seem to really drive the music).

Oaklands school

Oaklands caters for up to 30 young people aged 5 to 18 with autistic spectrum disorder and with particularly acute communication and/or social and emotional behavioural issues.

Only a few of the children start their school life at Oaklands. Others are transferred in or out, at any age, to or from other Enhanced Provision Units, which may stand alone or be within mainstream schools, in an attempt to provide the most appropriate facility for each young person. Such moves may entail significant emotional disturbance (as with Sam, see p.159), which has to be managed. Pupils new to the school tend to be particularly isolated, locked in their own world, may have minimal social interaction or communication skills, and quite limited verbal comprehension.

The role of music therapy at Oaklands

As I suspect is true of many establishments where music therapy is relatively unknown, staff generally have little knowledge of this intervention and how it can help such young people. Music therapy is so often viewed as giving the kids a good time. Staff education is thus an ongoing challenge. When I first arrived, I identified a prioritised list of pupils I felt could potentially benefit from music therapy, by means of initial observation of entire classes, and set about assessments. All referral forms were completed by the assistant head teacher rather than respective class teachers. This method had the advantage of a consistent experienced overview of each child's developmental needs.

Although individual referrals generally include a number of my current aims for this client group (see below), what I find striking is the consistent absence of *emotional security and stability*, which develop in the normal child benefiting from 'good enough mothering', and which, I believe, are key to positive social interaction and learning. My approach more recently has therefore been to give some priority to children exhibiting clear symptoms of emotional distress, manifesting as non-co-operation and challenging behaviour. This list often initially appears to surprise teaching staff, until they learn to appreciate how such aims actually support everything they try to achieve in class:

> *Establishing a supportive relationship with the therapist* – in which emotions can be safely expressed and understood.

Building emotional security and stability – through the developing therapeutic relationship.

Physical and psychological stimulation – through the propensity of music to affect our mental or emotional state (invigorating, exciting, calming, etc.).

Enhancing communication skills:

- turn-taking, waiting, sharing and interaction

- encouraging the reading of facial expressions – through their exaggerated use by the therapist in musical dialogue

- learning to read other non-verbal signals – gesture, body shape, sounds

- encouraging speech and eye-contact – through the use of interactive game-songs.

Aiding socialisation and self-awareness – through participating in a shared musical activity.

Increasing self-confidence:

- in learning to make musical connections with others

- (for less able clients) through a sense of achievement when even simple sounds or rhythms are produced.

Concentration and focusing ability – developed by learning about the instruments, listening to others, and learning to take one's turn.

Co-ordination, and development of fine and gross motor skills – through manipulation of the instruments.

CASE STUDY 10.1: SUSAN

Susan was one of my first clients at Oaklands, aged 14 and verbal. The deputy head teacher's referral specified a diagnosis of autistic spectrum disorder, and described her as a fearful teenager who had difficulty understanding her class peers and their responses. It was hoped that music therapy might improve her self-esteem and self-confidence, and enable her to develop some understanding of her own emotional responses through music. Susan found all new activities difficult, and if unsure or confused in a group situation found it very difficult to communicate her worries. She subsequently disclosed that she had an older sister, and a new baby brother who was drawing her mother's attention away from her.

Susan's early sessions were characterised by an initial paralytic fear of not knowing how to play even a tambourine during my usual hello song. However, through turn-taking on a drum, starting from just two or three beats each, she managed to match my basic phrases, building up confidence slowly. Similarly, using a metallophone, she succeeded in reflecting my single notes, short phrases and glissandi, but if I extended too far too soon she simply froze. This was a balancing act between security and stretching her out of her comfort zone.

In her first improvisation on metallophone, with me supporting on piano, she gradually overcame her fear of not knowing how or what to play, and was able to more or less follow my trial changes in tempo. In our next improvisation 'The Sea', using ocean drum and piano, Susan's playing became more robust and confident as a storm developed, eventually subsiding to a calm. She really enjoyed this. With hindsight, it seemed that Susan initially considered everything I played, in turn-taking, as a test for her, until she had learned to be free, using the vehicle of joint improvisation.

Over the weeks Susan's creativity blossomed and, unfettered by her early fear of the unfamiliar, her self-confidence and self-esteem seemed to grow. This was confirmed by her class teacher (after session 16): 'Susan now virtually never cries in class, is more confident, communicative, makes choices.' From session 18 onwards I had a double bass in my toolkit. This seemed to add a new dimension to our musicking through its versatility and a new subtlety, often causing Susan to express surprise at how much she enjoyed each new duet combination involving it, which I interpreted as the way she felt musically supported and contained by it.

Our work together included joint improvisations on piano, as well as using many combinations of instruments. She now initiated tempo and rhythm changes, was able to cope with my rhythmic syncopation, chose themes for our improvisations, and was able to comment on them afterwards. Difficult issues around tensions at home, and class peers, were also discussed verbally and addressed in our music-making. She seemed to find our ability to create musical improvisations around her themes and current emotional concerns reassuring and helpful.

One important ingredient of the therapy, which I introduced and pioneered with Susan and which I have subsequently used with a number of clients, was a wordless conversation, involving a semi-humorous 'dialogue', using gobbledegook with normal speech intonation, and in combination with exaggerated arm and body movements, and in which she was encouraged and learned to maintain eye-contact. This strand of our work seemed to have a strong impact on helping to build her self-confidence.

Her series of 48 individual sessions over five terms was followed immediately by weekly group sessions with her class peers, until she left school four terms later. The transition into group music therapy seemed absolutely right for her as I felt she now needed the peer-interactive element in her therapy. The double bass continued to figure in these group sessions but to a lesser extent, since a significant proportion of each session would involve turns at soloing and other group activities involving solely percussion instruments. The striking feature of Susan's presentation in group music therapy, apart from her creativity and rhythmic security, was her self-confidence in being able to suggest themes, in commenting on the group's improvisations afterwards, and increasingly her ability to stand up for herself.

To sum up, Susan made huge progress in music therapy over 32 months, and importantly this progress appears to have been reflected in her behaviour outside music therapy. Perhaps the ultimate endorsement of this work was how Susan won at audition, and carried off laudably, the principal part in her final school Christmas pantomime, including singing a solo in front of the entire school and many parents, including her mother and baby brother.

CASE STUDY 10.2: PAUL

Paul was a very large and strong African youth, approaching 18, whose referral described him as disordered, with very basic communication and comprehension. I initially found him quite unnerving as he darted around the playground, and yet he was harmless, stopping just short as he ran towards people. Paul found the demands of school very stressful, frequently chewing his shirt or hands, or sucking his thumb for comfort. It had, however, been noticed that in certain musical situations he relaxed and became more responsive, hence his referral for music therapy.

Escorted by a familiar adult throughout his first session, he initially sat, eyes covered with his hand, sucking his thumb. He managed two or three taps of a tambourine in the hello song, looking up at me a couple of times, for reassurance? However, with gentle and sensitive encouragement, Paul's confidence grew, and he soon seemed completely at home beating drums with his hands. On discovering how to play metallophone glissandi, he was clearly enchanted and his body started to sway periodically. As his excitement increased he would add his own vocal sounds and his body movements became increasingly pronounced. He used a wide range of instruments including piano in duets, his characteristic playing styles being continuous double finger rolls or alternate whole hand clusters when he was really getting carried away. He enjoyed initiating changes in dynamics and, increases in tempo, his foot often tapping quavers as he played. Despite the largeness of his hands he was also able to play his double finger rolls extremely quietly. It seems likely that his familiarity with the piano was influenced by his younger sister's piano playing ability.

From session 18 to 25, I had the double bass available, and we made extensive use of it. After inviting him to start playing on metallophone or other percussion instrument, I would gradually develop rhythmic riffs on a chord structure in support, basically providing a musical framework within which he was free to allow his creativity to flow, and flow it did, in every sense, as he was virtually jumping around on his chair with excitement when our music got into a real groove. At times, when he was beating drums loudly, I often wondered how he could hear the double bass, but his musical awareness, sensing tempo changes and endings, and meaningful glances at me, indicated that he clearly could. Paul was clearly attracted to strongly rhythmical warrior-like music (above, Section 1), which his own percussion playing helped satisfy.

To summarise, music therapy provided an important vehicle for Paul's emotional expression. The contrast between his static seated presentation, hands often shrouding his face, and his physical expression of fulfilling engagement, whilst musicking with the therapist, could not be more marked. Music simply brought him to life. He had learned to trust the therapeutic relationship and the musical structure enabled him to be himself, free from classroom curricular demands which he found so stressful. Sadly, the day-care centre he attended after leaving Oaklands was unable to fund music therapy provision. Six years on, speaking to his mother, I was pleased to hear that Paul is still attending a college of further education, has a drum-kit at home, and is learning to play the guitar. I find this news an endorsement of the importance of music in his life, and am heartened to feel that music therapy has perhaps played a part in his personal development.

CASE STUDY 10.3: KEITH

This child, aged nine, started at Oaklands in August 2009. He was physically strong, used to regular rough-and-tumble with his father, had some verbal comprehension but virtually no verbal language. He was aggressive in class, kicking, biting and scratching if denied his wishes, which he made abundantly clear, and was a highly accomplished escapist requiring absolute attention to door security. His referral hoped that music therapy could (a) help develop self-awareness of his body, his strength and its impact (b) stimulate his self-motivation to communicate and interact in more socially acceptable ways, including speech, and (c) achieve a level of calming and self-control, including redirecting his physical energy into more appropriate activities.

Keith spent most of his first session at the piano, playing full compass glissandi, loud fistfuls progressing slowly up and down, or playing with the keyboard lid. Occasionally he emitted long loud 'aaah' sounds which seemed to indicate enjoyment of what he was doing, and which I reflected. Meanwhile I provided heavy support on the piano, my arms reaching round behind him, except when he occasionally removed them. At no time did he attempt to stop my vocalisations though. He also briefly explored the bongos, the metallophone and the kokoriko, as well as twice being attracted to the double bass, which he fleetingly strummed on both occasions. When I announced the goodbye song during his last phase at piano he looked up when I sang our respective names, attempting to articulate them, then went to the door. My counter-transference feelings were of Keith feeling met and secure in this initial session. His class teacher, who had sat in on the session for safety reasons, also felt that some very promising interaction had taken place. As music therapy seemed to be one of the few activities that he was able to engage in, we agreed upon a strategy of an intensive two sessions per week for the remainder of the term. I mentioned earlier that I have a degree of freedom to allocate sessions, within my available time in the school, on the basis of my assessment of the priority of need of the various children, and I considered him a priority case.

Over the next few sessions, which I conducted alone, Keith became initially more boisterous, cyclically progressing around the room making glissandi sounds and pummelling the piano, beating the cymbal, the drums and the metallophone energetically and loudly, before returning to the piano, as before accompanied by his periodic long 'aaah' sound. It was imperative that I matched this acoustic barrage in my two-pronged support – from piano and voice. He seemed to approve, judging from the quality of his occasional grins and glances at me. Often we would be playing on the piano together, when suddenly he would lunge for the double bass, perhaps twice in a session, and want to use the bow briefly for long slow strokes followed by some tremolo scrubbing, before handing it back to me to use as he returned to the piano for a double bass/piano duet. The quality of interaction was continuing to grow, through his sharing of instruments, musical dialogue and joint musicking, and acceptance and awareness of the therapist. At the end of session 8, which happened to be observed, the teaching assistant commented that she had never seen him so focused for so long.

In session 15 he started using the rain stick as a hammer against part of the wall which had soft plaster. Finding that he could make indentations only fired him to continue at every opportunity, and with whatever instrument or beater he could muster. It was deemed essential thereafter to have another adult in the room ready to intercept any further destructive intentions so that I could continue to maintain my support from the piano in an uninterrupted way without having to divert him from making holes in the wall.

Keith's most recent sessions, 19 and 20, after a three-week gap over Christmas, suggest a possible landmark in his behaviour. He walked rather than ran to the music therapy room and for the first half of both sessions, each several minutes in duration, shared the piano with me without any attempts to push me or my hands away. His music, much more gentle than hitherto, comprised finger-walking up and down the keyboard including freely crossing my hands, some glissandi using the heel of his hands, and occasional gentle play with the two pedals and keyboard lid, after accepting my words of caution concerning the latter. He seemed very content with my reaching around him to play vacant sectors of the keyboard in support, and appeared to increasingly appreciate my intermittent vocal support too. In the second half of these two sessions, in contrast, he became more boisterous again. It seemed to me as if Keith oscillated between calm and energetic, like the natural ebb and flow occurring throughout nature, but significantly I now felt more included in his loud music-making. On both occasions he was able to calm himself down during the goodbye song, and managed to give our names on cue, after the usual prompts.

Keith has been learning to use music therapy as an effective vehicle for self-expression, interacting and communicating positively with the therapist, and has become less controlling and more willing to share instruments. The double bass seems to have a role, perhaps in terms of its paternal physicality, but certainly in the deep sonority of bowed open strings which Keith clearly finds satisfying and repeatedly returns to, possibly as an echo of the comfort of his mother's womb.

CASE STUDY 10.4: SAM

The case of this client is an example where I believe that carefully tailored music therapy has helped to counteract both the negative impact of well-meant attempts to provide the most appropriate education, and of the lack of stability thus engendered for the child. His profile, aged eight, was an Aspergers diagnosis, intelligent but socially isolated, with attention-seeking behaviours that escalated rapidly. In addition he was oppositional, becoming increasingly inflexible, and provocative and taunting to peers. Two years later, now aged ten, his negative interaction with peers left no alternative to individual learning, and meant that he was in isolation for much of the week. At this stage, we started one-to-one music therapy. Effectively free from challengeable verbal instructions, his musical awareness and creativity became immediately apparent along with strong senses of rhythm and pulse, giving him important opportunities for emotional expression. In parallel, he started group music therapy, with carefully selected participants, chosen because of their likely immunity to his provocations, to at least expose him to some social interaction. He subsequently became able to cope with being in a class of different, less able peers. However, a transfer a few months later to a theoretically more encouraging learning environment, a mainstream autism unit, appears to have adversely affected his emotional and mental health.

I became aware of this when Sam returned to Oaklands on a trial split daily between our school and the mainstream unit, and I witnessed the steep deterioration in his behaviour in three group music therapy sessions with his new class, compared to a few months earlier. He now had a hygiene sensitivity (apparent when someone sneezed over an instrument), was extremely touchy about requests to stop abusing instruments, and was generally in a highly strung emotional state. I reassessed him at this point, just after he was transferred once more, into another class (of more familiar peers) at Oaklands, to try to give him some stability. It was agreed with teaching staff to trial him on an intensive three sessions of individual music therapy per week, more along the lines of intensive psychotherapy, as this format had been so positive for him earlier. He was, at this stage, very difficult to engage in class, unable to cope with verbal reasoning (e.g. that the class computer had to be shared with others), often resorting to pacing the room and occasionally screaming, or lying on a table whimpering. Music therapy was effectively the sole activity he would willingly undertake, provided that I collected him from class.

Five school weeks and 15 sessions on, Oaklands staff report that his interactions and co-operation in class are becoming progressively calmer. Our current one-to-one sessions are long, around 40 minutes each, often comprising just three complex interactive joint improvisations. Speech hardly figures. Sam believes the music speaks for itself. In his case I largely agree. He invariably chooses to set up a large percussion kit of three metallophones (bass, soprano, and chromatic alto), conga, bongos and cymbal to choose from for most of his musicking, which I primarily support using double bass, because of its subtlety and versatility. It seems to me that the double bass' rhythmic and harmonic underpinning is providing essential framework in which he can comfortably and freely explore his emotions using his abundant musical creativity, whilst the structure of music arguably provides just the measure of non-verbalised order and stability he needs, in his current emotional turmoil of not knowing which is his school, or his class therein. I also suggest that the psychotherapeutic role of the double bass, played by a male therapist, should not be underestimated, in the sense of its gentle imposition of paternal (rhythmic) authority and discipline, and crucially for Sam, without having to resort to verbal intervention, to which he can react so adversely.

CASE STUDY 10.5: A TYPICAL GROUP SESSION, ILLUSTRATING THE USE OF DOUBLE BASS

This recent group session involved two 13-year-old verbal pupils with autistic spectrum disorder, Craig and Ben. They were from the same class, and were referred to help address the volatile dynamic between them. They were accompanied by a teaching assistant (Vincent). Both boys had received around 30 individual sessions each, and had shared nearly 30 class group sessions. The third pupil of their class was unwilling to participate in further sessions of music therapy and remained in class with his teacher. In his case staff agreed it was important to permit his opting out.

The session commenced with a familiar interactive hello song, followed by turns at simultaneously counting aloud and beating numbers of pulses (chosen by the boys) on a hand drum. Next we revisited 'Follow the Leader' (following the rhythm and dynamics) with each person taking a turn at leading. This activity really appealed to Craig, since he liked (a) directing and (b) trying to catch people out with dummy beats. For our first group improvisation Ben chose soprano metallophone. Craig, unusually promptly, chose a triangle, immediately changed his mind to xylophone but was told to remain with his original choice which, surprisingly, he accepted. Vincent took the cabassa, and myself the double bass. Ben needed no prompting to start playing steady crotchets. Vincent joined in with a quaver rhythm. I started with sustained bowed pedal Ds with contrasting leading semi-quavers, switching to D-minor pizzicato riffs after a few bars. From a fidgety, tentative start Craig gradually became more engaged, as if irresistibly sucked into the music, so much so that when I slowed to finish, three minutes later, he did not want to stop.

In our second group improvisation Craig was given the promised xylophone, Ben chose guitar, Vincent took bongos and I remained with the double bass. Ben confidently initiated, using open strumming, and was soon joined by Vincent's bongos and my double bass – tremolo initially, then sustained semi-breve 5ths with leading quaver 5ths one tone higher, going into five minutes of similar pizzicato riff 'frameworking' (Wigram 2004, p.117), D-minor once again feeling appropriate. This time Craig was motivated to join in from the start and remained unusually focused throughout with a continuous flow of music. Both boys periodically looked up at me as if seeking reassurance that all was well, and also wanting to share their enjoyment – a form of social referencing. This second improvisation had an even stronger groove feel which clearly helped maintain the momentum of the youngsters' musicking. When asked which group piece they preferred Craig characteristically did not know. Ben preferred the second piece. The session continued with the two boys taking turns on the groan tube, Ben commenting how it made monkey-like sounds. The session concluded with the familiar interactive goodbye song, and calmly sitting with hands on knees for a few moments.

On reviewing the video of the session I am struck by the way the double bass appears to provide a rhythmic and harmonic framework, or base, for the music, which is subtly transparent and hence not overbearing, and yet provides an essential, reassuring heartbeat pulse or underpinning which seems to encourage participant engagement – either by playing, or simply moving parts of the body in rhythmic sympathy with the music. With a larger and louder group I would probably opt for a bass guitar, if available, because of its greater power.

Conclusion

This chapter has described the delivery of music therapy to a variety of young people with autistic spectrum disorder and, specifically, the role of the double bass in this context has been explored. Although by no means the panacea for such clinical work, my aim was to demonstrate that it is worthy to take its place as an important part of the therapist's armoury. I have no doubt that the double bass has added an extra dimension to the experience of my clients and to the outcomes of the therapy, through what I believe is its ability to foster emotional security. My hope is that I have gone some way in stimulating interest in its use, and not just with this client group.

Chapter 11

'How Can I Consider Letting My Child Go to School When I Spend All My Time Trying to Keep Him Alive?'

Links between Music Therapy Services in Schools and a Children's Hospice

Órla Casey

Introduction

I hope to bring together in this chapter some thoughts arising from personal experience of working as a music therapist within both a schools' service and a children's hospice service. This work has highlighted the need to make links and manage cross-service transitions for children with life-limiting or life-threatening illnesses and their families. (For the purpose of this chapter and acknowledging associations to a *children's* hospice, I will use the term 'child' to refer to either a child or young person up to 19 years of age). For example, many children who attend special schools will, due to the nature of their complex health needs, access short breaks from a children's hospice. Should these children become ill, they may become life-threatened very quickly. School children using the hospice service may be living with a life-limiting or life-threatening condition or be in a palliative stage of care, i.e. where no further curative treatment is offered. Alternatively, a child who is under the care of the hospice service may require support with the transition into school if and when their health permits.

If the role of the music therapist in education is partly to support a child to access learning, my dual role has thus involved making links between schools and hospices where a child may need support with the transition into services or to cope within these different settings. This has included consideration of the experience of a life-limited child in school who may look different and behave differently to other children. Such a child may be a wheelchair user, use adapted equipment, wear a helmet, be susceptible to infection, need regular suction, carry a feed pump, have a physical disability as a result of an operation or of the side effects of medication (e.g. weight increase) or may not be noticeable at all as being 'different'. They may regularly miss school for extended periods of time and, along with their family, be dealing with increased anxiety during illness or hospitalisation. What, if any, support do these children need in reconciling their experience of the school and hospice settings?

Much of my approach in hospice music therapy work is informed by attachment theory. In this chapter I will examine child and family attachment and separation issues arising from childhood illness. I will also consider the role of the music therapist in promoting independence for the child as part of normal and healthy development. To this end, I will introduce the setting and theoretical context of my work before outlining two case studies: in the first of these I will seek to highlight the role of music therapy in providing psychological and attachment support for a teenage boy making the transition between home, hospital and school settings; in the second I will describe issues of teenage identity, complicated by illness, which are addressed through music therapy. Finally, I will conclude with thoughts and questions arising.

The children's hospice setting

Twelve in 10,000 children aged 0–19 years in the UK are affected by a life-limiting condition, with the number of young people aged 13–24 living under the threat of death and requiring symptom management and daily care estimated at between 6000 and 10,000 (ACT/RCPCH 2003). Children's hospice services provide specialist short breaks, family's pre-bereavement and bereavement support, palliative and end-of-life care for children with life-limiting conditions such as:

1. Life-threatening conditions for which curative treatment may be feasible, but may fail (e.g. cancer, organ failure).

2. Conditions where premature death is inevitable and where there may be long periods of intensive treatment aimed at prolonging life and allowing participation in normal activities (e.g. cystic fibrosis, Duchenne muscular dystrophy).

3. Progressive conditions, where treatment is exclusively palliative and may commonly extend over many years (e.g. Batten disease).

4. Irreversible but non-progressive conditions causing severe disability and leading to susceptibility to health complications, such as severe cerebral palsy or multiple disabilities. (ACT/RCPH 2003)

Within the hospice setting, music therapists working as part of specialist teams may offer one-off sessions in quality of life care as part of day services. In addition, they may offer short-term intervention to support families at times of crisis, for example, during times of change, deterioration of condition, transition and in pre-bereavement and bereavement care. Music therapists may work in end-of-life care to facilitate comfort, communication, spiritual care, memory making and funeral planning. They may support fundraising activities and also provide music for an annual memory day. Referrals to music therapy may come from family members and other professionals and be for any member of a family. As a result, therapists may work with individuals or several family members and may provide music therapy in hospice or hospital, at home or in a child's school. As the work is short term, links with other services are important and children may be referred on for longer-term music therapy if necessary, for example, if there is a music therapist in post at the child's school.

Theoretical framework – attachment theory

With reference to attachment theory, Harding identifies the roles of parents in normal child development as follows:

The maternal function in the child's development is complemented by the paternal function of separation and individuation, represented in psychoanalysis as the role of the father. Children need a 'third' in their lives to help them to separate from mother and to mediate the demands of external reality. When the father intervenes in the relationship between mother and child to 'reclaim' his wife and establish a relationship of his own with his child he offers the child 'a way out' of an exclusive dependence on mother. In order to develop an independent identity, the child needs help to separate from mother and encouragement to express their independent strivings, often in the form of angry protests. (Harding 2006, p.13)

In the light of these maternal and paternal roles for a well child, it is important to note that the experience of life with a life-limited or life-threatened child may lead to instances of disordered and disruptive attachment and separation within families. For example, when a child is life-limited or life-threatened it is likely that the mother may continue to experience the child as vulnerable, fragile and dependent on her for survival, i.e. over time her maternal instincts may become 'stuck' so that she continues to experience her growing child at an early infant stage. This will have implications for the role of the father, who may not have the opportunity to 'reclaim' his wife and may even himself take on more of a mother-type carer role with his sick child. Alternatively, if unable to find a role for himself with the mother–child duo he may become an absent figure and immerse himself in his role as a provider for his family. So also, other family members trying to identify a role in the family may find it necessary to take on a role akin to that of the mother figure, resulting in the whole family functioning in their own ways as a container for the life-limited child.

Where such a dynamic occurs, it seems that organisations involved in the child's care can take on some of the consequent missing functions. The hospice, in particular, may support the family as a unit when the child is sick and may take on the role for the family of both the nurturing, containing mother and the father promoting separation. As the child recovers and begins the transition back into normal life, the music therapist can also take on the father function and support development of healthy attachment and separation for family members. This may be through working with the child as an individual, with parent and child or with the whole family. The return of the child to school can likewise aid independence and represent both a literal and symbolic healthy separation.

Music therapy in the school and hospice setting

With the above in mind, I have been aware in my music therapy work of the implications of making links between schools and hospices where a child may need support with the transition into services or to cope within one or other setting. School settings can often provide an appropriate venue for sessions to happen in terms of boundaries and regularity of sessions, particularly if family life is chaotic and unpredictable. In addition, crossover of school and hospice music therapy can occur on various grounds:

- A need for emotional or psychological support for a life-limited or life-threatened child may be identified during a short break hospice stay and lead to input from the hospice music therapist within the school setting.

- Pre-school children who initially experience music therapy at the hospice may be referred for longer-term music therapy in school.

- Siblings who use the hospice services may also be referred for pre-bereavement or bereavement work in school with the hospice music therapist.

- The hospice music therapist may begin work with a child in need of immediate support which cannot be provided in school because there is no music therapy provision within the school or because it is felt that the relationship built up between the two of them must be maintained.

An advantage of the hospice model of music therapy work with a life-limited child is that the therapist can follow the child so that the work does not have to stop if he or she is in hospital or at home. The hospice music therapy service model thus arguably offers flexibility, most usually in the form of short-term intervention (generally up to 16 sessions). It also involves working with the whole family. This may be particularly relevant where attachment and separation are difficult between parents and children with life-limited illnesses or where family relationships become particularly enmeshed in the face of a crisis or the child's ill health. The hospice music therapist can support the holistic needs of the child during illness and then help him or her to separate and develop the confidence to return and function in an independent setting such as school. Often this work will continue after the child has returned to school.

I hope to illustrate within the following two case studies aspects of the type of reparative work for children and families that can take place across educational and health settings.

CASE STUDY 11.1: AARON

Aaron (all names have been changed to protect identity) is an 18-year-old young man with Duchenne muscular dystrophy and learning disability. He lives with his parents, an older brother (who also has muscular dystrophy) and a younger sister. He attends a special school and has also attended a children's hospice for short-break care and support with his complex medical needs since he was five years old. Aaron is a lively young man with a good sense of humour. He loves to whizz around in his wheelchair with his radio playing loud pop music. His ambition is to be a DJ. Aaron has little movement in his hands and arms, and he is quite weak and tires easily. In music therapy he is very engaged and uses a small keyboard or a computer to compose his own music. Reflecting his life, his music is busy with little space for thought or silence.

Referral and aims of music therapy

In the past, the hospice has supported Aaron by providing music therapy after sudden hospitalisation. A recent referral for music therapy is for support through several hospitalisations both for himself and his brother, to deal with changes in breathing and also feeding difficulties. At the time of referral, Aaron has missed approximately one month of the term's schooling due to repeated hospitalisation and recuperation at home. Aims for Aaron's music therapy are thus:

- to support quality of life in the midst of intense medical and care intervention
- to offer emotional and psychological support relating to recent invasive medical practices
- to offer this support whether he is in hospital, at home or during the transition back into school.

Aaron: music therapy in hospital

Aaron is having an emergency hospital stay resulting from a chest infection. I visit him in hospital as part of our weekly sessions. Aaron's mum is staying with him in a private room. Due to difficulties accessing his veins, regular procedures to site a syringe driver are proving very difficult. Both Aaron and his mum seem very anxious and are on high alert for physical symptoms and changes. I experience Aaron as asking lots of questions and showing detailed knowledge about procedures and bodily responses. He is demanding of his mum, who seems tired and anxious. Their relationship seems both that of carer and patient and of parent and vulnerable, fragile young man. After about 15 minutes, Aaron becomes somewhat settled and mum leaves us in order to take a necessary break.

Initially, Aaron's attention is diverted to see the instruments I have brought with me. A nurse has loaned him a 1980s CD and he is keen for me to see it. We begin to play music, with Aaron using the small keyboard and me supporting on bass guitar. Our improvisation seems busy, but fragmented, with lots of quick changes and little musical dialogue. I reflect this with words and narration, associating our music with Aaron's hospital experience. On several occasions, Aaron stops to ask me to settle his clothes, which he experiences as creased and uncomfortable. He chooses to listen to his selection of 'Indie' music on the laptop and this seems to offer containment and a means to increased interaction in singing and playful vocalisation. Suddenly Aaron stops singing and says that the music has distracted him: the cramp in his leg is gone and his bowels have opened. He comments that another teenager from the hospice is resident in the hospital and having invasive treatment to help him breathe. In our reflections about this, Aaron assures me that he is strong and will not lose his voice, which he needs to speak and to sing.

Aaron: music therapy at home

Our next three music therapy sessions are in Aaron's home. They take place in his bedroom for privacy and because this is where he has his computer and iPod. At home, Aaron is generally relaxed. The house and bedroom have been adapted to suit his needs. There is a predictable structure and routine to his day. Both his parents stay at home and, if he becomes uncomfortable, can provide immediate medical or physical assistance.

I bring the same instruments, i.e. midi-creator, amp and microphones, small keyboard, bass guitar and computer, with a range of backing tracks and software programs to facilitate composition and recording. Aaron is pleased to be home, but keen to revisit the experience of difficulties siting the syringe driver of the previous week. He seems immediately more relaxed to improvise today and has a greater musical awareness – his music is organised and structured phrases feed into an overall song pattern. Today Aaron is a DJ, playing loud pop music. He chooses to compose a birthday song for his mum and records a 'silly' birthday song during which he laughs and dances in his chair. Aaron's brother joins us and chooses to play midi-creator sensor with a one finger improvisation as Aaron sings. He has also been in hospital recently and Aaron remarks that it is good to have the family back together for mum's birthday. The improvisation, 'Here comes summer; gone is winter' reflects the teenagers' mood of hope and a new beginning which is discussed during listening back and reflection.

Aaron: music therapy in school

Aaron returns to school within a month. In school he is the only teenager in his class in a wheelchair and so is different to others. He has the support of a teaching assistant for daily needs such as toileting, feeding and suctioning. He comes for music therapy whilst others in his class have physical education. Aaron greets me with a wide smile and is keen to ask me how I am and about my drive to the session. He tells me how he is pleased to be back in school and how healthy he is now. He speaks of his future dreams of being a DJ, of going to college to study music technology and of his enjoyment of music therapy in the face of disappointment at no longer being able to access music in school. Today he is full of challenges to himself and explores a wide range of pitches during vocalisation to pop backing tracks. Whilst playing the small keyboard he is keen to see how many notes he can play at once and for how long he can hold notes down. He identifies further goals and challenges for our next sessions together.

The session is paused as Aaron's carer comes to give him suction. Following this, and towards the end of the session, Aaron chooses to sing a ballad and vocalises his disappointment about what the New Year has brought so far. He sings of his brother's return to hospital and the lack of fulfillment of the family wish for a new beginning where they would leave illness and hospital behind. I support him musically and reflect back his words of 'what a horrendous time, what a horrendous time'.

Thoughts arising from Aaron's music therapy

Much of my hospice work involves supporting people with anxiety relating to major life changes and the ongoing impact of episodes of loss. For this reason, I understood Aaron's anxiety in losing control of his body to present as a need to be in control, busy, constantly talking and needing adult attention for personal care. His hypervigilance for physical symptoms was manifest in poor concentration, fidgeting and difficulties in relaxing. In hospital, mum's attentiveness to his every request, alongside the need to make difficult decisions about operations and ongoing care, left her tired and experiencing difficulty in being a container for Aaron's own anxieties.

In our hospital session, Aaron initially projected onto me his need for emotional 'feeding' and containing, through requests to help him with physical comfort or in directing me about instruments and how to play. To the extent that Aaron had choice over instruments which he could access and play for short periods, for example, small keyboard and midi-sensors, music gave Aaron the experience of being in control and being heard. Singing on the microphone facilitated a space for us to meet each other in song and to engage in play and creative interaction. Musical expression also offered Aaron opportunities to express his anxiety, followed by a space to think about this. Time spent recording and listening back to music similarly enabled Aaron to experience himself in a different way and, over time, he developed confidence and a sense of identity in his music and the use of his voice. Through music, Aaron could experience himself as a separate person from his mum and he took the opportunity to give something of himself to her on her birthday. In identifying differences in their musical preferences and tastes, Aaron used the music therapy space to think about his mum as a person in her own right, allowing him to compose something which acknowledged and reinforced that musically. Finally, music and instruments were able to function as both containers and transitional objects, for example, Aaron's music helped to ground him and support embodiment (i.e. relaxation, so that leg cramp disappeared and bowels opened) so that the sick and well sides of him could come together.

I believe it was important for Aaron to have an attachment figure to support him in all three settings of hospital, home and school, to help him to integrate different aspects of himself and access the ongoing core of his personality across different environments. This was evident as, in school, even though Aaron assured me that he was better and became more goal focused to rise to the challenges of the environment, thoughts of hospital and ongoing health issues were still very much prevalent and needed an outlet. In summary, I believe that the fact that I had known Aaron across these settings was essential in allowing effective support for Aaron's continuous and integrated sense of self.

CASE STUDY 11.2: NATALIE

Natalie, a 17-year-old young woman had been diagnosed with a brain tumour two years before referral to the hospice. As a result of her tumour, she was visually impaired (she described herself as blind). She also had significant weight gain due to treatment. Natalie was an only child, who had been attending mainstream boarding school prior to her diagnosis, but now lived at home with her mum and dad. She was referred to the hospice when active treatment for her tumour came to an end. At this time, Natalie, a lively and sociable young lady, was spending lots of time at home, was very dependent on her parents and had become quite isolated. She had lost many of her friends upon leaving school, but remained in phone contact with one or two of them. On their first visit to the hospice, Natalie and her parents presented as a very outgoing family, living life to the full, but also very wary about coming to the hospice. After several weeks Natalie decided that she would come to the hospice one day a week for sessions of music therapy, lunch and art and craft.

Referral and aims of music therapy

The music therapy service had been mentioned to Natalie during her initial visit to the hospice. In conversation she had spoken about her desire to learn to play the guitar, having had to give up early lessons because of her tumour diagnosis. Aims for Natalie's music therapy were thus initially for her to learn to play the guitar. Other aims included:

- offering an opportunity for developing a relationship
- exploring Natalie's identity as a teenager and as a teenager with an illness
- offering an opportunity to explore issues of control and empowerment
- offering an opportunity to develop independence and confidence
- offering an opportunity for the expression of feeling.

Stage 1 – Telling her story (associations with school: Natalie's emphasis on educational aims and acquisition of musical skills)

Natalie arrived at her first music therapy session with her pink electric guitar. She seemed pleased to come and was eager to recount earlier experiences of school guitar lessons. Early sessions involved finding ways for Natalie to best access the guitar and we used plastic bump-ons on the guitar neck to indicate the most important frets. Natalie spent time remembering and playing Spanish pieces from school lessons, which I accompanied. She had been working towards a Duke of Edinburgh award in school and now wanted to work towards this with her guitar playing. Remembering and recounting stories about her life to date, and in particular as a well teenager in school, were important to her in telling her story and we often listened to songs on her MP3 player associated with these times. Natalie was very creative, engaging in poetry and songwriting to define and highlight experiences, many of which addressed themes of attachment. For example, she created 'The Revenge Song', played to the riff of Deep Purple's 'Smoke on the Water', which gave Natalie a place to express sadness about losing friends and relationships with her school 'family':

The Revenge Song

Where did she fall? Down a big hole
Never seen again – what a bloody shame
Do I really care? Oh no.

You weren't there, you didn't care
Totally unaware of me
Do I really care? Oh no.

Too much in a rush trying to find a brush
Do I really care? Oh no.

Natalie spoke of difficulties for her as a 'blind' teenage young woman dependent on her mum and dad, yet needing to find a new place (other than school) to rebel and be a teenager. An abandonment song helped express fears relating to separation (e.g. her mum having time away from the hospice while she was in sessions or the cancellation of play or music therapy sessions due to holidays), whilst music also offered an alternate means to address needs for separation and rebellion. When playing guitar, Natalie often assumed a 'rock chick' image, using distorted pedal sounds and turning up the volume as loud as possible. Keen to record her music and bring home a CD every week, Natalie seemed to find in this a way to share her story outside the sessions including, in particular, her story of her illness. While she wished to speak about feelings relating to her illness, her inclination was not to do so for fear of upsetting those close to her. Likewise, school friends had found it difficult to support Natalie or speak with her about her illness. Her CDs seemed to help bridge this gap in communication, opening up awareness and often discussion with others.

Stage 2 – Moving into the present (engaging with illness and exploring feelings about the hospice)

During the middle section of our work together Natalie continued to engage with her school identity, but began also to engage with current identity and change. Themes occurring through her music included friendship and independence, frustrations about her blindness and lack of control. She addressed her relationship with her tumour during a relapse by mastering Green Day's 'Do You Know the Enemy?' and in her own 'Georgie Porgie' song:

Georgie Porgie – (Natalie's tumour)

I am blind and I have no choice,
I may have a heart, but I have no voice
Every morning at half past eight
I must get up so I'm not late, late, late.

I fall out of bed, yes I do
I whack my head and go boo, hoo, hoo
I cry all day and I cry all night
Banging my head, it gave me an awful fright.

It takes me back – way back when
When someone hit me with a hammer and then
A few years later I was diagnosed
With a big fat tumour to the left of my nose.

'Bugger,' I said, 'oh why is it me?
Oh crap, now I can't see
Bollards and poles I do walk into
It's not my fault that's what I'm programmed to do.'

Georgie Porgie, pudding and pie
You came along and made me cry
And when all the boys came out to play
Georgie Porgie didn't go away.

Natalie had her 18th birthday around this time, so that birthday celebrations brought up further feelings of loss, unfairness and confusion regarding life expectations. Natalie appeared to deal with difficult feelings at this stage by planning to write a book for other teenagers to help them through similar illness. She was, however, having difficulty working out the final chapter. About this time, thoughts and questions also surfaced about the word 'hospice' and what that meant to Natalie. She still continued to enjoy her rock guitar, but during this period her music became more improvisational, with room for sadness, thoughtfulness and joint reflection.

Stage 3 – Ending (transition to college)

I continued to work with Natalie for approximately a year. During this time she brought a friend to visit the hospice and we had a session together. The two teenagers improvised together to music from *Friends* and *We Will Rock You*. They reflected on their friendship and were keen to record and make a CD together. At this stage, Natalie's sessions became much more focused on the music. Her interest in musicals had developed and she brought songs from *Cats*, *The Lion King* and *Phantom of the Opera* to sing as well as 'My heart will go on' from the film *Titanic*. Despite the fact that previously she had always chosen not to sing, Natalie now began to express herself in a clear and confident voice and seemed to enjoy taking risks and challenging herself vocally. Natalie also began to visit the hospice without her mum, who had until then always been her guide. Quite suddenly, Natalie announced that she was preparing for a move away to college. She had had a good result from a recent tumour scan and was planning to move on within the next month. She was excited, but also very apprehensive about moving away from home, adapting to a new life and physical environment as well as fitting in socially as a 'blind' person. The final two sessions of Natalie's music therapy therefore included time spent exploring some of these issues as well as holding on to her singing voice which was now confident and strong.

Thoughts arising from Natalie's music therapy

Defining the tasks of adolescence, Erikson refers to the need for teenagers to form a clear identity, to accept a new body image and to gain emancipation from parents. He also acknowledges, however, that 'each adolescent life task is supported by a psychosocial crisis. If it coincides with trauma then the life task may not be completed' (1968, p.15).

For Natalie, the trauma of her illness and blindness resulted in a loss of school as a symbol of Harding's (2006) 'third' in relationships, throwing herself and her parents back into earlier attachment relationship models. In coming to the hospice and engaging in music therapy, Natalie was supported to undertake separation tasks necessary for healthy adolescent development. Relationships developed with both the therapist and the music which could be seen as substitute 'third' elements, allowing for development of a new identity. To the extent that an important aspect of hospice work is facilitating a client to tell their story, stage 1 of the work acknowledged an identity very much rooted in Natalie's past and experiences of school prior to the diagnosis of her tumour. Stage 2 explored Natalie's changing identity, including a new attachment to her illness and tumour. Finally, time spent processing and formulating her thoughts, fears and experience into a format that could be safely shared with others led to a transition to a place which supported her needs as a normal teenager, as well as facilitating a healthier relationship with her illness. This integration of the sick and well sides of Natalie was evidently symbolised by renewed friendship and the hospice visit of her friend. In having been faced with the loss of musical skills from school, music therapy provided the opportunity for Natalie to re-engage musically according to her changing pace and abilities. The re-establishment of her confidence and identity allowed her to re-engage with her friend in normal teenage musical relations and her new-found singing voice seemed to represent a final link on the transition journey into a new independence and identity within college and student life.

Summary

I began this chapter by stating my intention to explore links for children's music therapy in school, hospice and hospital settings based on my experience as a music therapist within these environments. Therapists working in schools may or may not be aware of pupils who attend a children's hospice. My experience, however, is that schools often have very little knowledge of a hospice setting, of what happens there or why a student may be receiving hospice care.

The two case studies cited offer examples of the role of the music therapist in supporting integration of the sick and well person and of managing the transition between medical and educational settings. Indeed, in these two case examples, I would suggest that music therapy provided essential and unique support towards integration of the 'whole child' and promotion of an ongoing sense of self and identity across school, hospice and hospital settings at a time of change and trauma. I wonder how far this raises questions and carries implications for the school music therapist, i.e. whether there is not a demand for school music services to fulfil a similar role in providing more continuous, flexible and holistic support for students. For example, when a student who is having music therapy in school goes on extended absence due to exclusion, mental health breakdown or hospitalisation, is there not ideally a function for the music therapist in education to offer continued support in whatever form this might practicably be possible?

To conclude, as a music therapist working in both a school and a children's hospice, I feel that I have gained a greater understanding of what the period outside school might be like for students whose health has broken down and for their families. Parents of life-limited and life-threatened children may, understandably, be experienced by school professionals as difficult or overanxious. From my experience of working at a children's hospice, however, it is easy to comprehend why a parent whose 'raison d'etre' is ensuring the survival of her child (in the knowledge that she may have to intervene when he unpredictably stops breathing) poses the question, 'How can I consider letting my child go to school when I spend all my time trying to keep him alive?' With this in mind, difficulties of attachment and separation for the life-threatened child, their parents and wider family, are almost inevitable. Personal experience seems to have shown that the music therapist has an invaluable role to play in supporting healthier processes in these areas.

Chapter 12

Psychodynamically Informed Music Therapy Groups with Teenagers with Severe Special Needs in a College Setting

Working Jointly with Teaching Assistants

John Strange

What happens in a music therapy group for severely disabled teenagers? I shall describe and discuss an approach I have developed in a particular context, to provide a window on a setting with which readers may be unfamiliar.

CASE STUDY 12.1

Extract 1 is the start of a typical session, taken down from a video recording.

Members sit in a semi-circle, each student with a teaching assistant (name in italics). From left to right they are: *Karen*, Carole, Kathy, *Jenny*, Hugo and *Tessa*. (Students have the same teaching assistant each week except in case of staff absence).

I sing a hello song with keyboard accompaniment, greeting everyone together and then individual members. Carole makes singing noises and imitates some of Jenny's hand-signs. When Hugo (whom she only meets in this group) is named in the song, Carole looks at him. Kathy just turns her head slightly towards me at her name. Hugo at first makes no response, but when Tessa touches his arm and repeats his name he reaches for her hand and attempts to say his name.

Hugo kicks the footplates of his wheelchair. I mirror this with staccato chords. When Tessa taps the side of his wheelchair he looks for the source of the noise, then kicks his feet together. I sing 'look at his feet' and notice that Carole is watching him. Tessa imitates the movement. He then fiddles with his belt. As I sing about his actions, Carole turns towards Jenny, who signs my words and then prompts her to watch Hugo again. These are the first of many instances where the teaching assistants interact spontaneously with the students in ways that are helpful, with no prompting from myself.

Hugo is offered a glockenspiel, which he has enjoyed previously. Kathy's wheelchair is turned directly to face him. Tessa plays occasional notes on the glockenspiel, supported pianissimo by me on the keyboard, but Hugo silently taps his fists together and does not take the glockenspiel beater when it is offered. Jenny notices Kathy smiling at the music and smiles back. I accelerate my tempo to match Hugo's hand movement, and Tessa plays the glockenspiel in the same tempo. Carole, watching intently, starts to vocalise 'ah' with increasing emphasis and varying intonation, as though urging Hugo to play. He kicks his footplate and claps a little. I insert short bursts of clapping into my accompaniment and sing 'we can clap with this music'. Tessa continues to play the glockenspiel in time, no longer offering it to Hugo, as he clearly prefers clapping.

When Hugo stops, I leave the keyboard and ask what else people would like to play. I take some suspended wind-chimes to Kathy. Jenny supports her arm and sweeps her hand across the chimes. Carole is asked what she would like, and points at a metallophone on a trolley. It is brought to her place, as it would be rather awkward for her to carry it herself.

The following paragraph is transcribed at Figure 12.1, which follows.

When Carole has been given a beater, Hugo is again asked if he would like to hold his beater. He feels it but does not take it, humming on a downward sigh and withdrawing his hand. I gently imitate and extend this hum, harmonising with gentle flowing chords. Carole plays occasional accented single notes. When Jenny helps Kathy to sweep her hand outwards across the wind-chimes she smiles and co-operates with the movement. When Tessa (opposite Carole) borrows Hugo's glockenspiel and answers Carole's playing, Hugo immediately looks at Tessa and laughs. Jenny helps Kathy to synchronise her playing of the wind-chimes with this dialogue, and she vocalises with pleasure, a low glissando murmur which I imitate. Carole plays accented metallophone notes and is delighted when this elicits a clear response from my keyboard.

Hugo suddenly reaches over and grabs Carole's spare metallophone stick. Tessa places his glockenspiel on Carole's trolley so that he must face her to play it. Karen asks her to show Hugo what she is doing. She looks at him and plays several single notes. Despite Tessa's gentle suggestion and modelling, Hugo does not play in response. I sing 'Kathy's chimes', synchronising with

Figure 12.1 A relaxed atmosphere to encourage listening and responding

her assisted playing. She briefly turns her head towards me. Carole has stopped playing to watch her. Tessa plays glockenspiel glissandi to match the wind-chimes, and Hugo watches in silence. This is the first time in this session when he has become physically still and relaxed (a rare occurrence at this early stage of therapy) and thus able to attend in a more focused manner and perhaps realise that Tessa's music is now linked to Kathy's.

As I watch Kathy's assisted playing, although I know she is prone to involuntary spasms I feel that some at least of her arm movements are now voluntary responses to my music. I decide to offer her the chance of playing something by means of her finger movements, which always appear to be voluntary. After a brief discussion with Jenny, we offer Kathy an ethnic cabassa.

What is happening?

This is part of a longer section of the group's second session, in which I am trying to encourage everyone present to participate, as and when they feel inclined, in ensemble music-making. As the short musical transcription shows, my main contribution is to provide musical continuity by means of an unobtrusive keyboard accompaniment. Although the tempo is flexible, there is a clear enough underlying slow three-two metre during this extract to justify adding barlines and a time signature for ease of reading. Notes played by Carole or Tessa on pitched percussion often seem to fit the harmony, probably through a mixture of happy coincidence and my rapid accommodation to what they play. In transcribing members' vocalisations, including laughter and one spoken comment, I have notated pitches as precisely as possible in relation to the prevailing tonality, of which they may be implicitly aware.

The three students are very different and participate in contrasting ways. Carole is functionally fairly independent in this context, though she refers frequently to adults for recognition and reassurance. Kathy has very limited intentional movement and therefore requires physical assistance and carefully selected and positioned instruments in order to play, but her resistance at one point suggests that her relaxed compliance at other times is intentional, and her vocalisations of pleasure are clearly communicative. Hugo has recently changed schools and been moved from home to residential care, and tends to react angrily to any pressure or guidance that might feel like a further threat to his autonomy. Tessa therefore plays partly towards him, as a model and an invitation, and partly towards Carole on his behalf, to help him become aware that his and Carole's pitched percussion could have a dialogue.

The context

This is one of four music therapy groups for teenagers who have profound and multiple learning disability, or in a few cases severe learning disability. The groups are held in a further education college. Students from several nearby special schools come to college once a week for 30 weeks a year for a project known as 'College Link' which offers a range of activities including music therapy. The rationale for the project, which is quite complex to organise, is principally to accustom these vulnerable students to the hurly burly of life in a college setting with non-disabled teenagers.

The main consideration when choosing activities to include in the programme for the day is their contribution to quality of life rather than their educational benefit. From the variety on offer, participating schools select up to four they feel will best meet each student's needs, and then group the students so that each can attend the chosen options at some point in the day.

Many colleges provide courses for learning disabled students, but provision for those with severe or profound learning disabilities is often limited. In this particular college, provision for such students once they have left school does not match the College Link programme in quality or breadth, although large numbers of less severely disabled students are well catered for.

On College Link, nearly all students have continuous one-to-one support from school staff to help them participate. In most cases one-to-one support is also essential for personal care, mobility, and sometimes medical reasons. Although students miss an important aspect of educational 'inclusion' by not mixing socially with their non-disabled peers, at least they experience the lively ambience of college canteens and corridors and the challenges of an environment designed for the non-disabled, challenges they will have to face in adult life. For non-disabled students, despite minimal social contact with the severely disabled students, the College Link project is a reminder that such students have an equal entitlement to educational experiences. As non-disabled students grow used to their presence they may start to understand their needs and abilities.

Referral, reporting and accountability

Students do not arrive in my music therapy groups through a traditional clinical referral. College Link exists for broad educational, sociological, philosophical and even political reasons. Students often have needs which can be met by music therapy, and this is a factor in allocating some of them to my groups, but the main consideration is more often whether their developmental disabilities will *allow* them to participate (or perhaps rule out their participation in an alternative group). I issue retrospective referral forms on which staff are asked how they hope music therapy may help each student, but I may not have made the purpose clear enough, as staff tend to select, from the checklist provided, every special need which could possibly apply to the student, rather than focusing on those where music therapy might be beneficial.

The teaching assistants who attend the groups are convinced of their value and keep staff in the schools informed of students' encouraging and sometimes novel responses. In an attempt to raise awareness I write annual review reports for students and offer occasional training sessions for teaching assistants, school and college staff. In these I show video examples of students changing and developing and also mention relevant psychodynamic concepts to enhance teaching assistants' contribution to the groups and other staff's understanding.

I find myself in the unusual and liberating position of not having to demonstrate measurable progress in terms of reasons for referral. But whilst external demands for 'evidence' may feel oppressive and even distort therapeutic work, their absence can breed complacency, so it falls to me to ensure that I am providing a good service.

To plan or not to plan?

In *Music Therapy Groupwork with Special Needs Children* (2007) Goodman advocates a sequential process of determining and prioritising children's needs, considering which could be met by group music therapy and then forming groups whose members' needs, though varied, are mutually compatible. In the College Link situation this is not possible. Groupings are predetermined by the schools and the process of discovering which needs I can effectively address only begins once therapy is under way.

Goodman gives detailed advice on planning sessions. It will be clear from the above extract that the work I describe was not preplanned. Both my music therapy training and my clinical supervision have been psychodynamically based, and I view my clinical work from that perspective. It seems to me that to have a detailed agenda for a session would have two distinct disadvantages. It would detract from the attention I need to focus on how students are that day and what they are communicating, because I would be constantly wondering how best to introduce and implement whatever I had planned. It could also add an artificial strand of resistance, as students legitimately decline to co-operate with my plans, when the resistance on which I should focus is that which blocks their own expression and self-realisation. The only forward planning I allow myself is both provisional and very general in scope, as in the excerpt below, where I encourage students to participate co-operatively by the suggestion of building up from a solo (plus accompaniment) to a duet and then a trio.

I find reflection on what has occurred is the most effective tool for developing the work. By transcribing each session from video (not in such detail as in the short excerpts in this chapter but in a more general way) I re-experience the contributions of students, teaching assistants and myself to the group dynamic and also build up a picture of strengths and weakness, likes and dislikes and what works for whom. As the next session approaches, I do not re-read what I have written, trusting that I have internalised what I most need to know. Without an advance plan a session can still have structure, created in partnership with the group rather than imposed, and may incorporate pre-composed music and games when this is clinically indicated.

CASE STUDY 12.2

Extract 2: group 1, session 8 (Tim and Simon have had two previous years with me, in different groupings, and Zebedee one year).

Participants, from left to right: Sue, Tim, Greta, Simon, Kathleen, Zebedee.

At the hello song Tim turns briefly towards me and Simon smiles but Zebedee makes no response. As I move clockwise round the semi-circle to address both students and staff in order, Tim points to Kathleen and is reminded he has missed out Simon. Simon smiles at his greeting, then despite his very limited movement looks towards Kathleen and raises his arm. She takes his hand and says hello, and I extend the musical phrase to echo this. Zebedee looks at me at his name but his expression remains blank. In the silence following the song, Tim reaches and hits an ocean drum just within reach on a table. As I comment that this is a good idea, he is already trying to grab a second instrument. His first choice is placed on his lap and the second moved out of reach. I explain that first he will play alone.

The following three paragraphs are transcribed at Figure 12.2 which follows.

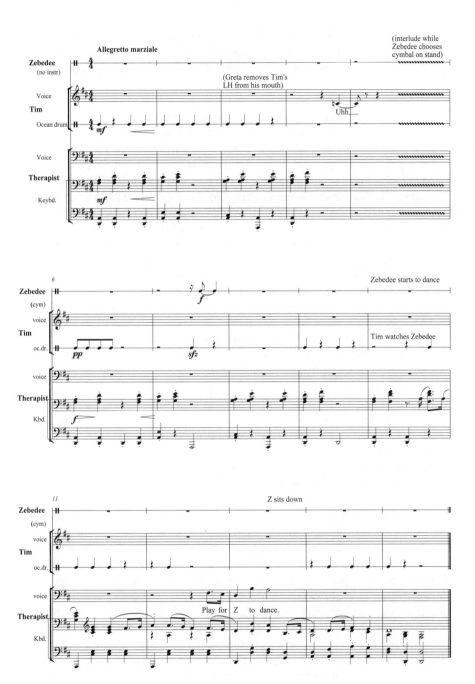

Figure 12.2 A rhythmic framework to encourage synchronised repsonses

Tim hits the ocean drum firmly with his right palm and I try to synchronise with strong piano chords. He stops abruptly when Greta removes his left hand from his face to prevent him chewing it or picking a sore spot on his nose.

When I say we will add music from someone else, Tim immediately points to Zebedee. I ask Zebedee what he would like to play and he points. I check which of two instruments he intends and he nods when I tap the cymbal. I explain that we will start with the same music as Tim played before.

I repeat the phrase with which I previously accompanied Tim, but he stops beating and waits until a rest in my part cues a single strong beat. Zebedee hits the cymbal so soon after Tim that I cannot tell whether he also responded to my musical cue or whether he was simply very prompt in imitating Tim. I continue with a balancing phrase and Tim responds in the rest as before then reverts to steady beating, though more quietly. Zebedee stands up and bounces on the spot so I extend my fourth phrase to fit the words 'play for Zeb to dance'. Zebedee immediately sits, so I bring the music to a clear final cadence, which Tim recognises and observes.

Zebedee then starts a regular beat on the cymbal, which I accompany. Tim quickly joins in, shaking the ocean drum in time. When Zebedee stops playing Tim reverts to beating the drum. At my next final cadence Tim offers his ocean drum to Greta, probably hoping to be given something else. I ask him to keep it so we can add music from Simon, who immediately raises his arms at his name. As I and the teaching assistants discuss which of Simon's preferred instruments will be loud enough to match the others, Tim beats his drum intermittently. Zebedee clicks his sticks together and then falls silent. I demonstrate the djembe and some rather hard-toned bongos. Simon chooses the bongos by smiling, his usual method of communicating a choice. I say 'well waited!' to Tim and Zebedee, who have been silent for some time, something Tim usually finds difficult.

Tim has found a small kabasa which he uses to beat his ocean drum. As this is not likely to harm it, it is ignored. On the piano I pick up Tim's initially hesitant beat and he plays more vigorously. As Greta holds the bongos on Simon's lap and supports his right arm ready to play, Kathleen crosses the room and plays a few beats on the bongos in time with Tim. Zebedee clicks his sticks together with a confidence which varies according to the decisiveness of my phrasing and accentuation. Tim uses the kabasa as an electric shaver in symbolic play. Greta moves the bongos to arm's length and supports Simon's arm, helping him to tap gently in time with my quiet staccato piano. I comment that the other two are playing quietly to hear Simon, at which point Zebedee plays more strongly on the cymbal and Tim joins in on his ocean drum in a faster tempo. Keeping the same style of playing, I accelerate to match Tim, and sing to Simon, 'they're telling you it's faster now'.

What is happening?

The three students are again very different. Tim is functionally independent but can be quite challenging and seldom accepts verbal guidance, though like Carole in case study 12.1 he refers frequently to adults for recognition and reassurance. Zebedee, though physically well co-ordinated, rarely plays until a steady tempo has been established by someone else, when he enjoys interacting musically. Simon has extremely limited range and speed of movement but more intentionality than Kathy in case study 12.1. His facial expressions of pleasure or disdain are highly communicative. He is sensitive to the music around him and can respond more decisively than he does in this extract. My keyboard accompaniment in the section transcribed is quite directive, in order to establish a strong enough framework to bring Tim's and Zebedee's music together, although after the transcribed section it does become more flexible in tempo and mood.

Music *in* therapy or music *as* therapy

Much has been written over the years about whether music merely supports processes from other disciplines (principally psychotherapy, but also speech and language therapy, physiotherapy and sensory integration as practised by occupational therapists). When these other disciplines provide the theoretical model of the therapeutic process we may speak of music *in* therapy. When, on the other hand, music itself is seen as the therapeutic agent we may speak of music *as* therapy.

Aigen (2005) makes a radical case for a wholly 'indigenous' music therapy theory. Jettisoning all imported theories of therapy, he makes novel use of theories of the formal, perceptual and sociological aspects of music and 'musicking' to account for the therapeutic effect of musical participation. As I understand him, the music therapist need not hold these theories in consciousness whilst providing therapy, but should rather use music intuitively within the boundaries of ethical practice. I find this last concept liberating, as the College Link work has made me more aware than ever before how much my musical improvisation, especially in ensemble music-making, is directed, at least at a conscious level, by a sense of where the music is leading, based on my experience as composer. This way of working has its dangers, as hinted in a recent presentation (Strange 2010), but I am reassured that the musical activities and experiences in the College Link groups are therapeutic when I see how music both relaxes and enlivens the students, often bypassing their communication difficulties and sometimes transforming their problem behaviours. In a more general sense I believe the groups contribute to quality of life and protect mental health and well-being.

The role of music therapy assistants

Most but not all teaching assistants have attended a training session in which I speak of the influence of the students' inner worlds on their interactions with others and their ability and motivation to communicate, musically or otherwise. I stress that all behaviours have communicative potential and cannot be understood and worked with if they are not permitted to occur. I try to avoid jargon, and to define any technical terms for which there is no everyday equivalent. I reassure staff that an approach to problem behaviours in the therapy room different from that adopted in school will not confuse the students or make them harder to work with. I present the task of running a therapy group as a collaborative exercise to which therapist and assistants bring complementary knowledge and skills and share insights into students' personalities and abilities.

I have been fortunate in the teaching assistants allocated to College Link groups. They know the students very well and are able to recognise attempts to communicate and pick up the idiosyncratic ways in which students indicate likes and dislikes and express varying moods. They are aware that challenging behaviours are a form of communication and should therefore be noted and acknowledged, rather than seen as a disruption to be stopped.

The teaching assistants' role in College Link groups is a complex one, not without tensions and ambiguities. They are group members who share in instrumental playing, both ensemble and solo. They are supporters who offer, demonstrate and hold instruments for students and physically support their playing when necessary. They are interpreters of the students' communication and they are co-therapists who interact musically with students. Each role may be required at any time, and they have to be able to move flexibly between them.

Each role carries within it its own tensions. As group members, and especially as co-therapists, teaching assistants should at times be able to express their own feelings in addition to focusing on the students' feelings. Being with profoundly disabled people can arouse strong emotions of pity, fear, anger and guilt. People who work with them all day, every day, have to find a way to deal with these feelings. They may repress them, but this can leave them feeling exhausted and flat, even depressed, and emotionally unavailable to the person in their care. They may deflect the feelings elsewhere, risking workplace or domestic tension. They may, usually unconsciously, hide intolerable feelings beneath their opposites, a defence known as reaction formation (Freud 1966). In order to minimise these stresses on teaching assistants I must provide them with sufficient emotional support, offering encouragement and appreciation and resisting the temptation to challenge their defences, provided the student is not harmed. I do, however, prompt teaching assistants to assert their right to be heard musically, to hang on to an instrument when a student tries to grab it, and to give safe musical expression to any angry feelings, just as students are allowed to do.

The role of supporter, which is probably all the teaching assistants thought would be asked of them when they took on the work, also has a tension within it. Does support mean trying to draw the most out of the student, or gently facilitating what students actually choose to express for themselves? I have found that as teaching assistants gain experience of the work they require less and less guidance on how to respond to students and help them participate. Many are skilled in giving physical support to a student without controlling how they play, by amplifying incipient movements, responding sensitively to varying levels of physical resistance, giving them time to respond and accepting non-responsiveness without showing disappointment. An interesting carry-over from their educational work with students is a tendency to give verbal prompts or verbal praise where a musical cue or a musical response to the student would be preferable, so I regularly remind them that whilst musical responses, whether by playing, vocalising or moving, are to be welcomed, the students need to respond as they feel, and not in order to please me or their teaching assistants, which can so easily become their strongest motive, fostering dependency.

There is tension also within the role of interpreter, between accuracy and wish fulfilment, both when translating the students' intentions and emotions to me and when reflecting these back to the student. One defensive reaction to unconscious guilt in the face of profound disability may be excessive optimism about students' understanding and a blandly sunny interpretation of the students' emotions.

A specific educational context for music-centred, psychodynamically informed group music therapy

The College Link work occurs in a specific context, whose determining features include the age of the clients (14–19), the severity of their disability, their allocation to groups without prior music therapy assessment, the duration of therapy (one or more academic years of 30 weeks) and the freedom accorded me to work as I see fit. There is no obtrusive line management, no set of targets to be met. Instead there is the opportunity for regular informal feedback to schools by teaching assistants who have actively participated in sessions, although the effectiveness of this depends on the teaching staff's eagerness to know, which can vary. Narrative annual reviews based on session notes are an ideal way to convey to staff and parents and carers an impression of the work and a sympathetic account of the young person's participation and progress.

There is an appropriate and consistently available room for the therapy, largely free from interruption and equipped with a wide variety of instruments purchased according to the therapist's specifications. Last but not least there are skilled teaching assistants who are willing to learn. These favourable working conditions are the result of enlightened hands-off management, mutual trust and the general philosophy of College Link.

My music therapy approach is strongly influenced by the fact that I am a composer and fluent improviser. I have so often been alerted by a series of clinical supervisors to the danger of letting music get in the way or take over that now my 'internal supervisor' (Casement 1985) usually intervenes to control any such tendency (Strange 2010). I have the ongoing support of clinical supervision and my own personal therapy.

To what extent can the College Link work be described as psychodynamically informed? I have never felt quite at ease with the reification of intra-psychic processes, but am in no doubt of the existence and powerful role of unconscious processes, in therapy and other helping professions, in caring roles, in management situations and in everyday life. The College Link students use many of the same defences and have the same need for a secure attachment and drive to self-fulfilment as anyone else, but are less able than those with greater verbal and intellectual ability both to introspect and to empathise – part of what Fonagy *et al.* (2004) term mentalisation – and thus not able to use verbal interpretation by the therapist. Nevertheless, my decisions as to whether and how to encourage, discourage, or comment on interactions during sessions are influenced by my private interpretation of what may lie behind them, and their meanings to the participants.

The majority of one-to-one interactions occur between students and teaching assistants and include many extra-musical elements, whereas interactions between students and myself are more often mainly musical. I strive to increase the frequency of inter-student interactions, including that of music-maker and listener, through my musical support and sung or spoken comments and suggestions, as the clinical extracts show. The final ingredient in the mix is supported ensemble music-making, which aims to integrate students' expression of their individuality with that of their group identity.

Chapter 13

'Yeah, I'll Do Music!'

Working with Secondary-aged Students Who Have Complex Emotional and Behavioural Difficulties

Philippa Derrington

Introduction

In this chapter I shall describe the development of music therapy at a secondary school, my practice and how it has been shaped by teenagers, and the set up of a system to monitor clinical practice in an educational setting.

Nearly all teenagers relate to music and are actively interested in it as a way of communicating with their peers and socially identifying themselves. The stereotype of a moody, monosyllabic and dreamy teenager is usually replaced by creative, communicative and dynamic play when music is the means of expression. I am particularly interested in using improvisation with this age group because it facilitates immediate and honest self-expression. However, there are lots of other ways too in which teenagers can engage in music therapy and their ideas and responses to music have informed and continue to challenge how I work. 'We are not what you think we are!' a chorus line by pop singer Mika (2009) suggesting that teenagers do not like to be 'worked out', highlights the need to engage in the culture of adolescence (Cobbett 2009) and understand its various forms of communication if therapy is going to be a successful intervention.

I am initially going to explain how music therapy has become established at a secondary school. This will be followed by snapshots of case work. I have used quotes from the students for each heading that I feel captures something of their identity.

Setting up music therapy at a learning support unit attached to a mainstream secondary school

I set up music therapy at Cottenham Village College in 2003, a mainstream college with about 1000 students aged between 11 and 16, which had a learning support unit attached to it aimed at helping students with special developmental, emotional and behavioural needs. This unit worked in a similar way to a pupil referral unit, which meant that it provided specialist education and support to students who were not able to learn in a mainstream environment. I worked with students in this unit, some of whom attended full-time and others who attended mainstream classes as well. The majority of music therapy referrals indicated that the students' learning was being affected by severe emotional difficulties, either as a result of one-off trauma or from ongoing emotional stress.

In November 2008, when the unit had over 50 full-time registered students, it became a school in its own right and was named the Centre School. What makes this school so distinct is that it is on the site of a mainstream secondary school so whilst the students are excluded and attend a separate unit, they are not isolated. The school's ethos is centred on the individual's learning and students follow personalised learning plans so that they all do what they are capable of and can reach their full potential. A student in the Centre can access mainstream classes with support and a mainstream student who needs extra help can be supported by the Centre. The college plays an important role in helping to reintegrate students from the Centre where possible and the schools are federated and continue to share resources so they remain firmly linked.

One of these resources is music therapy. The majority of the young people I work with attend the Centre School but I also work with students in the mainstream school, including those with hearing-impairment (Derrington 2010). I am employed by the Centre School (two days a week) and by Cambridgeshire's Hearing Support Service (one day a week), whose unit for secondary-aged pupils is based at the college. These two employers oversee all the referrals, which significantly may relate to students who do not come under their remit but whose referral they recommend. This illustrates how the schools work together in a co-operative and supportive way.

The Centre School

On the whole, students in the Centre are very troubled young people who have experienced failure in the educational system. Some have been excluded from primary school, others from mainstream secondary or special schools. The students are vulnerable and can exhibit challenging behaviour. They all come with complex needs and are battling against enormous difficulties, not just with learning but sometimes social and economic ones too. Most of the students have statements for social, emotional and behavioural difficulties, and many for associated learning difficulties. The school aims to provide a structure and routine for these students whose lives are in chaos so that they may begin to deal with these difficulties more independently.

The Centre's provision reminds me of Bowlby's (1988) concern for adolescents, as well as children, to have a secure base. As well as an emotional secure base and someone to keep them in mind, students need a constant and dependable space from which they can operate, i.e. a secure physical base and somewhere they can return to (Bombèr 2009). There is no separate staff room, which means that all the teachers and instructors share the same space at break times as the students and play games such as table tennis, pool, cards or board games together, allowing healthy and positive relationships to develop which are based on mutual respect and trust. From the cheese toasties and bacon rolls at breakfast to the reliable infrastructure of school, students can become more confident to try new things knowing that there is a place to return to and that there are people who will help them.

Garage music

At the launch of music therapy at the school, I was offered two possible places to work: a small room off the main area of the Centre, or sharing a slightly damp garage which was full of bikes. There was no question, I thought the garage was ideal. It was a separate building away from other classrooms but still very close to the school. It had been converted into a bike workshop so it had heating, power and windows. It was spacious with a graffiti logo across one wall claiming 'Wheel Fix It!' I began with just a few percussion instruments but soon afterwards bought a drum-kit and digital piano to help set aside one corner of the room for music therapy.

Within a few months, the school had increased my employment from half a day to two full days a week and I continued to collect instruments by finding bargains on eBay and responding to adverts for instruments which were being given away. I also managed to retrieve various items which the school was throwing away. With the gradual accrual of resources, including a piano, guitars, congas and a violin, cupboards, a table and chairs, I was gently able to extend the boundaries of the music therapy corner using old exhibition boards to mark out our space. The instructor who supervised the bike repairs was a keen drummer and understood the importance of music for the students. It was, however, easier when, after two years of sharing the garage, the time came for music therapy to have full use of the space and for the bikes to move on.

Colleagues in the Design and Technology department, who I also played with in a band, helped me clad the long back brick wall to provide sound-proofing and extra insulation. Then over another weekend, having recruited friends and my parents' help, the garage was transformed into a fully furnished and carpeted music therapy room, free from tools, bike chains and oil, and made from mostly recycled kit. Despite some suggestions to change its name to Sound Lab or Music Shed it is still known as 'the garage'. The 1990s genre of electronic dance music sharing the name seems to add kudos and appeal to the teenagers who use it because even the most resistant students admit the garage is cool.

Figure 13.1 Enjoying the freedom of improvisation

'Let's just play it'

Some students enjoy the freedom of jamming, the immediacy of making something up and making something sound good. They might set about imitating a band or learning a riff from a certain song but their spontaneity and energy can take the music in a new and improvised direction. Their eclectic taste and experience of music, from popular, rock, and drum and bass to children's songs and film tunes, can enter into the mix.

Improvising is also about making use of what is available and students are constantly finding new ways of playing instruments, such as beatboxing down a penny whistle or making the most elaborate drum-kit by hanging a ukulele or as many percussion instruments as possible on various stands. The enjoyment of setting up and preparing the ground for playing is important and certainly many want to test out the instruments' strength before they start.

CASE STUDY 13.1

Billy, 13, jammed for an entire year. He attended weekly sessions unstintingly. He either played the drum-kit, electric guitar or piano and each time, usually playing different instruments, we improvised together. It was difficult to discern who was following who at times as the music felt intrinsically shared. We usually got into a common groove before moving on to explore a range of dynamics and styles. With most improvisations exhaustively covering a multitude of moods the piece of music could sometimes last as long as 40 minutes, the length of the session itself. Billy hardly ever said a word and did not respond to my reflections on the music. If he took time out in a session, he liked to swivel on a chair or gaze out of the window. It was only as we approached the end of the first term, that the value and purpose of these improvisations really became clear. 'Is it gonna carry on after the holidays?' he asked. Knowing this student's background it was only too clear that his experience of good things was that they often ended abruptly.

Although he seemed to hear my assurances that music therapy was not finishing and that our work would continue, he still seemed agitated and, unlike his usual quietness, talked about death and unexpected disasters such as earthquakes and floods. We talked about looking ahead and the music we would play when we were back and then, just before we broke up, he asked if he could take one of the whistles home for the holiday. He promised to look after it and I knew it was important that he should take it. This physical object signified a transitional object as identified by Winnicott (1991). It was an object reminder that music therapy would continue, that I was holding him in mind and that school was a familiar and supportive place to return to.

After the holidays, our improvisations continued in the same way but now, having survived a break, seemed even more significant and communicative. Billy trusted the relationship that was formed through shared music-making and knew that he was expressing himself in a way that felt listened to and understood.

'That's sick, bruv, listen!'

For other students, the idea of making something up can feel far too random and precarious. A lot of students choose to use recorded music in their sessions and I encourage them to bring their own music with them, particularly at the start if I feel that they are slightly wary of playing instruments. The 'headphone generation' as described by Ruud (1998), able to listen to more music and on the move with the invention of the Walkman in 1980, can now access their music on flash drives, playstations and phones as well as the more obvious iPods and MP3 players. Listening to their choice of music and talking together can provide a really good launch pad for the therapeutic relationship. Through conversation and discussion of musical taste the therapist can facilitate development, by understanding the student's motivation and interest in music, as well as offer acceptance and establish an affiliation (McFerran 2010).

However hard I try I can never keep up with the massive variety of music which the students are listening to, but my ignorance can also be an advantage. Students need to know more, test our knowledge and look shocked when we've never heard of a band. However, an attentive and communicative response can match their enthusiasm and interest, provide ideas for further sessions and set up a rapport. Recorded music can act as a prop or precursor to playing live music, as in this following case example.

CASE STUDY 13.2

John, 14, had been excluded from two schools before he began at the Centre. His behaviour was difficult to manage, especially in groups, and he usually found it difficult to share in any activity with others, often becoming aggressive when he was not in control. In individual music therapy sessions we listened to songs together and he talked confidently about the bands he liked and respected. Each week he came prepared with a playlist of different music for us to listen to. John liked to drum along to his favourite bands and I tried to jam alongside, either on the electric guitar or bass, but it felt as if I was musically following him around and cut off from what he was doing, rather like sharing the same stage but being in a different band. His command over the recorded music, using the remote control to change tracks, made it difficult to keep up and I felt he wanted me to stop playing and listen to him, to acknowledge and affirm his drumming instead.

It was obvious that playing along to music like this was enjoyable for him and he was very settled and motivated by it, which strongly contrasted with his behaviour in school. Was it enough that he stayed in the room and was happy playing along to a CD? I could argue to myself that on one level music therapy was achieving its aims because he engaged in the activity and worked in a focused way, but his behaviour continued to be really challenging in other settings. John used recorded music in this way every week and rather than creating a barrier, I felt that his commitment to sessions was communication itself and that by listening I was able to share his music despite his resistance to playing together.

As well as actively listening and responding to his playing, I found other ways to join in. I held the microphone for him so that he could sing while he drummed, I worked meticulously on the PA system and even danced about playing the air guitar to his entertainment. I matched his energy, grabbed every chance to interact with him musically and gradually was allowed to join in with his band. John began to play in a more communicative and interactive way even to the extent of asking me what I thought of it afterwards, how we could improve the sound and asking me to take charge of the remote control.

Recorded music provided a necessary backing to live playing which moved from being a band and his audience to two players who shared one stage, who listened to each other's music and played in concert. John had learned to share his enjoyment and the experience of playing and begun to address issues of control.

'You've been mugged!'

Incorporating competitive games and activities can really help to engage and inspire teenagers, if they don't introduce them first! Simple games, such as who can play the loudest in a drum-off, turn-taking and copying rhythmic patterns, can be a good way to get started if they feel uncertain or nervous about playing. The addition of point-scoring and having mini competitions can add motivating factors and interest. Doing well and winning can be really important to these young people especially as many have known nothing but failure.

CASE STUDY 13.3

Tom was 13 at the start of music therapy. He had been excluded from primary school, had a difficult home life and tended to be isolated at school. He felt that there was not much that he could change in his life and he seemed resigned and sad. Initially Tom liked to sing songs with me which reminded him of primary school assemblies. He enjoyed listening to music and making up songs too, but it was important that everything was done together. Through regular sessions and sharing these activities Tom began to develop a greater sense of self and appreciation of what he could do. He started to talk about things he was doing outside music therapy and what he was achieving. At the same time within music therapy he started to make up games. He became increasingly competitive and enjoyed playing against me, bringing points into play which became particularly significant. Tom needed to win and do better than me, shouting 'You've been mugged!' every time he scored.

On one occasion we were playing a game, rather like musical statues where, if the player was spotted still moving after the other player had stopped drumming, he was given a number of minutes as points against him. The time related to the number of minutes Tom had had removed from his break at his old school as a form of punishment for his disruptive behaviour. Tom's new confidence allowed him to face the past and a time when he was not in control. Through this game he was able to win and instead of getting detention, could enjoy playing, feel independent and start to experience control in a playful way.

'Can I draw that?'

One of the items I salvaged from the school skip was a large whiteboard which was being thrown out as the school updated to interactive boards. I thought it would be particularly useful for writing up lyrics when the students composed songs and it has been good for this purpose, but it also provides a canvas for all sorts of art work. For some students, being able to doodle on the board can help them to focus, chat and think about how they are feeling. For others, printing their name or a gang's symbol at the start is their way of stamping out the space which is theirs for a time, or leaving a message of statement behind, for example, 'Music therapy. Be part of it!'

The whiteboard also re-creates an aspect of the classroom and has inspired some students to role-play. They adopt the part of a member of staff who can teach me, give me a detention or exclude me for bad behaviour. Such games further illustrate students' frequent need for playful control.

CASE STUDY 13.4

For one student in the Centre, who I shall call Sam, the whiteboard became the focus of many sessions when playing instruments just did not seem possible. She was 14 when she was referred to music therapy because of her very low self-esteem and poor social skills. She was quick to make the most of her time playing music, enjoying improvising and working out musical effects. Then, towards the end of the first year of therapy, her mother died. Over the weeks Sam's behaviour became erratic and dangerous and there was grave concern for her welfare. At the time she was attending music therapy twice a week and she needed to fill almost every moment of every session with very loud, recorded music and drawing on the board. She never missed a session and clearly trusted the therapy space but she no longer wanted to touch the instruments. All I could do was to be consistent and respond genuinely.

Setting up the amplifier and all four large speakers to their maximum volume, pop music blared out session after session. There was little way to engage with her in conversation although I did try and this occasionally resulted in a game with the volume control where she turned it down, as if to allow me airspace and then turned it back up just as I started to speak. Through such games though, however short, I was able to regularly achieve a meeting point with her in all the chaos and din. It reassured me that she knew I was sharing the noise and confusion and that I was always listening.

The turning point came when Kylie Minogue's song 'I can't get you out of my head' was playing. Sam had covered the board in drawings and, looking at one sketch (see Figure 13.2), said that her mother was always in her head: 'What a shame we don't have brains like computers with a button you press for shut down.'

She started to play certain songs on repeat which made the lyrics more noticeable and pertinent. She clearly wanted me to hear them as they blared out and she occasionally allowed me to pause the CD to talk to her and reflect a little on what was being sung. One song by Pink called 'Who Knew' (2006) was about grief and disbelief. The lyrics are based on the loss of a friend to an overdose and the loss of a friendship. For this student, the words expressed her sudden change in circumstance, the pain, devastation and her feelings of anger. It was very hard to listen to these words together but absolutely crucial.

Sam initially used recorded music as background and noise to match her feelings, at times to block them out and certainly to try to prevent us from thinking about anything. She was able to draw on the board to express herself without words until she arrived at a point where the songs were allowed to the foreground and we could both hear and begin to acknowledge the lyrics. The board continued to play an important part in music therapy sessions but, crucially, had provided her with another way to communicate with me when her feelings had felt overwhelming and chaotic.

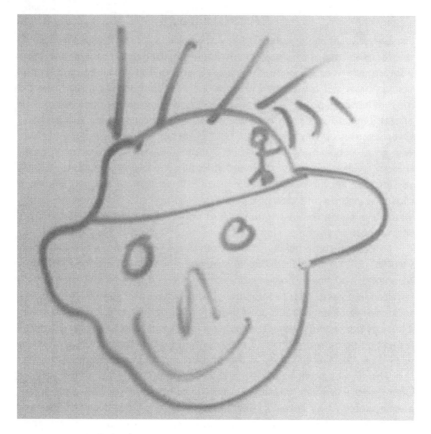

Figure 13.2 Sam's sketch

'Can I have your skateboarding magazine?'

I have found that having a variety of books and magazines about subjects such as skateboarding, biking and go-karting lying around in the music therapy room can sometimes instigate ideas and themes for musical play and songwriting. Working with teenagers is constantly a fine balancing act between making suggestions and actively enabling them to come up with their own ideas. Having magazines and books, as well as the more obvious supply of music books in the room, can provide prompts without leading.

CASE STUDY 13.5

Jacob, a 15-year-old student in the Centre, had very low self-esteem when he was referred to music therapy. He had suffered neglect and been moved away from his family. At the time of his weekly session he was often overexcited and seemed to relish music therapy as a chance to be noisy, leap about and hit cymbals and cowbells with wooden beaters for maximum volume. He was moving about in this way one day, hitting as many different surface areas as he could find with a drumstick and always in time to the heavy metal music which he had brought with him on CD. I followed him to create moments of interaction, by mirroring his playing or holding brief conversations through rhythmic patterns. He always moved away from me if I went near to him and it was difficult to introduce change to this play. It was loud and quite boisterous but it felt important to keep up with this slightly frenzied activity and support his mood and, most importantly, react to his playing.

He then hit upon a children's book *Giraffes Can't Dance* (Andreae and Parker-Rees 2001) on one of the shelves and was immediately drawn to it. He stopped playing, took the book and started to read out loud. He continued to wander around the room as he read, but was engrossed in the pictures and story so I lowered the stereo's volume, wandered over to the piano and gradually introduced a musical accompaniment to his reading. Then, like Gerald in the story, the most remarkable change occurred. Jacob came over to the piano where I was, stood in front of me facing the piano and continued to read and sway as he read the words in time to the music. The story had introduced a different way of being in music therapy and, whilst sessions continued to be loud and chaotic at times, they could also contain periods which were quieter and unruffled. Jacob used the tale of the giraffe, who felt different to the other animals in the jungle, to start to address his own feelings. The story helped him to stop rushing around, stay with himself and consider his own feelings of being different and not accepted. This occurred in his own time when he was ready to do this. A few months later Jacob chose to make up his own song and he asked if we could write it up like a story and do all the pictures. He no longer needed to identify with Gerald, but had his own story to tell.

'I'm gonna do the X-factor!'

The use of recording equipment has increased over the years that I have worked at Cottenham. Audio recordings are now made on computer rather than on minidisc, which allows students to mix and make their own arrangements. Originally I used the video camera to record sessions for my own observation and for my own learning through supervision, but it has gradually become evident that the camera is also an important tool for teenagers to observe and learn from *during* their sessions. I now consider the video recorder almost as invaluable as any musical instrument in the room. It is a source of much inspiration and has made us into pop stars, musical lead singers, not to mention politicians, newsreaders and weathermen. Making videos for a song can be just as important as the song itself and I purposefully keep one wall clear of pictures and shelves as it provides a versatile backdrop for such filming.

Away from peer pressure and the call to conform, students' plans are boundless. So much can be about fantasies and the video camera seems to foster playful and imaginative pretending, of being in a band, being famous or being a cameraman. Needless to say, X Factor and other television talent shows make a huge impression on this age group and many of the students are keen to re-create their own version of such a show, participating either as judge or performer. With the aid of the camera in sessions, students can listen and become reflective learners. It can really boost students' confidence and help them to think about the music, as well as how they look and perform. Sharing DVDs with staff, friends and family members can give students a new way of presenting themselves, their opinions and feelings and enable them to be seen in a different light (Powell 2004). They can be really proud of the outcome and the CD or DVD is a tangible record of their achievement which they can take away from the music therapy session.

CASE STUDY 13.6

John, 15, had moved foster homes many times before finally settling at a children's home. He had very low self-esteem and was difficult to motivate but was willing to try music therapy. As well as talking, he liked to sing along with a microphone to recorded music, mostly by boy bands. He sung quite quietly and only if I joined in. Unexpectedly for me, he was keen to use the video camera which acted rather like a video diary of his therapy. Even though he did not want to be heard on his own, he enjoyed looking back at the recording and having a laugh about his performance! Watching the video together was an excellent way to reflect on what he was doing and getting ideas for the next time. It was an obvious step forward when John decided to record singing on his own, still accompanied by either a karaoke DVD or CD, but with the microphone turned up a little bit louder. Gaining confidence and encouragement from the regular pattern of filming and watching it back together John began singing without the CD backing. Once he was familiar

Figure 13.3 Singing with feeling

with the songs he started to enjoy taking more responsibility for the music and would chose to sing to a piano accompaniment.

Using the camera seemed to add tenability to his performance and on one occasion inspired him to make up some movements to create a dance video to one of these songs. As I was accompanying his singing on the piano, I naturally began to improvise around his movements which led to a new song – his song. He added some of his own words, beginning to improvise with his voice, and the music took on a completely different feel. Having found his musical identity in pop music and filming his performances, he had developed huge self-confidence and was able to make the music his own.

'This is my song, man!'

Songwriting can be a very effective way for teenagers to communicate their story and their ideas, as a social activity and within a structure which feels predictable and purposeful (Derrington 2005). For some it is a natural progression from improvising and for others it may be their aim from the outset. Either way, it is 'a powerful use of the existing relationship between teenagers and songs' (McFerran 2010, p.110).

Ben, 14, would come over to the music therapy garage, talk and fiddle with the instruments but find it hard to stay for the whole session and after ten minutes or so, usually ask if he could go back to the Centre. I would accompany him back to the Centre and continue the session, talking to him and sharing jokes as we played umpteen games of table tennis. This carried on for a few weeks. As I gradually developed his trust, he started to share more of his experiences and be more interested in staying in the garage and using the instruments. Improvisations felt far too uncertain and embarrassing for him so they were usually short-lived. The idea of writing a song, however, felt much more controllable and Ben liked the idea. He wrote his words on the board, told me how to drum and, ready to play the electric guitar with the amplifier turned up on distortion, he got up onto the cajon drum and precariously balancing announced at the top of his voice: 'To anyone…it's better to not be afraid' and sang his song:

> When you know that
>
> You did not do nothing
>
> Wrong so why are you
>
> Afraid of him
>
> You know you did
>
> Nothing wrong to me
>
> So why are you afraid. The End.

'Have I done well in music therapy?'

Sessions are confidential and students know that I do not talk about their work in any detail with other teachers. However, it is important to feed-back on a student's attendance and general well-being, for example, as collaborative working in a school, as in any team, is essential.

One way in which the school promotes personalised learning and reinforces achievement is by using the Assessment and Qualifications Alliance, an English examination board which offers a unit award scheme. This gives students of all abilities formal recognition of success in short units of work. After working at the Centre for a couple of years it was clear to me that music therapy should not stand apart from one of the school's systems of assessment but link in and also acknowledge students' achievement. Whilst my way of working and my aims of each session may be different to other lessons and activities, I could see how important these awards were to the young people I was working with and how their work in music therapy could be equally validated. As well as learning to use music as a way to connect and express themselves, students can learn musical skills along the way.

To date I have written five unit awards (see Appendix 4) which have been validated by the Assessment and Qualifications Alliance and are available on their national database for any assessment centres such as schools, pupil referral units, or hospital education services, to use. The units are: Exploring self-expression through music (2007); Communicating through music (2007); African drumming (2007); Expression through African drumming (2008) and Songwriting (2009). The certificates are awarded after the work has been completed and I only talk about them in sessions if it seems important and useful for that student. The awards form just part of the monitoring of music therapy that has been set up at this school. Other means of evaluation include photo and video evidence, song compositions and recordings if appropriate. This sort of evidence is parallel to other subjects and the students' practice-based learning. I also write regular reports and update monitoring forms every half term.

The aims which I set for half-termly monitoring, such as helping to improve communication, concentration or motivation, link in with the student's individual behaviour plan and individual education plan. These aims, like the unit awards, do not interfere with a student-centred approach which underpins my work but add guidance and constructive thought to the process. Being able to use and connect through music is always my primary aim and these other goals develop only as a result of this. However, as many of these students can seem directionless and the provision has to be time-limited due to the level of need at school, this sort of monitoring helps me to think really clearly about how music therapy is benefitting each student. Relating work to the individual education plans does not lessen the therapeutic value of the work but adds to the student's social and emotional aspects of learning which is key to success in school. This regular monitoring helps promote the work in evaluation-biased educational settings as they encounter Ofsted inspections, struggle with overstretched budgets and reasonably question the value and effectiveness of music therapy in their school. This is why documented research and records of music therapy work play a far-reaching part in the development of the profession in mainstream, as well as special, secondary schools.

Figure 13.4 Exploring self-expression playing the drums

'I couldn't be bothered when I came into school... but I can now'

In conclusion, there are a number of ways of engaging teenagers in music therapy including a varied use of improvised and recorded music. It is important to be dynamic and reactive, to work with the energy and ideas that are brought to sessions and to always be consistent and genuine. Although I have to be flexible and not have an agenda in mind for the session, I am very clear on the needs of each student and my aims for our work together. Teenagers tend to vote with their feet so their attendance, in itself, is credit to their commitment and motivation to use music when they actively grab the opportunity and respond: 'Yeah, I'll do music!'

Looking Back on the Development of a Service

Personal Reflections of Three Heads of Service of Cambridgeshire Music

Jo Tomlinson, Kathryn Nall and Órla Casey reflect on the development of music therapy within Cambridgeshire Music and their roles whilst head of the team.

Jo Tomlinson writes

Music therapy was set up as part of the county peripatetic music service in 1995. At this time there was no organised system for music therapy in schools in Cambridgeshire and very little clinical work with children in the county.

In 1995 the first intake of music therapy students had completed their training at the newly established music therapy training course at Anglia Polytechnic University in Cambridge, and the course leaders had discussions with the head of Cambridgeshire Music (formerly known as Cambridgeshire Instrumental Music Agency) about setting up music therapy in schools. The agency was responsible for supplying peripatetic instrumental teachers to mainstream schools in the area but had not previously had any links with music therapy. All the special schools in the area subsequently received letters about the possibility of buying in music therapy hours and there was considerable interest in this. Initially, three music therapists were employed for a few hours in a variety of special schools.

There were many advantages to creating an organised system of music therapy provision in the county. At the outset we were able to set up a service level agreement, which presented the needs of the schools and also the working requirements for music therapists, for example, instrument and room provision and the need for time to write up notes, liaise with staff, attend annual reviews and other meetings. This meant that music therapists setting up work in schools had these guidelines to work from, and both schools and therapists had similar expectations for the organisation of the work. In addition to this, a system of pay and travelling expenses was established.

In 1995 I had just qualified as a music therapist and responded to the advertisement in the Association of Professional Music Therapists' job list for a music therapist to work for Cambridgeshire Music. It was unclear how much work would potentially be generated but I was taken onto the team alongside two other music therapists. I was allocated four special needs schools to work in. This involved a lot of travel and it was very challenging setting up new pieces of work in each school, none of which had previously had music therapy or understood much about what it could offer. At this early point in the development of music therapy in schools it was essential for me to communicate clearly with staff, to meet regularly with teachers and learning support assistants, to set up workshops and give talks with video examples of work, and to be as clear as possible about the benefits of music therapy.

Over the following few years I was gradually able to expand my work in two schools. The music therapy team expanded rapidly as well and before long we were having regular business meetings, which reduced the sense of isolation that peripatetic work can create. In 2001 I became head music therapist. It has been very exciting to see the team developing and evolving over the years. Being under the Cambridgeshire Music umbrella has meant that the work has remained consistently organised and that we have met regularly as a team, both to discuss work issues and to meet socially.

The expansion of the music therapy team has been largely due to the commitment and hard work of the therapists and their capacity to successfully establish themselves within school communities. When working in a school it is essential to be flexible and adaptable according to the needs of the staff and children and the individual environment. Each school has its own system and cultural identity. Music therapy can only successfully develop if the therapist has the ability to fit into this context.

Money is always restricted in schools but generally music therapy hours do increase the longer the therapist works there.

Some schools have been extremely limited in terms of providing a suitable space for therapists to work in. Often therapists have had to work for a certain length of time in a room that may not be ideal, for example, the school hall or library. Once positive relationships with staff and children have been established it has then sometimes been possible to negotiate a more appropriate working space. Generally if schools have the experience of a therapist working on site they become aware of the requirements of the therapist and children, in terms of space and instrument provision. The essential factor has always been positive communication with staff at the school, as has been mentioned in music therapy literature:

> Several (education) authorities in the UK employ music therapists... The settings where children are seen for therapy vary from dedicated spaces in music therapy centres to shared spaces in pre-school nurseries and rooms of varying quality in schools. The provision of suitable space for therapy is usually improved when there is clear explanation about the work and close liaison between the visiting music therapist and other staff in these settings. (Bunt and Hoskyns 2002, p.17)

Auriel Warwick also described the need for communication with staff in schools when she wrote about the development of music therapy in schools in Oxfordshire:

> Music therapists must take on the responsibility for dispelling... suspicion and anxieties by being open about their aims and methods: talking in seminars to colleagues in schools, school governors, running workshops and presenting videos of individual and group work with children so that the value of the therapy can be seen in the context of the whole curriculum for the child. (Wigram, Saperston and West 1995, p.209)

Another element of the school system that has impacted on our work has been Office for Standards in Education (Ofsted) inspections. Music therapists working in the school context have to communicate with inspectors about their work and, on occasion, allow sessions to be observed. I have been involved in several Ofsted inspections where inspectors have pre-arranged some appropriate music therapy observation and have been very sensitive to the nature of our work. One observation culminated in positive feedback within the schools report, and this in turn led to an expansion of my hours at the school. The inspector had not previously observed any music therapy but was a musician and could appreciate the powerful effect of music-making on the children. In more recent years we have been part of the Ofsted process but have not been included in the written report from the inspectors, as the primary focus now is on evaluation systems and assessing teaching and learning.

Kathryn Nall writes

I took on the role as head of the music therapy team in Jan 2006 having previously taken on this role for a year while Jo was away on sabbatical leave. I started out with a commitment to enabling more children with identified needs to benefit from a professional music therapy service.

Whilst I was head of the team, four special schools serving Cambridge were closed and were replaced by two new special schools, as discussed in Jo Tomlinson's Chapter 7. It was important to find ways of ensuring we would take music therapy into these new schools and that the level of service, which had already been established in some of the feeder schools, was not compromised. This process involved meeting with new heads, governors and those responsible within the local government for planning the schools. After a lot of negotiation, we were able to secure full-time music therapy at both schools.

At the same time, other music therapists within the team also managed to increase the music therapy provision in the schools where they worked. For example, in one special school the hours increased from two to four days, and in a mainstream secondary school a three-day post was created for students who presented with challenging behaviour and were at risk of exclusion.

An example of how new work was established in mainstream schools was when two young people I had been working with in a special school were transferred into supported places in mainstream settings. Interventions needed to be put in place to support their inclusion. I gave presentations to special educational need co-ordinators (SENCOs), teachers and assistants to highlight the needs of these individuals and, as a result, music therapy was set up in both these schools.

Alongside these initiatives liaison was needed with student assessment services, access to learning and inclusion services. It was through their interest that funding later became available for work at a unit for children with Aspergers' syndrome attached to a mainstream secondary school.

The policy of national trend towards inclusion (Department for Education and Skills (DfES) 2001) which gives parents the right to choose the type of school they would like their child to attend regardless of disability, enables students to be placed within mainstream schools. This means that there are some schools where there is only one student with particular disabilities. As a result we had to adjust our ideal of having a music therapist working a minimum of two hours in any school to just one hour. This work required particular skills and energy but therapists on the Cambridgeshire Music team responded to the challenge, showing how working in this way could be successful. As the work developed in special schools, mainstream primary and secondary schools, nurseries and children's centres, more music therapists were employed.

Our work can be seen to fulfil requirements of the government's agenda *Every Child Matters* (DfES 2003) through which we have a duty to help enable all children and young people to achieve the five key outcomes of being healthy, staying safe, enjoying and achieving, making a positive contribution, and economic well-being. There is also an emphasis on providing creative therapeutic interventions for those with special needs. As practitioners registered with the Health Professions Council we have good reason to be part of these interventions and assessment processes. Music therapy has a place within Children and Young People's Services in Cambridgeshire (CYPS) and it is essential that we continue to be part of the process of identifying, assessing and meeting children's needs.

Órla Casey writes

At the time that I became head of the music therapy team at Cambridgeshire Music in 2009 the team was well established and existing services were securely developed. Increased management hours allowed for opportunities to develop new areas of work; this included setting up music therapy in children's centres and mainstream schools. Additionally we were able to make better links with other services, both in health and education, and to develop systems for referral and liaison, as well as improving marketing, evaluation and information tools.

By 2011 the team covered work in 37 schools of which the work divided into approximately 49 per cent special schools, 13 per cent units attached to schools, 5 per cent children's centres, 18 per cent mainstream primary schools, 15 per cent mainstream secondary schools. Recent trends have seen a small decrease in demand in special schools as a result of reduced school budgets, but work to support children with additional needs in mainstream continues to grow. Local authority budgets are limited so I see one aspect of my role as to protect the service that has been built up to date. Strategies to support this include the development of robust evaluation tools, built in as standard processes in every piece of work and which can give information about the relevance of music therapy intervention in improving learning outcomes. This information should help to challenge perceptions that music therapy is an added luxury. Software programs to support report writing and statistical evidence are essential to this. I have found it beneficial to liaise with other music therapy heads of service towards sharing of resources to this end.

The value of the therapist informing about and promoting music therapy work at a local level with school professionals and with parents cannot be underestimated. It is important to share skills and resources and have opportunities to reflect on the work with other therapists too. Music therapists from the Cambridgeshire Music team regularly present papers about their work at conferences both in the UK and abroad.

Arts therapists often have to adapt or rethink their practice to fit with the overall philosophy of the school and the needs of their clients (Karkou 2010). Music therapists in the team, while adopting mostly traditional music therapy approaches, have at times had to adapt their work and roles to include playing for assembly; using a 'psychodynamically informed' approach for one part of the day and a 'community' music therapy approach for another part of the day; running a lunchtime school choir; participating in 'Proms in the Playground' and community arts projects in schools.

In 2010 music therapy was identified as one of the main strengths of the Cambridgeshire Music service. I would like to conclude with a quote from the Federation of Music Services Report:

> The approach used to demonstrate and promote the benefits of music therapy has contributed to the service's growth in this area…The increases which have taken place in the provision of music therapy demonstrate the value that schools place on its impact on children and young people. With 14 therapists delivering 189 hours a week, this represents a significant contribution to vulnerable children and young people. (Smith 2010)

Appendix 2

Questionnaire for Parents

Feedback for Community Music Group

Thank you for taking the time to give some feedback on your experience of the community music group.

None of these questions need to be answered – they are more of a guide, if helpful, for you to write about your and your child's experience of the community music group.

Please don't feel constrained or limited by the questions but feel free to write as much or as little as you'd like to.

How long have you attended the music group with your child?

What do you particularly like/dislike about the group?

Do you feel that your child benefits from the group? If so how?

What is helpful and/or difficult about the group for your child?

And for you?

What is it about the music that makes this different to other groups that you attend?

Any other comments surrounding your experience of music at the centre?

Appendix 3

Interview Questions for Teachers

1. What were your first impressions of music therapy?

2. Have your views on music therapy changed over the years? If so, how and why?

3. What did you think music therapy tried to achieve?

4. How do you feel it fits in with the general curriculum of early year's education?

5. How do you feel about the inclusion of parents and carers in children's music therapy sessions?

6. Has your experience of music therapy changed the way you think about and introduce music into your classroom planning?

Appendix 4

Assessment and Qualifications Alliance Unit Awards

AQA UNIT AWARD SCHEME
CODE NO: 83767

UNIT TITLE: EXPLORING SELF-EXPRESSION THROUGH MUSIC
CURRICULUM AREA(S): MUSIC
DATE OF VALIDATION: 03-10-2007

UNIT DESCRIPTION: Through music therapy, the student will learn different ways of expressing him/herself through playing live and mostly improvised music.

PROCEDURES FOR MAKING AND RECORDING ASSESSMENTS: Assessed by the teacher through observation (1–6). All assessments recorded on an AQA Summary Sheet.

LEVEL: Entry Level   **NOTIONAL LEARNING TIME:** 10 hours

OUTCOMES TO BE ACCREDITED
In successfully completing this unit the student will have experienced
1. creating live music;
2. using music as a means of self-expression;

demonstrated the ability to
3. play at least three different instruments at a basic level;
4. interact musically;
5. choose instruments for at least two different styles of music;
6. use at least two social skills, such as turn-taking, listening and responding.

EVIDENCE TO BE OFFERED
Teacher checklist (1–6), itemised (5, 6)

AQA UNIT AWARD SCHEME
CODE NO: 83768

UNIT TITLE: COMMUNICATING THROUGH MUSIC
CURRICULUM AREA(S): MUSIC
DATE OF VALIDATION: 03-10-2007

UNIT DESCRIPTION: Through music therapy, the student will develop emotional and social skills by learning to interact musically. S/he will gain confidence in using music as a way to communicate with others.

PROCEDURES FOR MAKING AND RECORDING ASSESSMENTS: Assessed by the teacher through observation (1–6) and discussion (7). All assessments recorded on an AQA Summary Sheet.

LEVEL: Entry Level   **NOTIONAL LEARNING TIME:** 10 hours

OUTCOMES TO BE ACCREDITED
In successfully completing this unit the student will have experienced
3. using music as a means of self-expression with both manual and electronic instruments;
4. listening and being listened to;

demonstrated the ability to
7. use at least three social skills which can help when communicating with others;
8. use at least four different styles of music using a variety of dynamics, rhythms and tempi;
9. co-operate in a shared setting;
10. use song composition to articulate thoughts and feelings through music;

shown knowledge of
7. how different forms of music can communicate emotions.

EVIDENCE TO BE OFFERED
Teacher checklist (1–7), itemised (3, 4)

AQA UNIT AWARD SCHEME
CODE NO: 83775

UNIT TITLE: AFRICAN DRUMMING
CURRICULUM AREA(S): MUSIC
DATE OF VALIDATION: 07-12-2007

UNIT DESCRIPTION: Through group music therapy sessions, the student will learn to lead and follow drum patterns. S/he will gain further techniques to play djembe.

PROCEDURES FOR MAKING AND RECORDING ASSESSMENTS: Assessed by the therapist through observation (1–6). All assessments recorded on an AQA summary sheet.

LEVEL: Entry Level   **NOTIONAL LEARNING TIME:** 10 hours

OUTCOMES TO BE ACCREDITED
In successfully completing this unit the student will have experienced
5. drumming solo and as part of a group;
6. listening and responding to others through drum patterns;

demonstrated the ability to
11. use at least three different drum strokes;
12. follow a taught song;
13. be 'the caller' in call and response songs;
14. play a rhythm in a three-part drum song.

EVIDENCE TO BE OFFERED
Therapist checklist (1–6), itemised (3)

AQA UNIT AWARD SCHEME
CODE NO: 83774

UNIT TITLE: EXPRESSION THROUGH AFRICAN DRUMMING
CURRICULUM AREA(S): MUSIC
DATE OF VALIDATION: 04-02-2008

UNIT DESCRIPTION: Through group music therapy sessions, the student will learn basic techniques and rhythms of African drumming.

PROCEDURES FOR MAKING AND RECORDING ASSESSMENTS: Assessed by the therapist through observation (1–6). All assessments recorded on an AQA Summary Sheet.

LEVEL: Entry Level   **NOTIONAL LEARNING TIME:** 10 hours

OUTCOMES TO BE ACCREDITED
In successfully completing this unit the student will have experienced
7. drumming in a group;
8. listening to drumming and being listened to whilst drumming;

demonstrated the ability to
15. use at least two drum strokes appropriate for African rhythms;
16. keep a pulse;
17. follow a caller in 'call and response' phrasing;
18. play a rhythm in a two part African drum song.

EVIDENCE TO BE OFFERED
Therapist checklist (1–6), itemised (3)

AQA UNIT AWARD SCHEME
CODE NO: 84089

UNIT TITLE: SONGWRITING
CURRICULUM AREA(S): MUSIC
DATE OF VALIDATION: 30-06-2009

UNIT DESCRIPTION: Through music therapy sessions, the student will learn to write a song and to use a song as a means of self-expression.

PROCEDURES FOR MAKING AND RECORDING ASSESSMENTS: Assessed by the teacher through observation (1, 3, 4), inspection (2) and discussion (5). All assessments recorded on an AQA Summary Sheet.

LEVEL: Entry Level **NOTIONAL LEARNING TIME:** Less than ten hours

OUTCOMES TO BE ACCREDITED
In successfully completing this unit the student will have experienced
1. playing a wide variety of different instruments;

demonstrated the ability to
9. write lyrics for a song;
10. choose and play at least two appropriate musical instruments, including voice, to fit the style of song;
11. play the song from memory or from a score;

shown knowledge of
5. how a song can express ideas and feelings.

EVIDENCE TO BE OFFERED
Teacher checklist (1, 3, 4), itemised (3)
For outcome 3 checklist to be itemised into 2 parts to show that 2 musical instruments have been played Student's lyrics (2)

References

ACT/RCPCH (2003) *A Guide to the Development of Children's Palliative Care Services*, 2nd edn. Bristol: The Association for Children with Life-threatening or Terminal Conditions and their Families and The Royal College of Paediatrics and Child Health.

Aigen, K. (1998) *Paths of Development in Nordoff-Robbins Music Therapy*. Gilsum, NH: Barcelona Publishers.

Aigen, K. (2005) *Music-Centered Music Therapy*. Gilsum, NH: Barcelona Publishers.

Allen, J. (2005) 'Both sides of the wall.' Unpublished study review of the ongoing music therapy intervention undertaken in five primary schools located in high profile interface areas of Belfast.

Alvin, J. (1966) *Music Therapy*. London: Stainer and Bell.

Andreae, G. and Parker-Rees, G. (2001) *Giraffes Can't Dance*. London: Orchard Books.

Ansdell, G. (1995) *Music for Life: Aspects of Creative Music Therapy with Adult Clients*. London: Jessica Kingsley Publishers.

APMT (2009) *Directory for Members 2009–2010, Association of Professional Music Therapists*. Available at www.apmt.org/

Austen, D. (2006) 'Songs of the Self: Vocal Psychotherapy for Adults Traumatised as Children.' In L. Carey *Expressive and Creative Arts Methods for Trauma Survivors*. London: Jessica Kingsley Publishers.

Bion, W. (1967) 'Attacks on Linking.' In W. J. Bion, *Second Thoughts: Selected Papers on Psychoanalysis*. London: Maresfield. (Original work published 1959.)

Bombèr, L.M. (2009) 'Survival of the 'fittest'... Teenagers find their way through the labyrinth of transitions in schools.' In A. Perry (ed.) *Teenagers and Attachment. Helping Adolescents Engage with Life and Learning*. London : Worth Publishing.

Bowlby, J. (1988) *A Secure Base: Clinical Applications of Attachment Theory*. London: Routledge.

Brackley, J. (2007) 'Music therapy on a pupil referral unit: What does music therapy have to offer pupils aged 5–9 on a behaviour support programme?' Unpublished Master's thesis, Anglia Ruskin University, Cambridge.

Bull, R. (2008) 'Autism and the Family: Group Music Therapy with Mothers and Children.' In A. Oldfield and C. Flower (eds) *Music Therapy with Children and their Families.* London: Jessica Kingsley Publishers.

Bunt, L. (1994) *Music Therapy: An Art Beyond Words.* London: Routledge.

Bunt, L. and Hoskyns, S. (2002) *The Handbook of Music Therapy.* Hove: Brunner-Routledge.

CAIN (2010) 'RUC/PSNI statistics: Table NI-SEC-05: Persons injured (number) due to the security situation in Northern Ireland (only), 1969 to 2003.' Available at http://cain.ulster.ac.uk/ni/security.htm#05, accessed on 16 January 2010.

Cairns, K. (2002) *Attachment, Trauma and Resilience.* London: British Association for Adoption & Fostering (BAAF).

Carey, L. (2006) *Expressive and Creative Arts Methods for Trauma Survivors.* London: Jessica Kingsley Publishers.

Carter, E. and Oldfield, A. (2002) 'A Music Therapy Group to assist Clinical Diagnoses in Child and Family Psychiatry.' In A. Davies and E. Richards (eds) *Group Work in Music Therapy.* London: Jessica Kingsley Publishers.

Casement, P. (1985) *On Learning from the Patient.* Hove: Brunner-Routledge.

Cobbett, S. (2006) 'Therapeutic teaching music therapy for excluded adolescents with challenging behaviour: Finding the right language.' Unpublished paper presented to the BSMT/APMT annual conference 17/18 March: 'The Sound of Music Therapy'. London.

Cobbett, S. (2009) 'Including the excluded: Music therapy with adolescents with social, emotional and behavioural difficulties.' *British Journal of Music Therapy 23,* 2, 15–25.

Department for Education and Skills (2001) *Special Educational Needs Code of Practice.* London: HMSO.

Department for Education and Skills (2003) *Every Child Matters.* London: HM Treasury Green Paper.

Department of Education Northern Ireland (2009) 'Enrolements at Schools and in Funded Pre-school Education in Northern Ireland 2008/2009'. Available at www.deni.gov.uk/enrolments_at_schools_and_in_funded_pre-school_education_2008_09.pdf, accessed on 16 January 2010.

Derrington, P. (2005) 'Teenagers and Songwriting: Supporting Students in a Mainstream Secondary School.' In F. Baker and T. Wigram (eds) *Songwriting. Methods, Techniques and Clinical Applications for Music Therapy Clinicians, Educators and Students.* London: Jessica Kingsley Publishers.

Derrington, P. (2010) 'The sweet escape: Hearing-impaired students in a mainstream secondary school get out of lessons to go to music therapy.' Unpublished paper to the Anglia Ruskin University conference: The Music of Music Therapy.

Department for Children, Schools and Families (2008) *The Early Years Foundation Stage.* London: DCSF Publications.

DHSSPS (2004) *Inequalities and Unfair Access Issues Emerging from the 'Equality and Inequalities in Health and Social Care: A Statistical Overview' Report.* Belfast: DHSSPS.

Drake, T. (2008) 'Back to Basics: Community Based Music Therapy for Vulnerable Young Children and their Parents.' In C. Flower and A. Oldfield (eds) *Music Therapy for Children and their Families.* London: Jessica Kingsley Publishers.

Equals Schemes of Work Creative Development Part Two. In *Music PMLD,*1999.

Erikson, E.H. (1968) *Identity: Youth and Crisis.* New York: Norton.

Fay, M-T., Morrissey, M. and Smyth, M. (1999) *Northern Ireland's Troubles: The Human Costs.* London: Pluto Press.

Fonagy, P., Gergely, G., Jurist, E.L. and Target, M. (2004) *Affect Regulation, Mentalization, and the Development of the Self.* New York: Other Press.

Fraser, G. and Morgan. V. (1999) *In the Frame – Integrated Education in Northern Ireland: The Implications of Expansion.* Coleraine: University of Ulster. Available at www.cain.ulst. ac.uk/csc/reports/fraser99d.htm, accessed 23 June 2011.

Freud, A. (1966) *The Ego and the Mechanisms of Defense: The Writings of Anna Freud, Vol. 2.* New York: International Universities Press. (Original work published 1936.)

Gaston, E.T. (1968) *Music in Therapy.* New York: Macmillan.

George, M. (1998) 'Being and identity: A Winnicottian approach to the mother/infant relationship.' Unpublished master's dissertation, Anglia Ruskin University, Cambridge.

Gibson, K. (2001) 'Healing Relationships between Professional Psychologists and Communities: "How Can we Tell them if they Don't Want to Hear".' In M. Smyth and K. Thomson (eds) *Working with Children and Young People in Violently Divided Societies.* Belfast: Community Conflict Impact on Children and INCORE.

Goodman, K.D. (2007) *Music Therapy Groupwork with Special Needs Children: The Evolving Process.* Springfield, IL: Charles C. Thomas.

Hadley, S. (2000) 'Early developmental processes and the facilitative role of music therapy.' Unpublished keynote paper presented at 4th International Music Therapy Conference, Toronto, Canada.

Haire, N. and Oldfield, A. (2009) 'Adding humour to the music therapists tool-kit: reflections on its role in child psychiatry.' *British Journal of Music Therapy 23*, 1, 27–34.

Harding, C. (2006) (ed.) *Aggression and Destructiveness. Psychoanalytic Perspectives.* London: Routledge.

Heal, M. And Wigram, T. (eds) (1993) *Music Therapy in Health and Education.* London: Jessica Kingsley Publishers.

Healy, A. (2007) In D. Hill, 'Breaking the silence.' *Guardian,* 21 March.

Hibben, J. (1991) 'Group Music Therapy with a Classroom of 6–8 Year-Old Hyperactive-Learning Disabled Children.' In K. Bruscia (ed.) *Case Studies in Music Therapy.* Phoenixville, PA: Barcelona Publishers.

Hill, D. 'Breaking the silence.' *Guardian* 21 March.

Hillyard, P., Rolston, B. and Tomlinson, M. (2005) *Poverty and Conflict in Ireland: An International Perspective.* Dublin: Institute of Public Administration/Combat Poverty Agency.

Horgan, G. (2005) 'Why the Bill of Rights Should Protect the Rights of Children and Young People in Northern Ireland. The Particular Circumstances of Children in Northern Ireland.' In G. Horgan and U. Kilkelly *Protecting Children and Young People's Rights in the Bill of Rights for Northern Ireland. Why? How?* Belfast: Save the Children and Children's Law Centre.

Howden, S. (2008) 'Music Therapy with Traumatised Children and their Families in Mainstream Primary Schools: A Case Study with a Six-year-old Girl and her Mother.' In A. Oldfield and C. Flower (eds) *Music Therapy with Children and their Families.* London: Jessica Kingsley Publishers.

Jamieson, R. and Grounds, A. (2002) *No Sense of an Ending: The Effects of Long-term Imprisonment amongst Republican Prisoners and their Families.* Report of a study commissioned by the Ex-Prisoners Assistance Committee (Expac). Monaghan: SEESYU Press.

Joy, I. (2005) *Valuing Short Lives: Children with Terminal Conditions: A Guide for Donors and Funders.* London: New Philanthropy Capital.

Karkou, V. (2010) (ed.) *Arts Therapies in Schools: Research and Practice.* London: Jessica Kingsley Publishers.

Kilkelly, U., Kilpatrick, R., Lundy, L., Moore, L., *et al.* (2004) *Children's Rights in Northern Ireland: Research Commissioned by the Northern Ireland Commissioner for Children and Young People.* Belfast: NICCY.

Knox, C. (2002) 'See no evil, hear no evil. Insidious paramilitary violence in Northern Ireland.' *British Journal of Criminology 42*, 164–185.

Kortegaard, H.M. (1993) 'Music Therapy in the Psychodynamic Treatment of Schizophrenia.' In M. Heal and T. Wigram (eds) *Music Therapy in Health and Education.* London: Jessica Kingsley Publishers.

Leitch, R. (2000) *A Millennium Vision: Issues and Ideas for the Future of Education in Northern Ireland.* Belfast: Blackstaff Press.

Leonard, M. (2004) *Children in Interface Areas: Reflection from North Belfast.* Belfast: Save the Children.

McCallum, R. (2007) 'Anti Rioting Poster.' Available at North Belfast Interface Network website: www.nbin.info/index.php?option=com_content&task=view&id=14&Itemid=2.

McCown, W., Keiser, R., Mulhearn, S. and Williamson, D. (1997) 'The role of personality and gender in preference for exaggerated bass in music.' *Personality and Individual Differences 23*, 4, 543–547.

McFerran, K. (2010) *Adolescents, Music and Music Therapy. Methods and Techniques for Clinicians, Educators and Students.* London: Jessica Kingsley Publishers.

McKittrick, D., Kelters, S., Feeney, B., Thornton, C. and McVea, D. (2007) *Lost Lives.* Edinburgh: Mainstream Publishing.

McMahon, L. (1992) *The Handbook of Play Therapy.* London: Routledge.

McTier, I.S. (2003) 'Why use a bass in music therapy?' Unpublished diploma dissertation, Anglia Ruskin University, Cambridge.

Muldoon, O. (2007) 'Peace treaties end fighting but can't cure PTSD.' *Psychiatric News 42,* 19, 14.

Muller, P. and Warwick, A. (1993) 'Autistic Children and Music Therapy.' In M. Heal and T. Wigram (eds) *Music Therapy in Health and Education.* London: Jessica Kingsley Publishers.

Murray, N. (unpublished) 'The Therapeutic Use of Music with Children Affected by the Troubles in Northern Ireland and the Challenges Faced by the Therapist.' In M. Smyth and K. Thomson (eds) *Working with Children and Young People in Violently Divided Societies.* Belfast: Community Conflict Impact on Children and INCORE.

Nordoff, P. and Robbins, C. (1971a) *Music Therapy in Special Education.* New York: John Day.

Nordoff, P. and Robbins, C. (1971b) *Therapy in Music for Handicapped Children.* Victor Gollanez.

Nordoff, P. and Robbins, C. (2007) *Creative Music Therapy: A Guide to Fostering Clinical Musicianship,* 2nd edn. Gilsum, NH: Barcelona Publishers.

North and West Belfast Trust (2001) *Caring Through the Troubles: Health and Social Services in North and West Belfast.* Belfast: North and West Belfast Trust.

Northern Ireland Social Services Inspectorate (1998) *Living with the Trauma of the Troubles.* Belfast: Northern Ireland Social Services Inspectorate.

Ockelford, A. (2008) *Music for Children and Young People with Complex Needs.* Oxford: Music Education Series.

Ofsted (2000) *Inspection Report 223669,* 40.

Oldfield, A. (2006a) *Interactive Music Therapy – A Positive Approach: Music Therapy at a Child Development Centre.* London: Jessica Kingsley Publishers.

Oldfield, A. (2006b) *Interactive Music Therapy in Child and Family Psychiatry: Clinical Practice, Research and Teaching.* London: Jessica Kingsley Publishers.

Oldfield, A. and Flower, C. (2008) *Music Therapy with Children and their Families.* London: Jessica Kingsley Publishers.

Pavlicevic, M. (1997) *Music Therapy in Context: Music Meaning and Relationship.* London: Jessica Kingsley Publishers.

Pavlicevic, M. and Ansdell, G. (2004) (eds) *Community Music Therapy.* London: Jessica Kingsley Publishers.

Powell, H. (2004) 'A Dream Wedding: From Community Music to Music Therapy with a Community.' In M. Pavlicevic and G. Ansdell (eds) *Community Music Therapy*. London: Jessica Kingsley Publishers.

QCA (2009) *Music. Planning, Teaching and Assessing the Curriculum for Pupils with Learning Difficulties*. Coventry: Qualifications and Curriculum Authority.

Radford, K. (2010) '"And Stay Out!" Hoods and Paramilitarised Youth, Exiles and 'Punishment Beatings.' In D. Ford (ed.) *Fragmenting Families*. Chester: Chester University Press.

Robarts, J. (1996) 'Music Therapy for Children with Autism.' In C. Trevarthen, K. Aitken, D. Papoudi and J. Robarts (eds) *Children with Autism. Diagnosis and Interventions to Meet Their Needs*. London: Jessica Kingsley Publishers.

Ruud, E. (1998) *Music Therapy: Improvisation, Communication and Culture*. Gilsum, NH: Barcelona Publishers.

Schlindwein, H. (2002) *Community Healing – Community Development Approaches to Political Trauma*. Derry: Yes! Publications.

Smith, G. (2010) Cambridgeshire Music Service Report, Federation of Music Services, Self Evaluation and Peer Moderation of Music Services. Review Report.

Smyth, M. (2002) 'The Role of Creativity in Healing and Recovery of One's Power after Victimisation.' In J. Sutton (ed.) *Music, Music Therapy and Trauma: International Perspectives*. London: Jessica Kingsley Publishers.

Smyth, M., Morrissey, M. and Hamilton, J. (2001) *Caring Through the Troubles: Health and Social Services in North and West Belfast*. Belfast: NWBHSS.

Stern, D.N. (1985) *The Interpersonal World of the Infant*. New York: Basic Books.

Stige, B., Ansdell, G., Elefant, C. and Pavlicevic, M. (2010) *Where Music Helps: Community Music Therapy in Action and Reflection*. Farnham: Ashgate Publishing.

Strange, J. (2010) 'Facility in improvision – a mixed blessing?' Unpublished paper presented to the Anglia Ruskin University conference: The Music of Music Therapy. 27 February. Cambridge.

Trevarthen, C. (1996) 'What Causes Autism?' In C. Trevarthen, K. Aitken, D. Papoudi and J. Robarts (eds) *Children with Autism. Diagnosis and Interventions to Meet Their Needs*. London: Jessica Kingsley Publishers.

Twyford, K. (2008) 'Collaborative and Transdisciplinary Approaches with Children.' In K. Twyford and T. Watson (eds.) *Integrated Team Working*. London: Jessica Kingsley Publishers.

Tyler, H.M. (2003) 'Being Beverley: Music Therapy with a Troubled Eight-year-old Girl.' In S. Hadley (ed.) *Psychodynamic Music Therapy: Case Studies*. Gilsum, NH: Barcelona Publishers.

Ware, J. (2003) *Creating a Responsive Environment for People with Profound and Multiple Learning Difficulties*. London: David Fulton Publishers.

Warwick, A. (1995) 'Music Therapy in the Education Service: Research with Autistic Children.' In T. Wigram, B. Saperston and R. West (eds) *The Art and Science of Music Therapy: A Handbook.* Chur, Switzerland: Harwood Academic Publishers.

Wengrower, H. (2010) '"I am here to Move and Dance with You." Dance Movement Therapy with Children with Autistic Spectrum Disorder and Pervasive Developmental Disorders.' In V. Karkou (ed.) *Arts Therapies in Schools – Research and Practice.* London: Jessica Kingsley Publishers.

Wigram, T. (2004) *Improvisation: Methods and Techniques for Music Therapy Clinicians, Educators and Students.* London: Jessica Kingsley Publishers.

Wigram, T., Pederson, I.N. and Bonde, L.O. (2002) *A Comprehensive Guide to Music Therapy: Theory Clinical Practice, Research and Training.* London: Jessica Kingsley Publishers.

Winnicott, D.W. (1964) *The Child, the Family and the Outside World.* Harmondsworth: Penguin Books.

Winnicott, D.W. (1990) *The Maturational Processes and the Facilitating Environment.* London: Karnac. (Original work published 1965.)

Winnicott, D.W. (1991) *Playing and Reality.* Hove and Philadelphia, PA: Brunner-Routledge. (Original work published 1971.)

Wood, S., Verney, R. and Atkinson, J. (2004) 'From Therapy to Community: Making Music in Neurological Rehabilitation.' In M. Pavlicevic and G. Ansdell (eds) *Community Music Therapy.* London: Jessica Kingsley Publishers.

Wright, K. (1991) *Vision and Separation: Between Mother and Baby.* London: Free Association Books.

The Contributors

Chris Achenbach qualified from the Nordoff-Robbins London course in 1985 and since then has lived and worked in Scotland. His career has included 13 years with the NHS in East Lothian and the Scottish Borders, and nine years with the Scottish Nordoff-Robbins charity. In 2007 he became a freelance music therapist. He is a supervisor tutor on the MSc Music Therapy (Nordoff-Robbins) training course at Queen Margaret University, Edinburgh. A pianist, organist and composer, he is author of a music group work manual and has a particular interest in music improvisation. He is married and lives in Galashiels.

Jane Brackley has worked as a music therapist since 2003. As a member of the Bedfordshire music therapy team, she has worked on pupil referral units and at a Child Development Centre with children who are at risk of exclusion from mainstream primary school due to their social, emotional and behavioural difficulties. This work is the focus of her current PhD research project which seeks to investigate how music therapists work with such children's aggressive behaviour. Jane also works with adults with learning disabilities within the Cambridgeshire Learning Disability Partnership and as a clinical supervisor.

Ann Bruce (née Woodward) qualified as a music therapist in 1996. Since then she has worked with children and young people in a variety of settings, including both mainstream and special schools. More recently she has begun working with adult stroke survivors. Ann has been the Co-ordinator of the APMT Education Group and the Deputy Chair of the APMT. She is currently the BAMT Newsletter Editor, and a registrant assessor for the Health Professions Council. Having worked in London and the south-east of England for over ten years, Ann relocated to Cumbria in 2007, where she now works in three schools.

Órla Casey is head of the music therapy team at Cambridgeshire Music and currently works with children and young people in schools and children's centres in Cambridgeshire. She also works at East Anglia's children's hospice with children, young people and their families. She provides music therapy supervision and is a guest lecturer at Anglia Ruskin University, Cambridge, and Limerick University, Ireland.

Emma Davies (née Carter) read music at Oxford University before training as a music therapist at Anglia Ruskin University in 1999. For almost eight years she was based at the Croft Unit for Child and Family Psychiatry with Dr Amelia Oldfield. Emma has set up a variety of music therapy posts within Early Years settings and schools. She has a particular interest in working with young children and families and has written and lectured on the subject both in the UK and abroad. She is currently taking a career break to care for her two children aged one and three.

Philippa Derrington taught modern languages in the UK and abroad before training as a music therapist at Anglia Polytechnic University. Since qualifying in 2001 she has worked predominantly with children and adolescents with emotional and behavioural difficulties in schools and pupil referral units and has established a permanent music therapy post within a federated mainstream and special secondary school. The Music Therapy Charity is funding her doctoral research, which investigates the effectiveness of music therapy for young people at risk of underachieving or exclusion and describes an approach with this client group. Philippa has presented at conferences nationally and internationally and is a guest lecturer at Anglia Ruskin University. In her free time she enjoys playing a lot of clarinet and tennis.

Karen Diamond is the head music therapist with the Northern Ireland Music Therapy Trust where she has worked for over 20 years. She has specialised in the areas of severe learning disabilities, brain injury and trauma. In addition to her clinical work she regularly facilitates workshops and seminars on music therapy, supervises students in training, and advocates for the improved strategic development of music therapy in NI representing the profession on the Northern Ireland Allied Health Federation. Dog walking, singing in a gospel choir and cooking are the activities she uses to keep herself amused when not working.

Jan Hall first trained as a music teacher and worked as head of music in mainstream secondary schools. She qualified as a music therapist from Roehampton in 1983. Since then she has worked in Sheffield and Northamptonshire, mainly with the role of music therapist and teacher. She has worked primarily with children and young people from 2 to 19. In 2007 she co-founded Thomas's Fund, a charity which provides music therapy at home for children and young people with a life-limiting condition or disability which, for medical reasons, means that they are too ill to attend school for extended periods.

Angela Harrison enjoyed a career with the Hallé Orchestra before becoming a music therapist. She joined the North Yorkshire Music Therapy Centre in 1995, now Angela manages the service and works mainly with children with emotional and communication difficulties. Angela has presented her work at conferences in the UK, Europe, Canada and Argentina. She lectures at three universities in Yorkshire and has contributed to two books. In 2010, Angela took the chair of the UK professional body, overseeing the establishment of the British Association for Music Therapy. Angela is married to a farmer and plays viola in local chamber groups.

Suzie High is head of Early Years foundation stage at a special school for children with severe or profound and multiple learning disabilities in Cumbria. She has been teaching for 15 years. Suzie originally trained as a mainstream primary teacher in Manchester. She gradually moved into teaching children with special needs where she found she could work in a more person-centred way. Suzie developed her interest in the person-centred approach by studying and qualifying with a counselling diploma. Her counselling work involves using expressive arts therapy and discovering ways of being creative.

Ian S. McTier qualified as a music therapist in 2004, having been an active classical and jazz musician for many years, whilst maintaining a string instrument teaching practice, specializing in double bass. His music therapy work has taken him into a number of special schools and out-of-school facilities for children with learning difficulties and complex communication disorders. The potential of the double bass in this field became clear to him during training, and remains an important ingredient of his approach. Ian also acts as a placement supervisor for music therapy postgraduate students at Queen Margaret University, Edinburgh.

Kathryn Nall first studied Economic and Social Studies, then gained a diploma in social work. She was a social worker in both residential and field work settings within Local Authorities and the voluntary sector. At the same time, Kathryn pursued her interest in music and achieved a diploma in singing (LGSM). In 1995 she decided to train as a music therapist at Anglia Polytechnic University and was awarded her Masters in 2001. Whilst working at a children's hospice Kathryn developed a 'Hospice to Home' Project in conjunction with Jessie's Fund. She continues to work as a music therapist for Cambridgeshire Music in a mainstream secondary school. Over the last couple of years she has successfully combined this with a return to social work within a looked after children's team.

Amelia Oldfield has over 30 years' experience as a music therapist and has provided regular clinical supervision to music therapists working in schools for the past 16 years. She currently works as a music therapist at the Croft Unit for Child and Family Psychiatry. She also lectures at Anglia Ruskin University, where she co-initiated the two-year MA Music Therapy Training in 1994. Amelia has completed four research investigations and a PhD. She has written and edited five books and has produced six music therapy training DVDs. She has run workshops and given papers all over Europe and in the USA, Canada and China. She is married with four children and, in her free time, plays clarinet in local chamber music groups in Cambridge, UK.

Nicky O'Neill graduated from Nordoff-Robbins London in 1990, with a diploma in music therapy. In 2002 she obtained a Masters, in which she focused on one of her areas of speciality, which is working with children in an acute medical setting. Her clinical experience covers a wide age range of people within a variety of settings including acute hospitals, educational and community venues. Between 2005 and 2010 she was a group work tutor on the Nordoff-Robbins Masters Music Therapy programme. She joined the Greenwich Community Health Services Music Therapy Department in 1999, where she specialises in working with children with complex needs. Nicky also lectures on other music therapy training courses in the UK, as well as presenting regularly at music therapy and other health related conferences.

Clare Rosscornes worked as a teacher in mainstream and special education for ten years before training as a music therapist. Since qualifying in 2006 from Anglia Ruskin University she has worked with children and teenagers in Cambridgeshire. She currently works in schools, a children's centre, the children's wards of Addenbrooke's Hospital and her recently completed MA dissertation compares the provision of music therapy in these different settings. She is particularly interested in working with children and their families within the community. Clare is a keen ukulele player and enjoys playing and singing with a local band.

John Strange taught music in secondary schools until retraining as a music therapist in 1985. From 1986 until 2010 he worked with children and adults with a range of learning disability in the education and voluntary sectors. He supervised postgraduate students on clinical placement throughout that period, and also qualified music therapists from 2004. Since 1995 he has provided expert evidence on music therapy to the High Court in over 20 medical injury cases. He was chair of the Association of Professional Music Therapists and UK representative on the European Music Therapy Confederation from 1995 to 1998. He spent three years as external assessor in improvisation on the Aalborg Universitet undergraduate Masters training programme in Denmark. Since early childhood John has observed and tried to predict the weather, and for relaxation he composes songs, musicals, cantatas, chamber and orchestral works.

Jo Tomlinson (née Storey) has worked in special needs and mainstream schools in Cambridgeshire since 1995, employed by Cambridgeshire Music. Within the school setting she has worked with a high proportion of children with autistic spectrum disorder. Jo lectured on the music therapy training course at Anglia Ruskin University from 2001 to 2002 and was Head Music Therapist for Cambridgeshire Music from 2002 to 2006. She has presented papers at numerous music therapy conferences. Jo lives in Cambridge with her husband and two young children, and also tries to find time to perform locally as a piano accompanist.

Subject Index

Author Index